IMAGES
of America

NORTH SACRAMENTO

On the Cover: Two citizens of North Sacramento confer with the city's zoning commission in a c. 1960 meeting with officials.

IMAGES
of America

NORTH SACRAMENTO

V. Ehrenreich-Risner

ARCADIA
PUBLISHING

ISBN 978-0-7385-8003-6

Published by Arcadia Publishing
Charleston SC, Chicago IL, Portsmouth NH, San Francisco CA

Printed in the United States of America

Library of Congress Control Number: 2010926128

For all general information contact Arcadia Publishing at:
Telephone 843-853-2070
Fax 843-853-0044
E-mail sales@arcadiapublishing.com
For customer service and orders:
Toll-Free 1-888-313-2665

Visit us on the Internet at www.arcadiapublishing.com

For J. R., my beloved

In memory of Raymond Brewer, Chief Erskin Fish, and Officer Francis M. (Jack) Rhea, whose tragic deaths left a void in the community; and my recently passed parents, Veronica and Carl Kanowsky

To Fay Graf, historian of the North Sacramento School District

Contents

ACKNOWLEDGMENTS

I wish to thank the first contributor to *North Sacramento*, Robert Kent, and the members of the Rancho Del Paso Historical Society. Charlene Van Allen, publicity coordinator for the North Sacramento School District (now Twin Rivers School District), who entrusted me with the research compiled by Fay Graf. A heartfelt thanks to Tim Risse for sharing the photographs of his fortuitous discovery of the Betty "Ollie" Bryan bomb shelter documents. To Clare Ellis, curator of the Sacramento Room, and to her staff whose expertise were invaluable in the production of this book. To MaryAnn Stanek, current librarian and past supervisor of the North Sacramento branch of the Sacramento Public Library. To Edwina Minor and Wendell Echols for sharing their knowledge of North Sacramento and Del Paso Heights. Randy Wootton, firefighter and collection manager for the Pioneer Mutual Hook and Ladder Society, for sharing the Edward Gardiner Collection of the North Sacramento Fire Department. To Leora Matranga, director of the Grant Union High School Museum, who shared the wealth of documents collected and processed by the school's alumni. To North Sacramento Chamber of Commerce's Doug Austin of Uptown Studios on the Boulevard, who kindly photographed the existing maps of the Rancho Del Paso and North Sacramento. Most sincerely, I wish to thank the archivists and staff of Sacramento Archives and Museum Collection Center (SAMCC) for their invaluable expertise and for allowing me the use of the collection.

In addition to the above individuals, and due to limited space, I would like to thank in alphabetical order the following individuals and organizations: Carlos Acalala, Doug Austin of Austin's Uptown Studios, Buddy Bergstrom, Bob Blymyer, Franklin Burris, Dale Cook and the people of Cook's Hardware, David Crane, Susan Drake, Nadia Halawe, Grantland Johnson, Rob Kerth, Eloise Leong, Jo Alice Erickson Nastal, Lois Hansen Nickless, North Sacramento Chamber of Commerce, North Sacramento Rotary, Kathy Raines, Bob Roth, Linda Roth, Sandy Sheedy, Robert Slobe, Margaret Fish Smith, Fred Steinkamp, Eleanor Strongman, Subway Truck Parts, Richard Taber, Catherine Taylor, California State Parks, Pete Tellers, Jean Tranum, North Sacramento United Methodist Church (NSUM), and Woodlake Garden Club.

Thanks to my sons, Ian, Ryan, and Kevan, and my daughter-in-law, Hannah, and my editor, John Poultney, for encouragement. A special thanks to James for his deep affection and devotion.

INTRODUCTION

Every house and business was a landmark and had a shared history. Children of families in the community married their neighbors down the block and many chose to stay, work, and raise their families on the familiar soil of their birth. In researching the past of North Sacramento, I was struck by the consistency of the community and the gaps, which yearned to be filled. Like connecting the dots on a child's coloring book, many dots of history were in place, but other critical ones were missing. For example, the exact location of the open-air theater on Del Paso Boulevard where Max Baer trained and able youngsters climbed the oaks to view a "free movie" is unclear. Only two residents are of an age to remember the 1910s. Possible locations for the theater where Harry Erickson, the tallest of the Erickson brothers, would pull down the screen, is remembered as being either next to the bowling alley, behind the Grand Theatre or in today's Taber's Furniture location. By interviewing second- and third-generation families, many of those missing pieces were placed in the correct order, yet, always leading to the next gap. Never complacent, often contentious, North Sacramentans did not wistfully watch the demise of their Frank Kapra city. Like an urban legend, stories are still told of the night "fire" set by opponents of the merger to burn the city's records before annexation with the big fish of the City of Sacramento. Councilman Strongman's daughter, Susan Drake, recounts her father's preparation for imprisonment the night of December 30, 1964, as he would refuse to vote for the merger as the courts ordered him. The City of Sacramento (*A Sacramento Saga*) began its campaign to annex North Sacramento even before she became a city. Holding the wolf at bay, North Sacramentans were able to reign over their own city from 1924 to December 31, 1964. In his wishful farewell statement to the North Sacramento City Council, Mayor Joseph Schlegel urged all residents of the city,"now that the civil war is over and the merger is concluded," to put aside their disagreements and renew friendships. In 2008, residents still remember, knowledge was passed down through generations, who voted for and who voted against the merger. But let us go back to the beginning, before North Sacramento was a twinkle in the eye of vertical developer Daniel W. Johnston.

Thousands of years ago, groups of ancient Californians lived in small, defined areas, about 10 miles across. Each tribe respected the boundaries of their neighbor and lived in harmony on the lands where the worlds of the living and the supernatural intertwined and the seasons defined the harsh cycles of life. Around 500 B.C., when Miwok-Costanoan groups moved from the bay region and settled along the rivers in the Sacramento region, complex landscapes of large shell mounds developed. The people existed on a staple of acorns, fish, and waterfowl. The Miwok and the Nisenan, or Southern Maidu, were the major tribes in the Sacramento Valley. The plain of North Sacramento provided the Nisenan a hospitable land to raise families. Food was abundant—deer, elk, beaver—the American River on the southern boundary provided water. Yet as today's North Sacramentans know, the summer can be ruthlessly hot, parching the ground and destroying crops. Likewise, the winter can be relentlessly cruel, causing flash flooding over villages. With no levee system along the river, the Nisenan built their huts on higher ground.

Just outside of Sacramento and southwest of North Sacramento where the Sacramento River breaks from the American River, the Brazil site, known to archaeologists as CA-SAC-43, is an open space controlled by the Bureau of Land Management. The closest known site to North Sacramento, the Brazil settlement was named after Manuel Brazil, the farmer in 1924 who, upon digging a foundation for his house, noted the presence of a large village mound and human burial sites on his acreage. Eventually he notified archaeologists at Sacramento Junior College who excavated the property. The Brazil mound, according to charcoal samples, existed between 450 B.C. and A.D. 1350. Like today's developments in North Sacramento, the settlement was built on higher ground to avoid flooding of the village. For nearly 2,000 years, the mound grew as descendants lived on the site. In A.D. 1350, a severe drought, harbinger of present hardships, occurred which is the probable cause for the abandonment of the site. Same as today, too little water, or too much water dictated movement of communities.

In the 16th century when the first Europeans arrived in California, over 300,000 Native Americans of the Miwok and Nisenan tribes lived in the northeastern portion of California. Spain claimed title to California around 1602 but did not settle in the region until 1769 with the founding of the missions along the California coastline. Spanish forays did not penetrate into the interior of California until 1808 when Lt. Gabriel Moraga set out from Mission San Jose to explore the Sacramento Valley for potential mission sites. Moraga crossed what is today's southern boundary for North Sacramento, the American River, and named it Rio de las Llagas (the wounds or river of sorrows) in honor of Christ's suffering on the cross. Moraga found more than 20 Native American communities but no suitable mission sites due to the steep riverbanks. In 1837, the American River was permanently named "Rio de los Americanos" by Governor Alvarado because the area was frequented by "trappers of revolutionary proclivities (called Americanos)."

After the mountain man Jedediah Strong Smith sent reports to the Hudson Bay Company of the abundance of pelts in the Sacramento Valley, trappers populated the river regions and decimated the Native American population with their malaria. In 1833 alone, nearly 20,000 Native Americans died in the valley from the disease. A year later, to escape debtor's prison in Switzerland, John Augustus Sutter would abandon his wife and child and sail for the United States. Creating his own myth, Sutter became Capt. John Sutter of the Swiss army (later the Mexican government actually conferred upon him the title of captain). On a circuitous journey to California by way of Hawaii, Sutter recruited men and supplies for the empire he planned to build. Landing in Monterey, Sutter became a Mexican citizen and then approached the Mexican governor who gave him permission to colonize a location of his choice.

Arriving in the Sacramento Valley in 1839, Sutter and his party were driven off by Native Americans along the Feather River but found the dwindling tribes along the American River offered little resistance to his occupation of their lands on which he deemed to build his settlement. In an interview with Bancroft the historian, Sutter claims that upon crossing the river in 1839, he (not Governor Alvarado in 1837) named the stream the American River for the pass or ford 3 miles north of Sutter's Fort where trappers, called Americanos by the Spanish-speaking Native Americans, crossed the stream.

On September 13, 1910, North Sacramento Land Company (NSLC) was formed with seven directors: Marshal Diggs, James F. Elliott, Charles G. Hollister, D. W. Johnston of Los Altos, G. A. Richardson of Placerville, Ray C. Waring, and M. N. Williamson.

One

BEGINNINGS

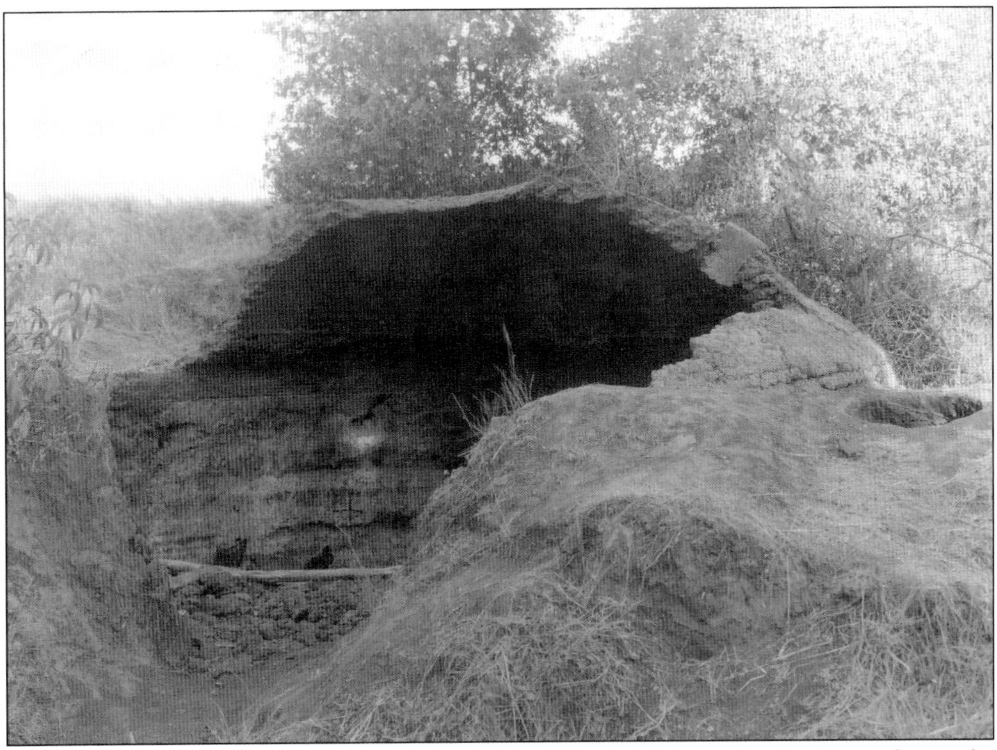

This mud structure was set into an embankment and used as a kiln or charcoal oven during the Gold Rush era. Located on old Sinclair Ranch in Rancho Del Paso, the kiln was built by John Sinclair. The photograph was taken around 1922. (Sacramento Archives Museum and Collection Center, hereinafter cited as SAMCC.)

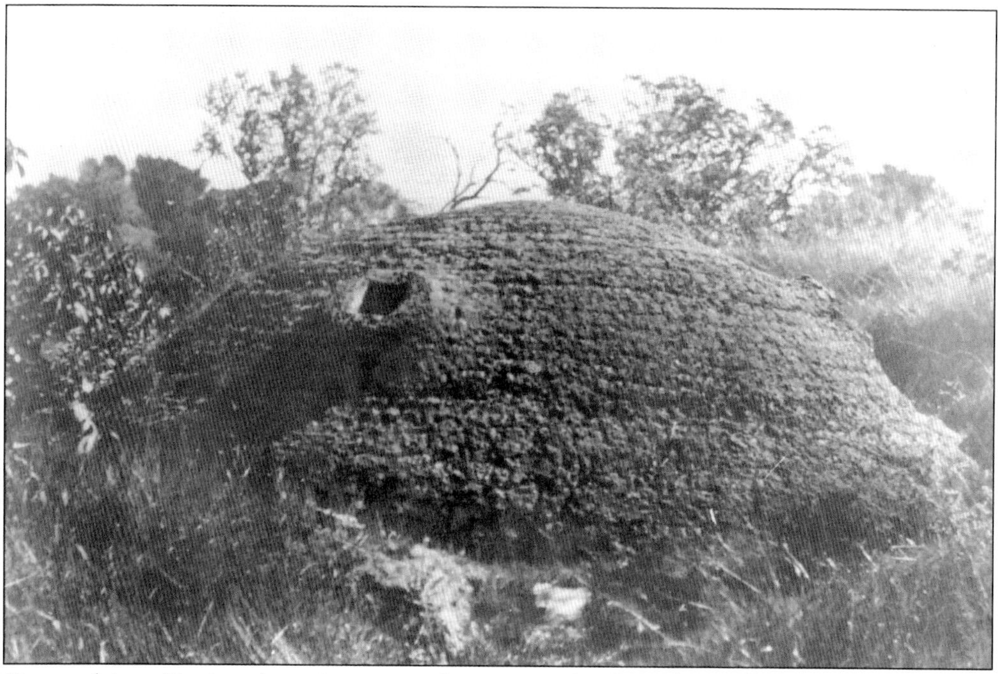

Pictured is a Native American sweathouse on the Rancho Del Paso Grant around 1911. (SAMCC.)

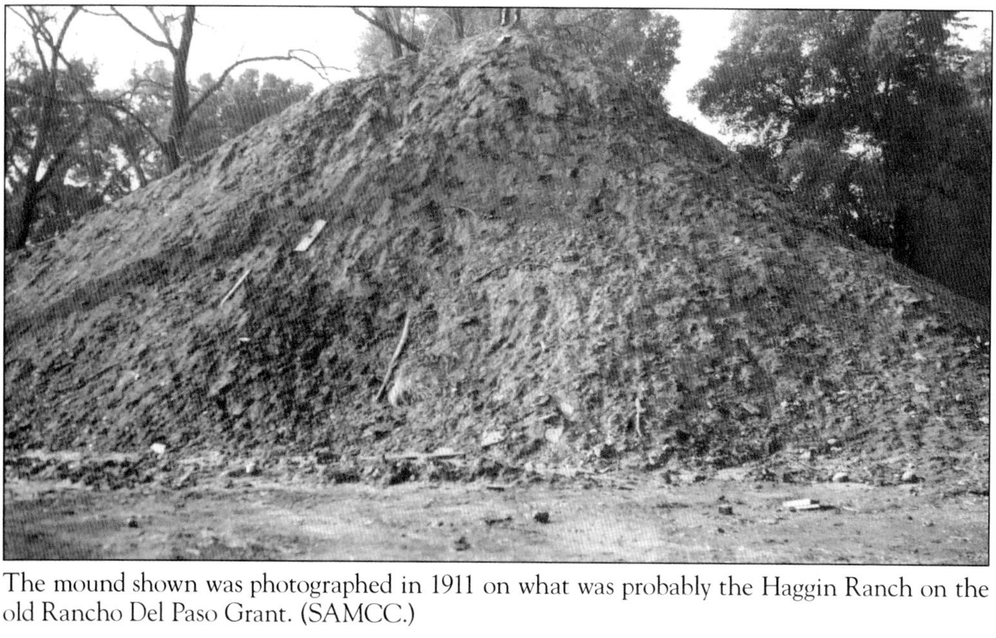

The mound shown was photographed in 1911 on what was probably the Haggin Ranch on the old Rancho Del Paso Grant. (SAMCC.)

In this 1910 North Sacramento Land Company advertisement, in which an acre of land goes for $500, the countrified gentleman grows his own food and laughs at old HCL (High Cost of Living). (North Sacramento Land Company.)

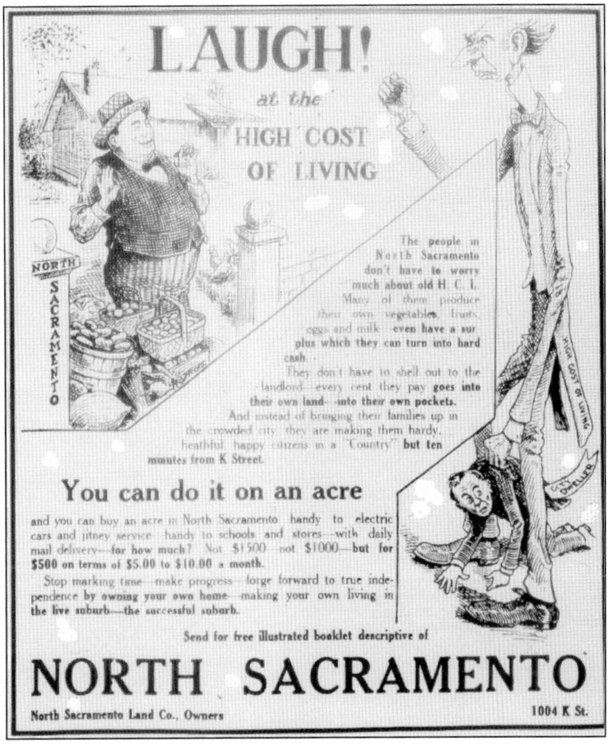

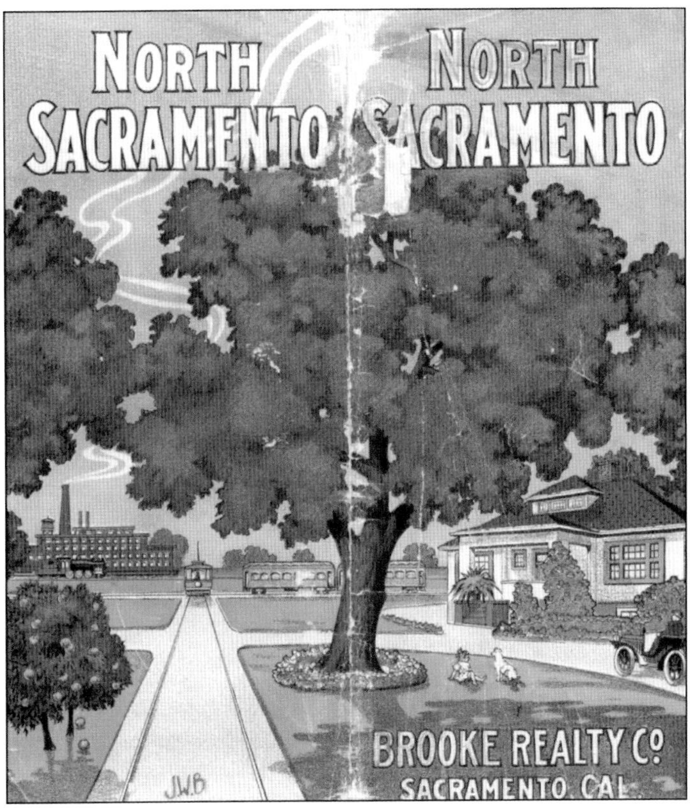

In this idealized pamphlet, North Sacramento's Globe Iron Works sits at left with the Southern Pacific Railroad loading. The electric cars abut the residential area where families plant orange trees and children with their pets, while a Model T sits in every driveway. The Brooke Realty Company sold lots to prospective buyers. A train stops in front of the Globe Iron Works (later Liberty Iron Works) factory depicting the Globe station depot. (Sacramento Room, Sacramento Public Library.)

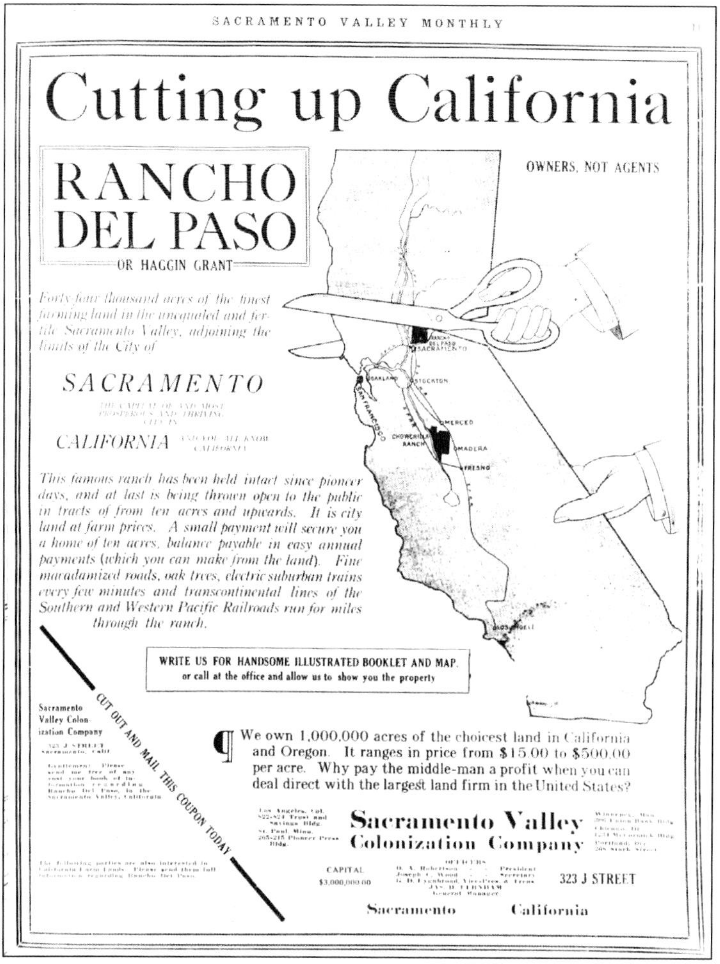

After the death of his son, Haggin lost interest in horse breeding. Development north of Sacramento had been stalled as Haggin and Tevis wished to sell the Rancho Del Paso (ranch of the pass) intact. Although the racehorses had been sold by 1905, the partners waited until 1910 and sold the entire rancho to the Sacramento Valley Colonization Company. (Sacramento Room, Sacramento Public Library.)

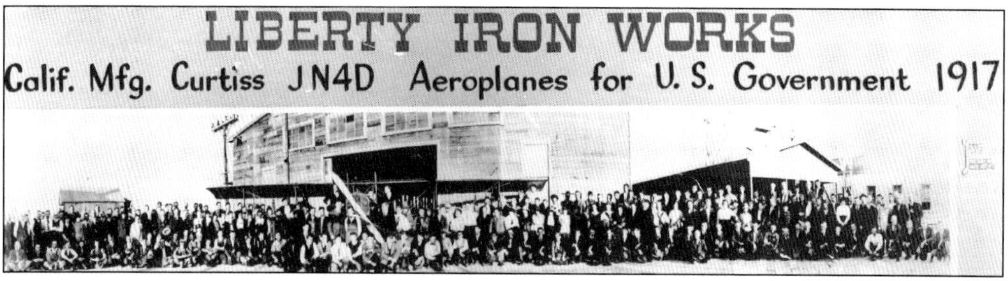

Formerly known as Globe Iron Works, on Globe Avenue at the base of Del Paso Boulevard, Liberty Iron Works brought in an $18-million government airplane contract to build Curtiss JN4D airplanes for the U.S. government. Employees of the company pose in front of the foundry building around 1918. (SAMCC.)

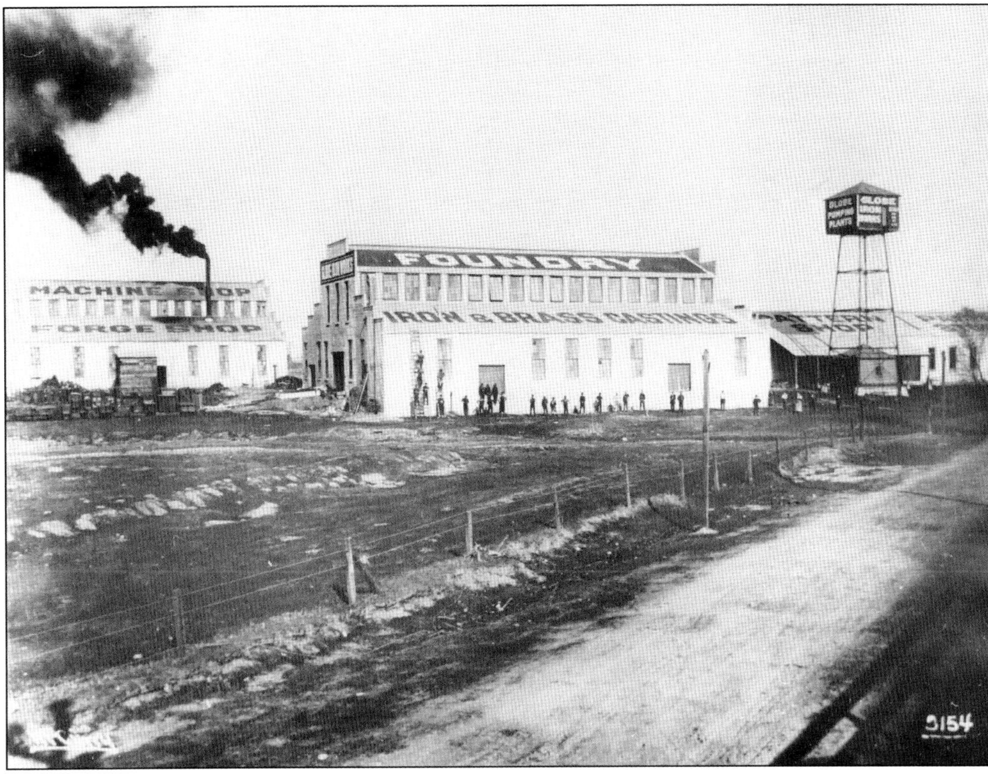

This is a 1918 photograph of the exterior of Liberty Iron Works (formerly Globe Iron Works). Note the water tower in the right side of the picture, which became a familiar landmark for North Sacramentans for generations to come. The dirt road was later paved with macadam, and to the right is Del Paso Boulevard. (SAMCC.)

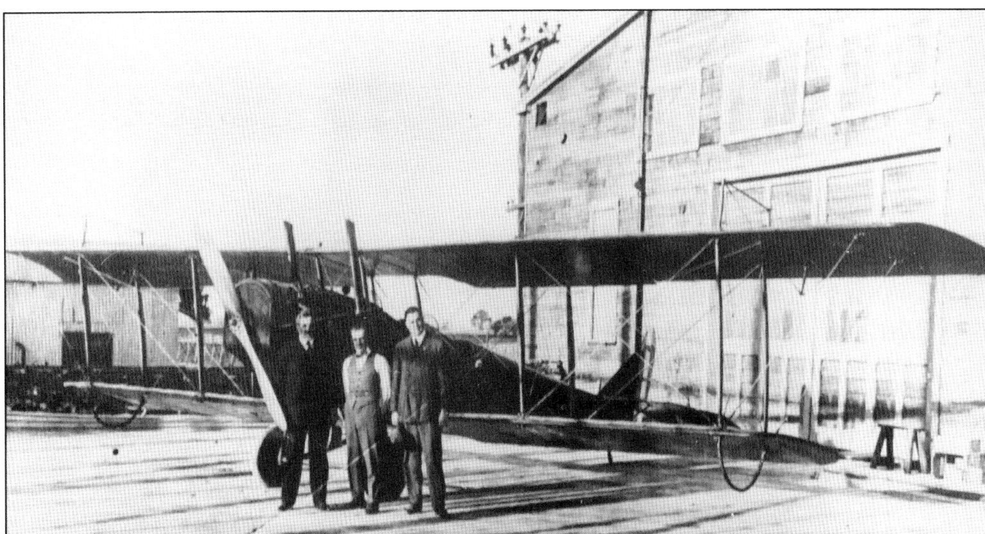

Three Liberty Iron Works employees stand proudly in front of a Jenny airplane. This 1918 interior shot of Liberty Iron Works plane assembly area is from an early publication, *Air Currents*, for December 1918. (SAMCC.)

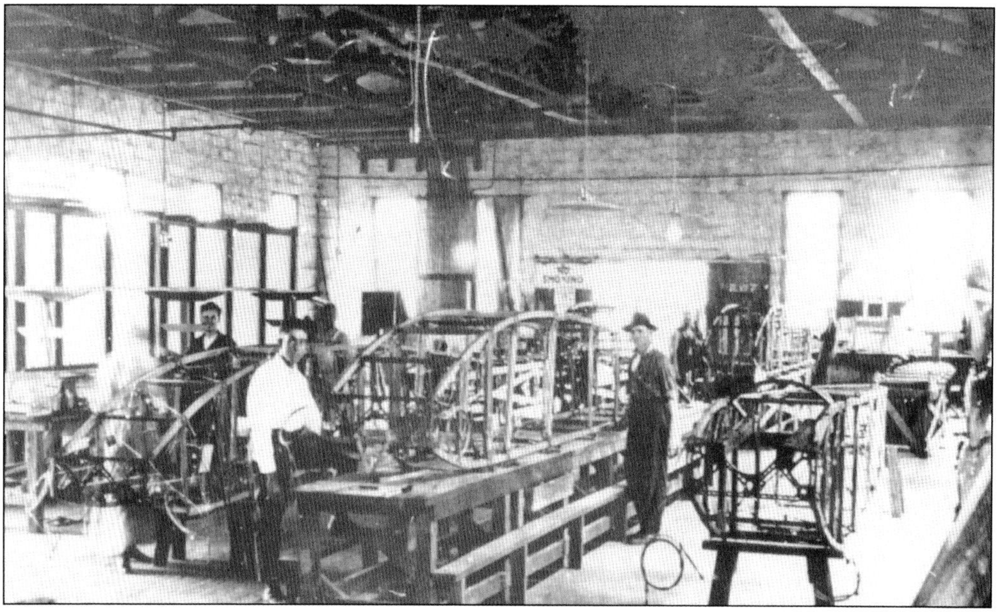

Inside the foundry of Liberty Iron Works on Globe Avenue and Del Paso Boulevard, workers assemble the Jenny airplane to contribute to the war effort around 1918. (SAMCC.)

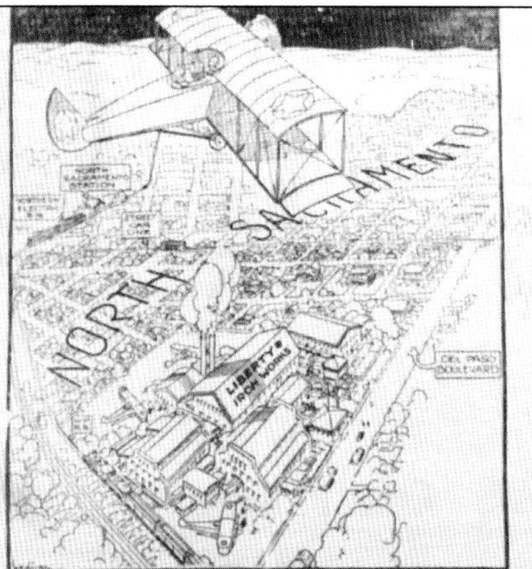

What Does This Picture Tell You?

Study it closely.

Note the Liberty Iron Works—the business buildings on Del Paso Boulevard—the many homes in the surrounding district.

All of this splendid development is not there—YET.

But—**the Liberty Iron Works with an $18,000,000 Government airplane contract is a reality and operating; four more business buildings are under construction on Del Paso Boulevard and many modern homes are built and building.**

It is difficult to estimate the tremendous effect the Liberty Iron Works will have on North Sacramento. Its employees will number into the thousands—its payroll will approximate $3,000,000 annually. And the Liberty Iron Works is here to stay—irrespective of the duration of the war. Its manufacturing possibilities are unlimited.

North Sacramento, already the largest community in Sacramento County outside of Sacramento City, is certain to be developed in a phenomenally short time to an even greater degree than the artist has pictured above.

Now—look again at this picture. Within less than 2 blocks of the Liberty Iron Works and in that section where the home development is indicated and where homes are now being built, **you can buy a big 50-ft. lot for the surprisingly small sum of $500 and for as little as $10 monthly.**

In this 1918 newspaper clipping of an investment advertisement for Liberty Iron Works, North Sacramento real estate agents promise secure jobs and low-priced property for prospective buyers. The ad reads, "Within less than 2 blocks of the Liberty Iron Works and in that section where the home development is indicated and where homes are now being built, you can buy a big 50-ft. lot for the surprisingly small sum of $500 and for as little as $10 monthly." (SAMCC.)

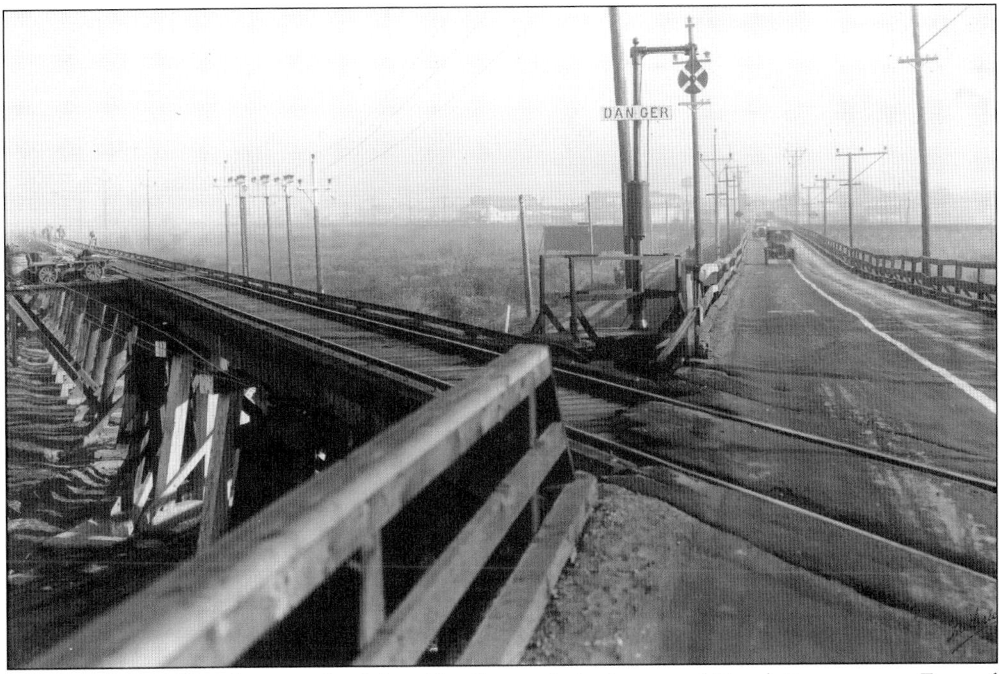

Shown in 1910, this photograph of the old mile trestle looks toward North Sacramento. Erected in the early 1890s, the trestle was torn down in 1925 and replaced by a highway. (SAMCC.)

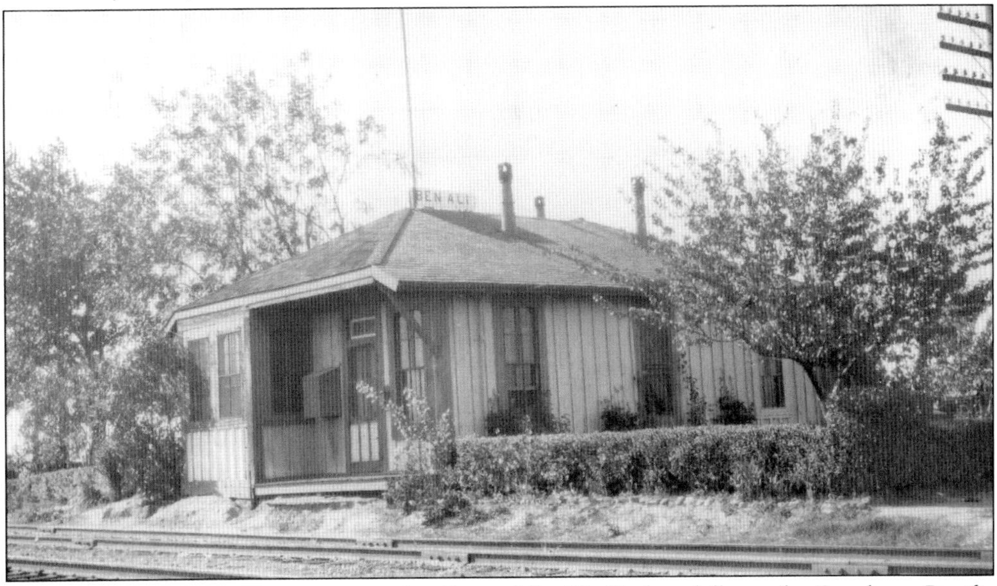

With Haggin's monetary incentive, the Central Pacific Railroad (later the Southern Pacific then the Union Pacific) provided a railroad depot, called Ben Ali Station, for transporting thoroughbreds back East. Ben Ali Station was named after James Ben Ali Haggin, the co-owner with Lloyd Tevis of the Ranch Del Paso Grant. Haggin contracted with the railroad to have this stop built to convey his racehorses back East. The Southern Pacific Railroad Station depot at Ben Ali Station, later the end of Highway 160, is shown here on November 5, 1939. This station was east of North Sacramento and named when this district was known as Haggin Grant. The site is now a flag station. (SAMCC.)

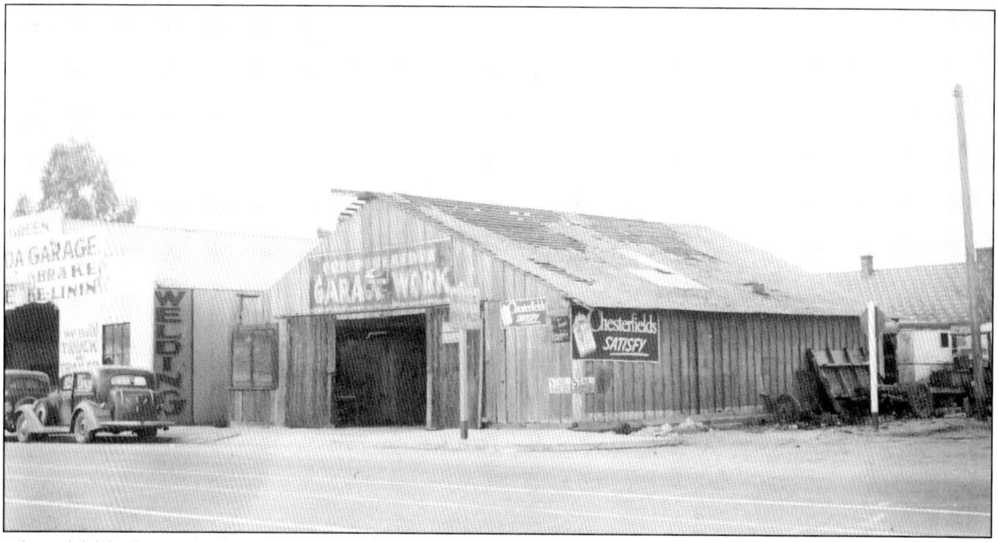

The old blacksmith shop on East El Camino and Ninth Avenue, just before the overpass, was one of the first buildings in North Sacramento. Erected in 1923, the building was photographed on January 28, 1940. Green's Garage is next to the blacksmith. (SAMCC.)

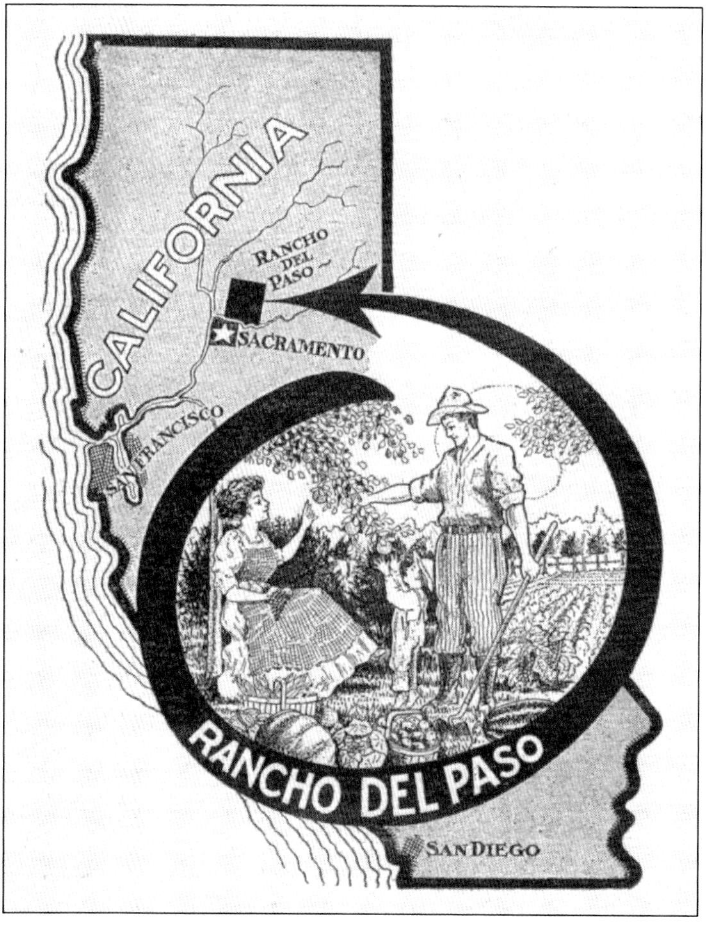

Touted by Sacramento Valley Colonization Company as California's gardenland or Rancho Del Paso, the actual name for the subdivision, North Sacramento, attracted prospective eastern buyers. (Sacramento Room, Sacramento Public Library.)

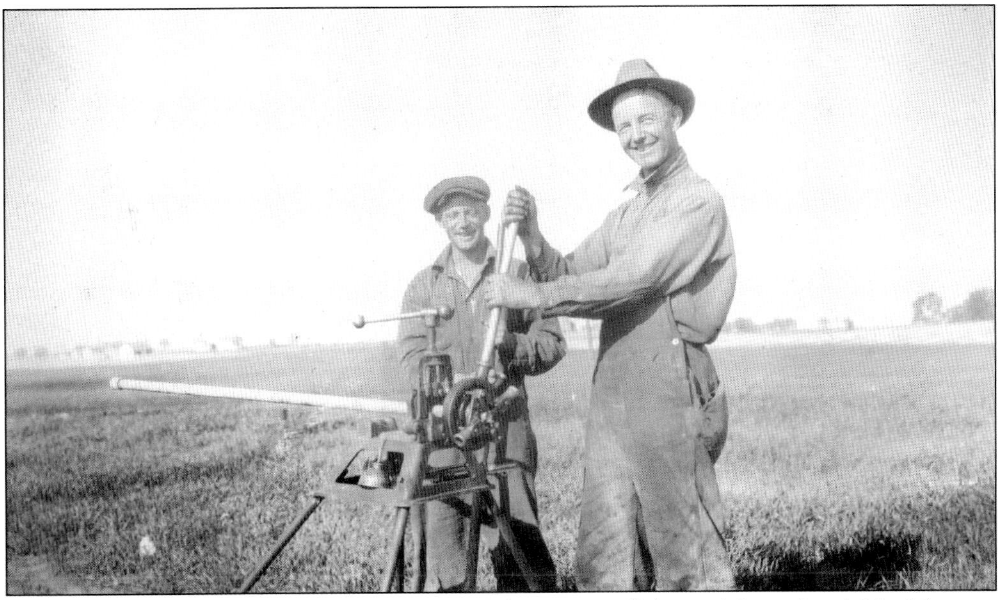

Pictured on the right in this 1913 image is Mr. Johnson, a well digger. Married to Addie Johnson, he was the father of three Johnson girls: Alice (Johnson Erickson), Evelyn (Johnson Missall), and Mildred (Johnson Roundtree), and one son, Bob Johnson. When he passed away, Addie was left to raise the four children and found compassionate support within the North Sacramento community. Note the undeveloped expanse in North Sacramento, with houses in the background. (Erickson-Nastal.)

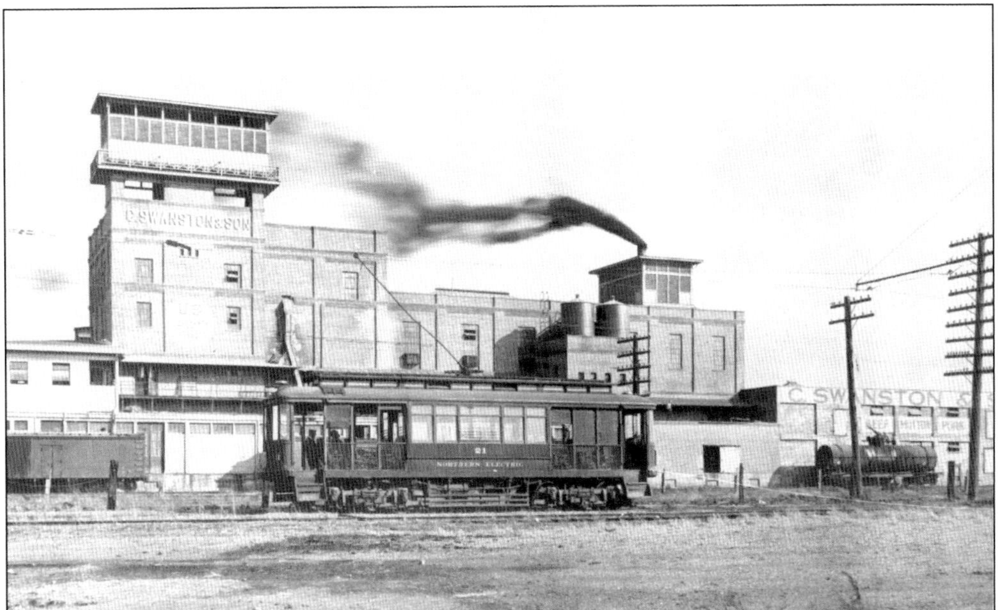

In 1910, Swanston Meat Packing Company had its own terminal. The No. 21 Northern Electric Railcar stopped in front of the plant where many North Sacramentans worked. (Bill Blymer.)

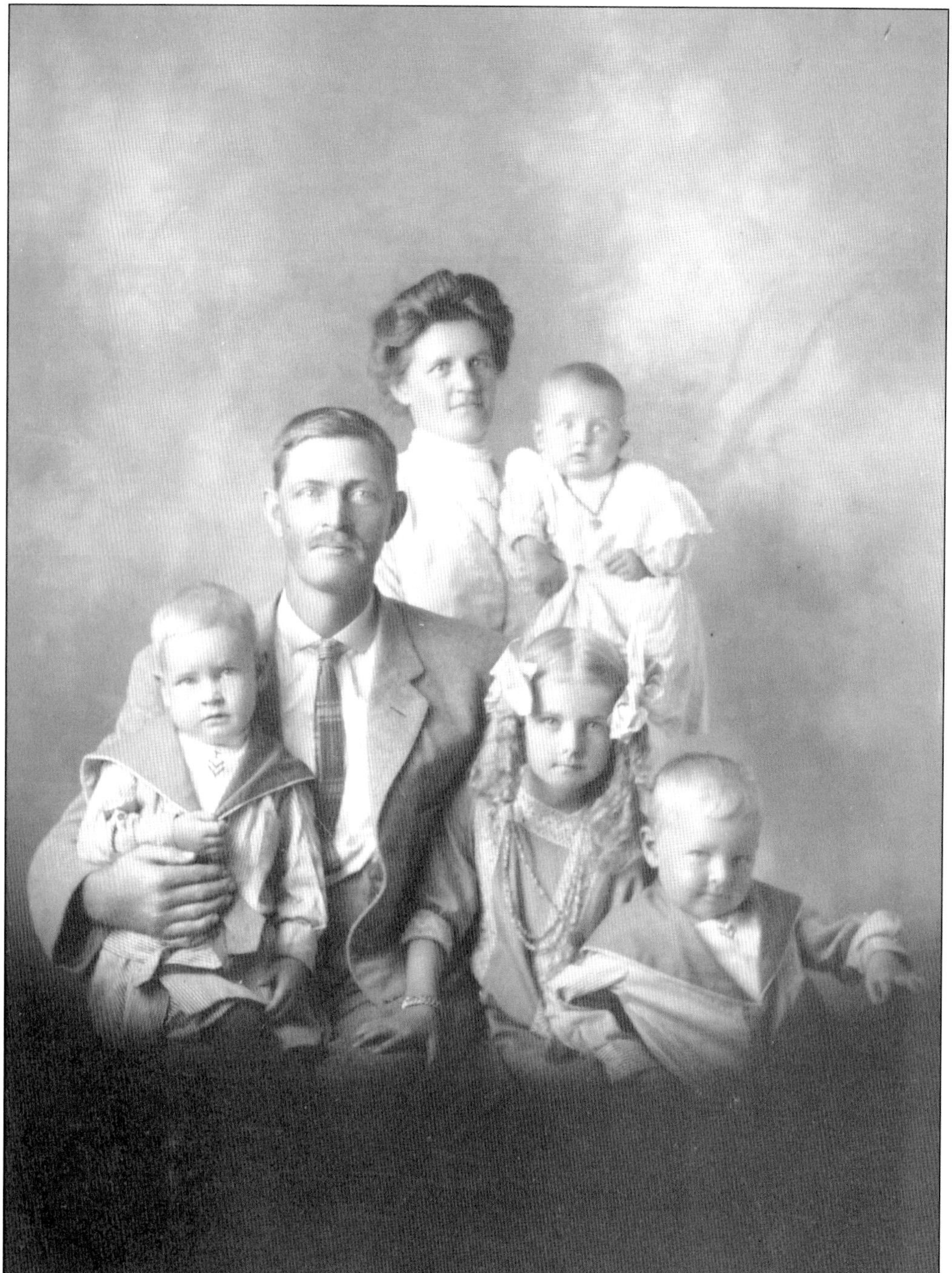

The Erickson brood grew to three sons and a daughter, Nell. They lived near Auburn Boulevard and later built a home behind the Del Paso Country Club at Arden Arcade. In 1913, posing for a family portrait are, from left to right, Frank (in Pop's lap), Axel ("Pop"), Olga holding Auburn ("Babe"), Nellie, and Harry Erickson. (Erickson-Nastal.)

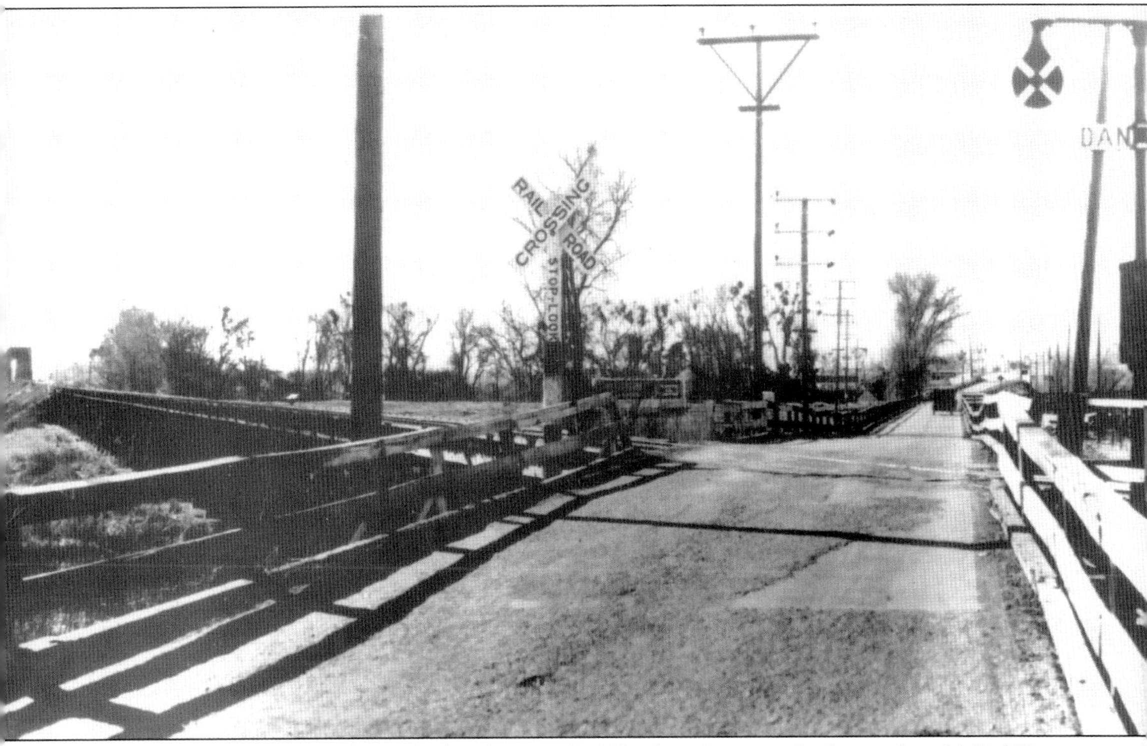

Looking northwest toward Gardenland around 1910, the photograph shows the old Del Paso Boulevard causeway crossing at the Northern Electric Mainline just north of the American River. The old mile trestle was erected in the early 1890s. A freeway now crosses this intersection well above the much-flooded location. The gypsies camped at this site as well as Arcade Creek along the old trail between the Southern Pacific tracks and Haggin Oaks Golf Course. Before North Sacramento incorporated, Sacramento City attempted to tax the gypsies for fortune-telling but was largely unsuccessful. (SAMCC.)

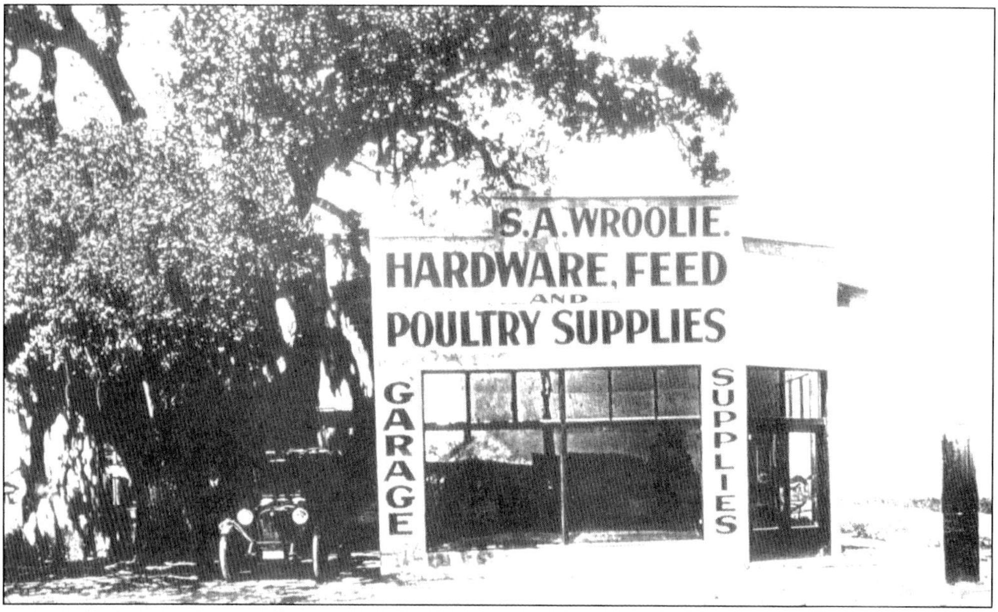

Originally known as Wroolie's corner, the corner on Del Paso Boulevard and Rio Linda changed businesses from Wroolie's Hardware to McDowell's Grocers and then to Cook's Auto Supply. Cook's moved to its current location 2125 Del Paso Boulevard in 1936. (Cook.)

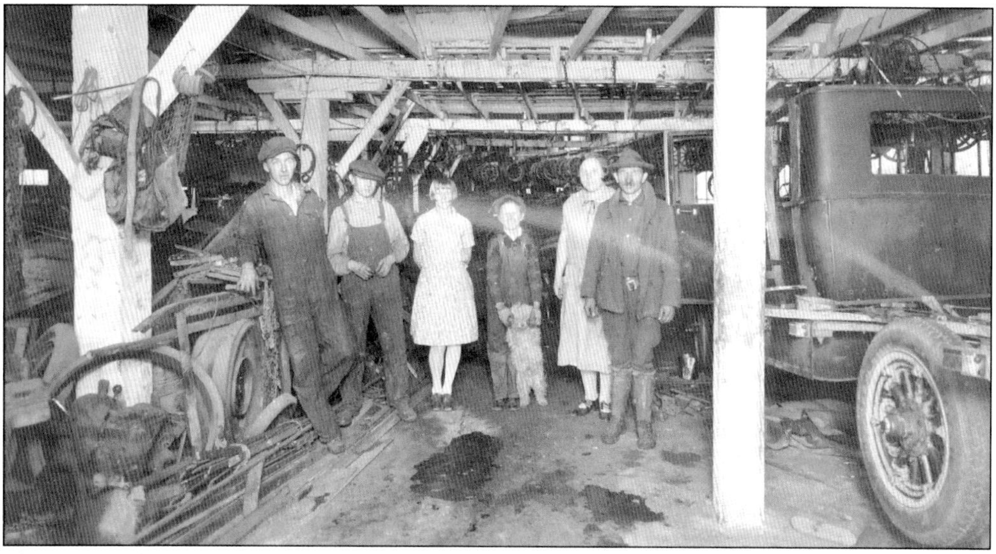

The Lauszus family opened Subway Truck Parts in the early 1920s at the base of Del Paso Boulevard just south of Liberty (Globe) Iron Works. Brad Martin, a fourth-generation owner by marriage, operates the business today. The fourth-generation family-owned business sells guaranteed used automotive parts for domestic pickups, mini-pickups, vans, minivans, and SUVs. Pictured here in 1923, the Lauszus family is at Subway Truck Parts, which was under the subway at Twelfth Street and North B Street, (hence the business was named subway). In the center with the dog is Herman Lauszus Jr., who was born November 6, 1914, in Portland, Oregon, to Herman Lauszus (far right) and Marie Lauszus (second from right) of Russia. In 1923, the Lauszus family moved to the fringe of North Sacramento at Twelfth and North B Streets, then four years later moved into their auto parts business to 795 Del Paso Boulevard. (Lauszus.)

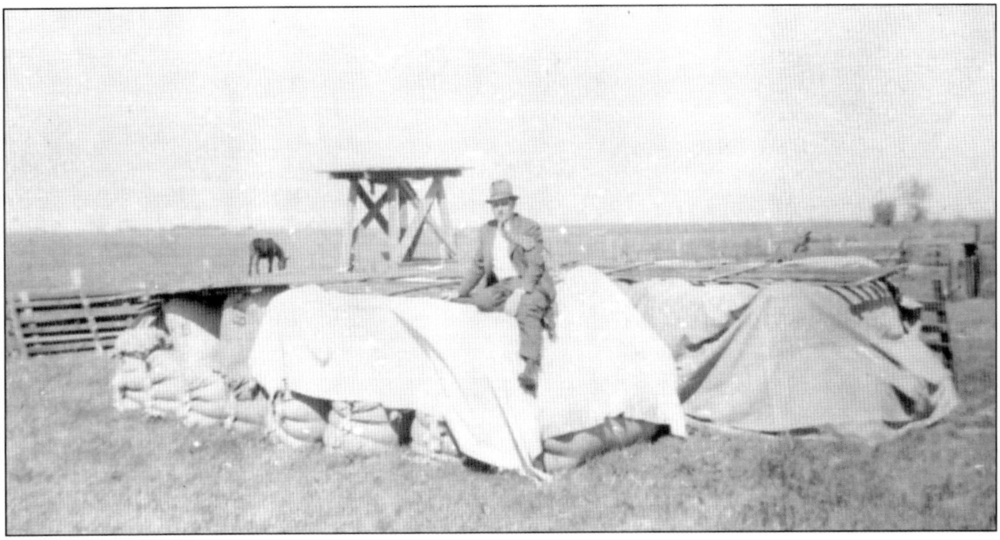

E. W. Boudier sits on bags of wool during sheep-shearing time at the Diamond Bar ranch in the North Sacramento area in March 1938. (SAMCC.)

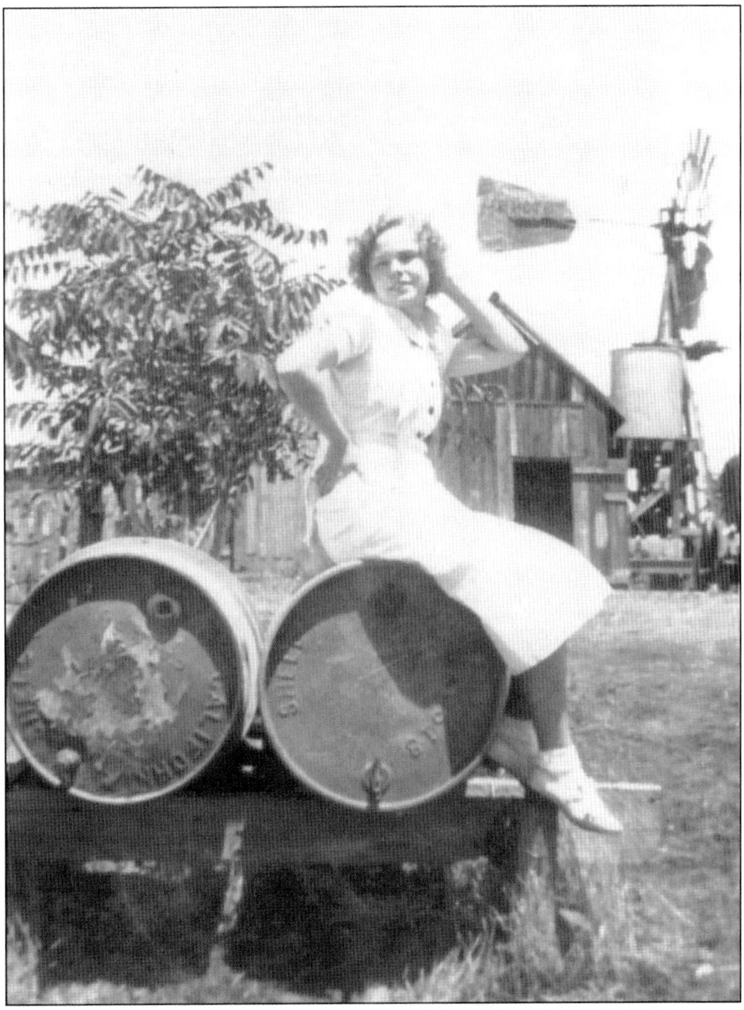

Evelyn Boudier sits on "Shell of California" cans at Diamond Bar ranch in June 1934. (SAMCC.)

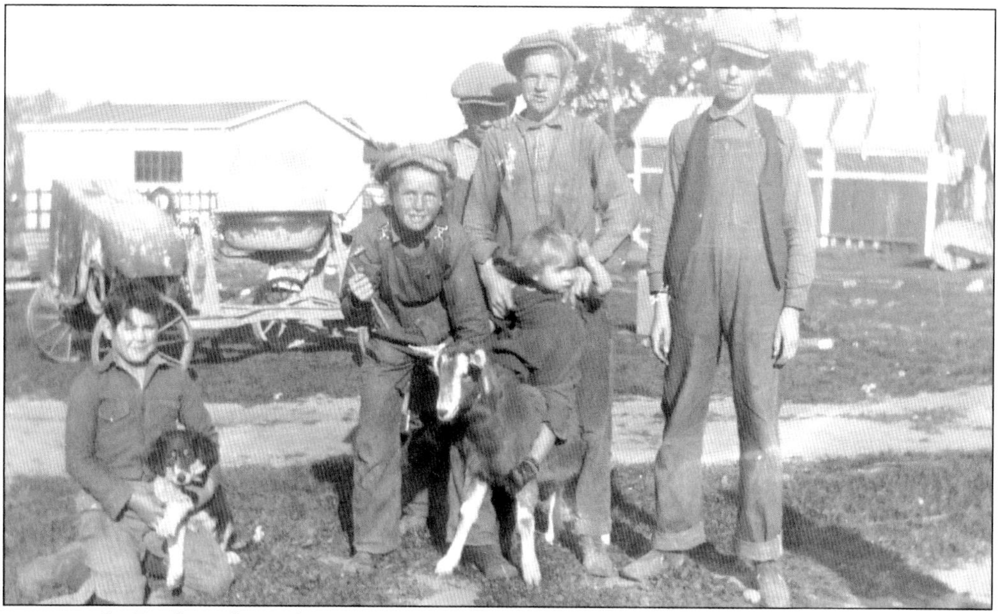

In 1922, the Erickson boys clown around with the neighbors on "a vacant lot west of our home at 1918 Del Paso Boulevard, where Ben Franklin store is [was] now." From left to right are an unidentified boy with a dog, Auburn "Babe" Erickson, Frank Erickson (holding baby Edreen on a goat), and Harry Erickson. Carl Harder is behind Frank. (Erickson-Nastal.)

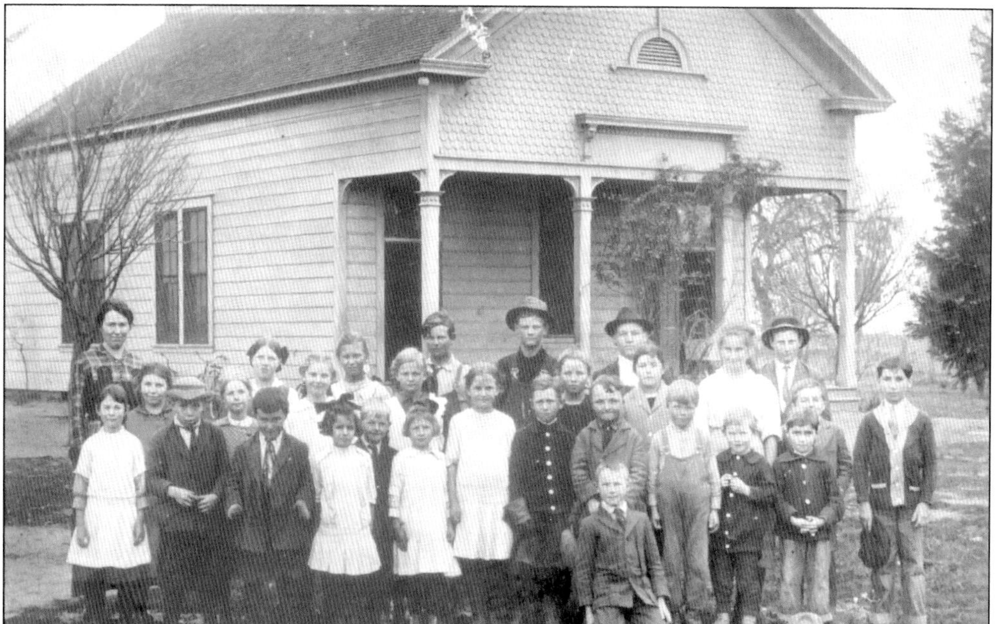

The Erickson kids are among the children at the one-room Arcade schoolhouse near Pope Avenue in the north area around 1914. (Erickson-Nastal.)

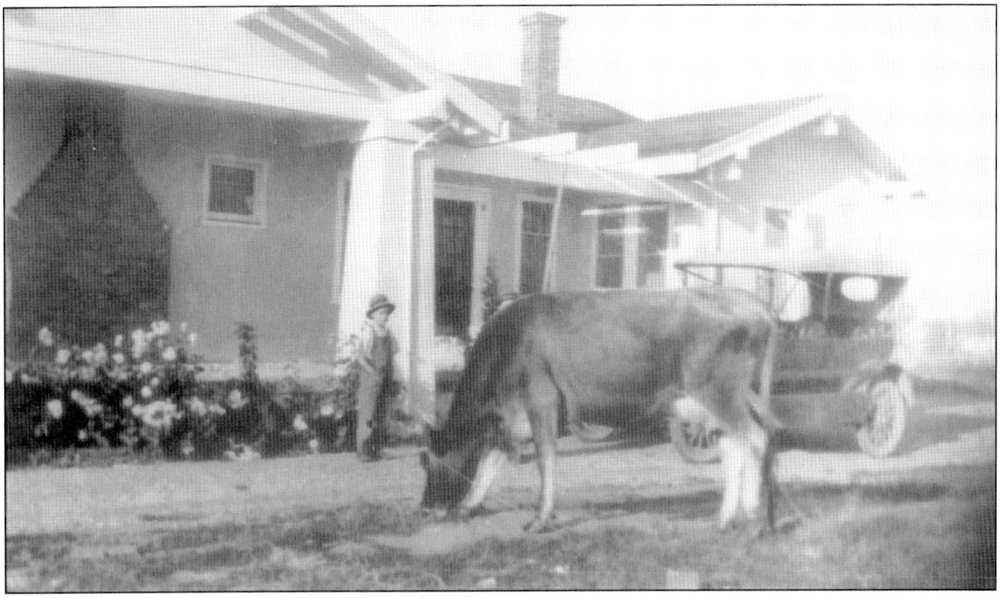

At the Arcade Avenue house built in 1915, pictured around 1918, Babe (Auburn) Erickson grazes the neighbor's cow, which was one of his early morning chores. (Erickson-Nastal.)

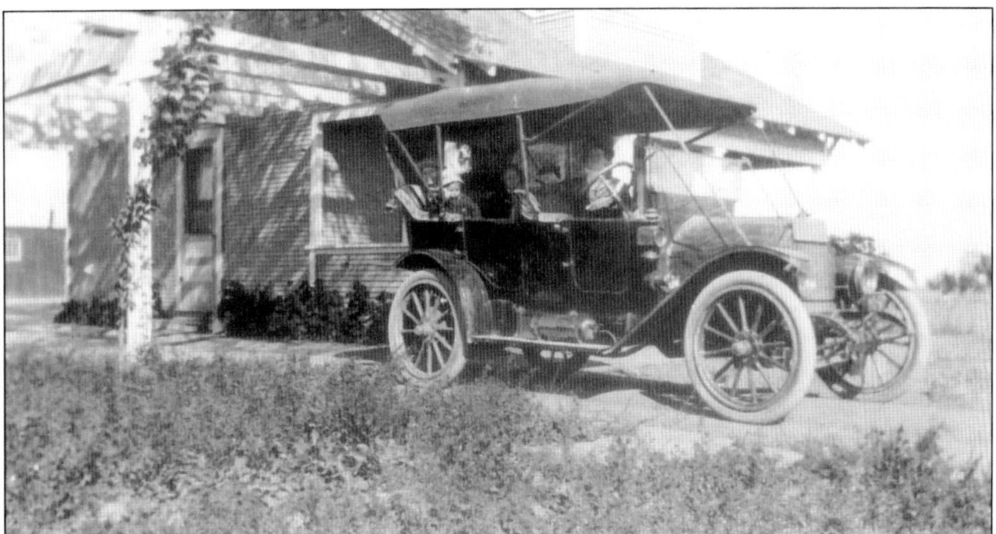

In 1914, Axel "Papa" Erickson built this house on Pope Avenue behind the Del Paso Country Club. The Erickson brood waits in the family car. (Erickson-Nastal.)

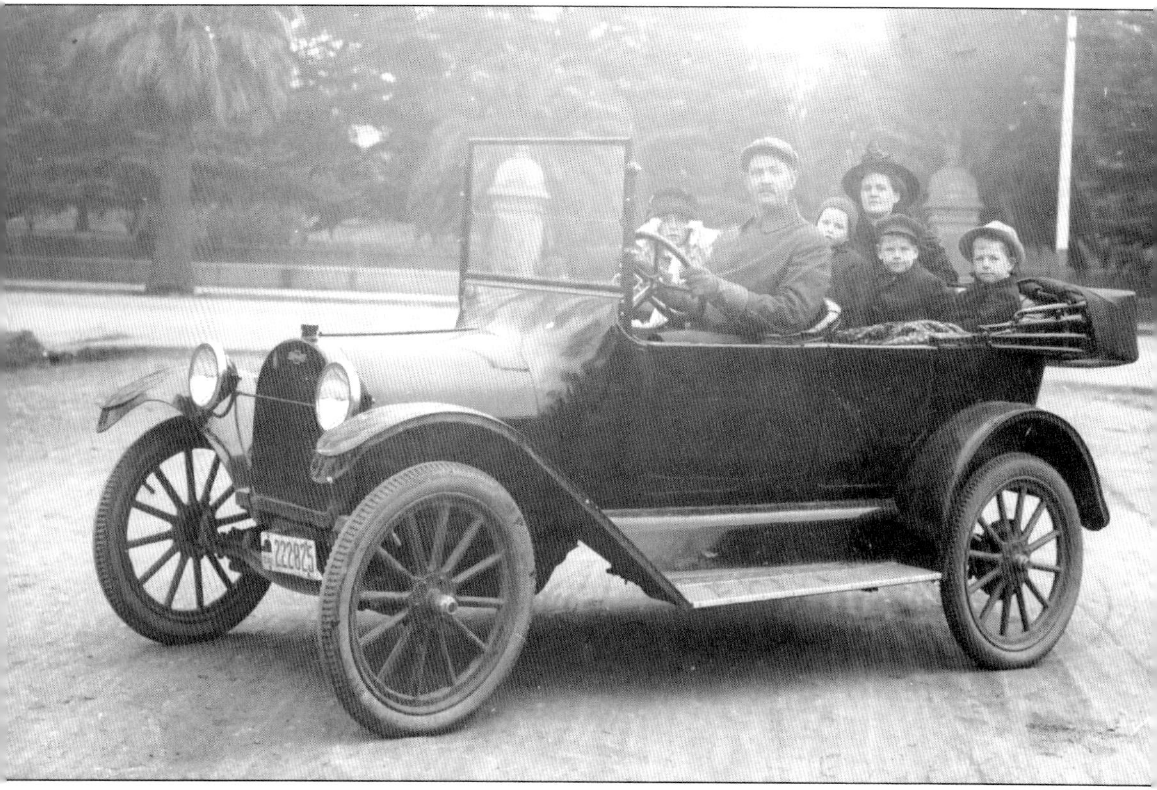

Pictured here around 1914, the Erickson clan park in the roundabout in front of the capitol in downtown Sacramento. (Erickson-Nastal.)

Two

WHERE THE HECK IS NORTH SACRAMENTO?

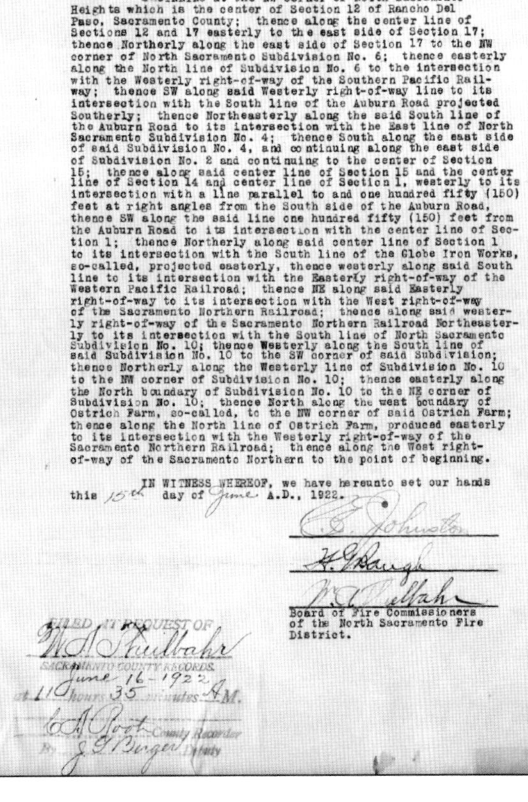

WE, THE BOARD OF FIRE COMMISSIONERS of the North Sacramento Fire District do hereby describe and define the fire limits of said town or village as follows:-

BEGINNING at the NW corner of North Sacramento Heights which is the center of Section 12 of Rancho Del Paso, Sacramento County; thence along the center line of Sections 12 and 17 easterly to the east side of Section 17; thence Northerly along the east side of Section 17 to the NW corner of North Sacramento Subdivision No. 6; thence easterly along the North line of Subdivision No. 6 to the intersection with the Westerly right-of-way of the Southern Pacific Railway; thence SW along said Westerly right-of-way line to its intersection with the South line of the Auburn Road projected Southerly; thence Northeasterly along the said South line of the Auburn Road to its intersection with the East line of North Sacramento Subdivision No. 4; thence South along the east side of said Subdivision No. 4, and continuing along the east side of Subdivision No. 2 and continuing to the center of Section 15; thence along said center line of Section 15 and the center line of Section 14 and center line of Section 1, westerly to its intersection with a line parallel to and one hundred fifty (150) feet at right angles from the South side of the Auburn Road, thence SW along the said line one hundred fifty (150) feet from the Auburn Road to its intersection with the center line of Section 1; thence Northerly along said center line of Section 1 to its intersection with the South line of the Globe Iron Works, so-called, projected easterly, thence westerly along said South line to its intersection with the Easterly right-of-way of the Western Pacific Railroad; thence NE along said Easterly right-of-way to its intersection with the West right-of-way of the Sacramento Northern Railroad; thence along said westerly right-of-way of the Sacramento Northern Railroad Northeasterly to its intersection with the South line of North Sacramento Subdivision No. 10; thence Westerly along the South line of said Subdivision No. 10 to the SW corner of said Subdivision; thence Northerly along the Westerly line of Subdivision No. 10 to the NW corner of Subdivision No. 10; thence easterly along the North boundary of Subdivision No. 10 to the NE corner of Subdivision No. 10; thence North along the west boundary of Ostrich Farm, so-called, to the NW corner of said Ostrich Farm; thence along the North line of Ostrich Farm, produced easterly to its intersection with the Westerly right-of-way of the Sacramento Northern Railroad; thence along the West right-of-way of the Sacramento Northern to the point of beginning.

IN WITNESS WHEREOF, we have hereunto set our hands this 15th day of June A.D., 1922.

Board of Fire Commissioners of the North Sacramento Fire District.

FILED AT REQUEST OF

SACRAMENTO COUNTY RECORDS.

June 16 - 1922

at 11 hours 35 minutes A.M.

County Recorder

By Deputy

Discerning the boundaries of North Sacramento was cumbersome. The Board of Fire Commissioners of the North Sacramento Fire District used the Ostrich Farm as a landmark for the northwest corner of the boundary of North Sacramento. Note the signature of C. E. Johnston of the North Sacramento Land Company on this 1922 fire-limits document. (Sacramento Room, Sacramento Public Library.)

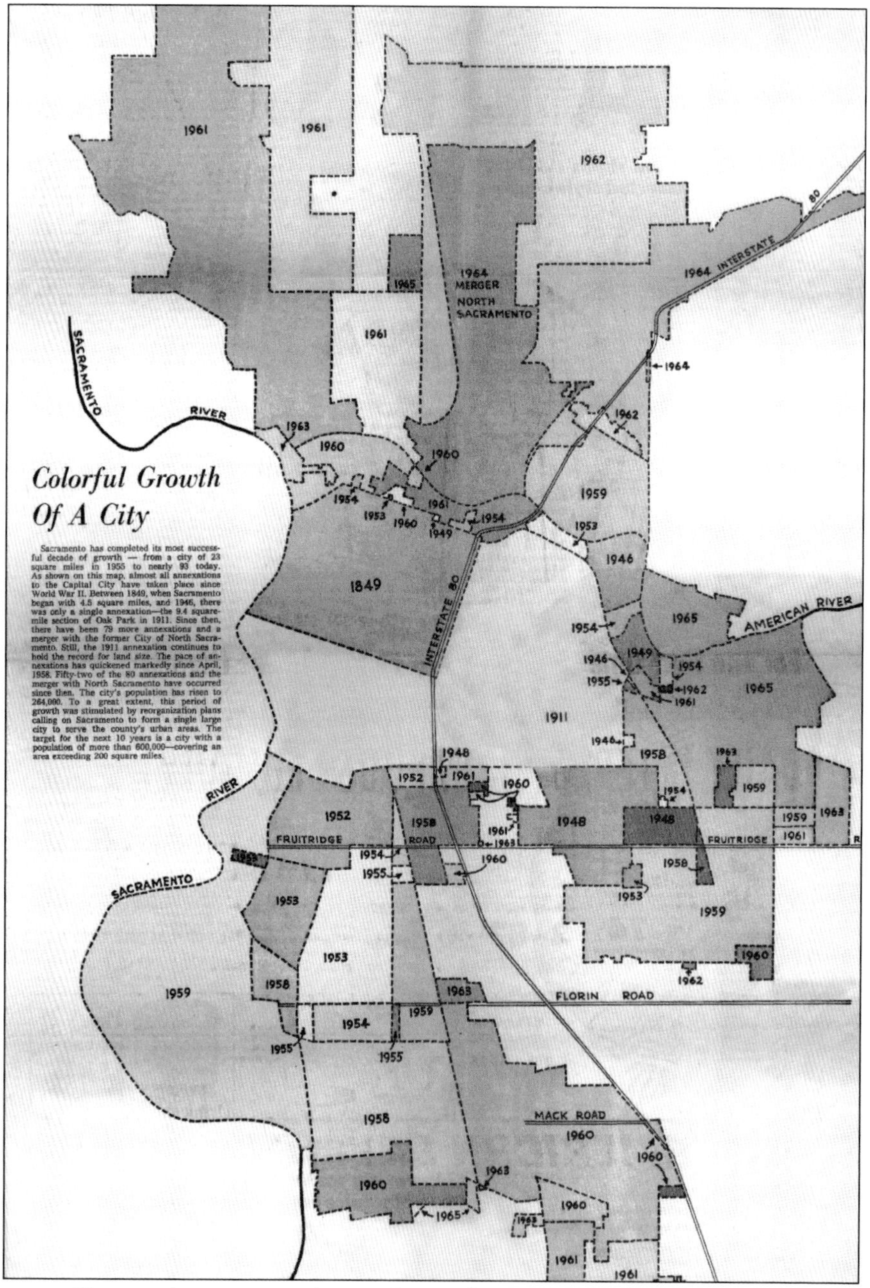

Sacramento City sought to annex the north area beginning in the early 1920s, according to *A Sacramento Saga*. The renegade North Sacramento refused to be caught in the net of the big fishermen of the Sacramento City Council. As the caption on this map states, the City of Sacramento annexed 80 areas before capturing North Sacramento. After several elections and a court fight, the big fish (Sacramento) successfully merged (not annexed) the "Frank Kapra" city of North Sacramento on December 31, 1964, at 11:59 p.m. Jean Tranum, North Sacramento resident and historian for the North Sacramento United Methodist Church, says that the draw for the merger was no water meters. Citizens to this day remember who voted for and who voted against the merger. (SAMCC.)

A division of Township 9 North Range 5 East, North Sacramento is located in Section 12 of the Rancho Del Paso early subdivision map, which includes the subdivisions of Arcade, Arden, Del Paso Heights, Fruitdale, and Robla. (SAMCC.)

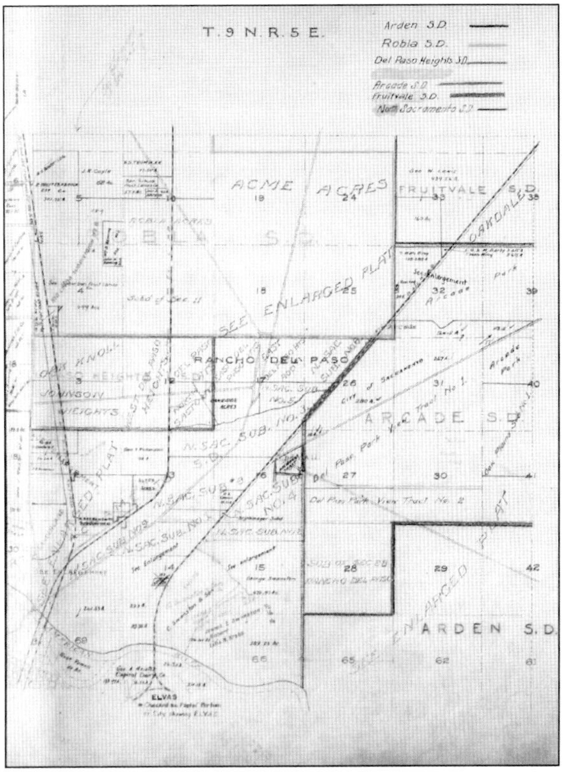

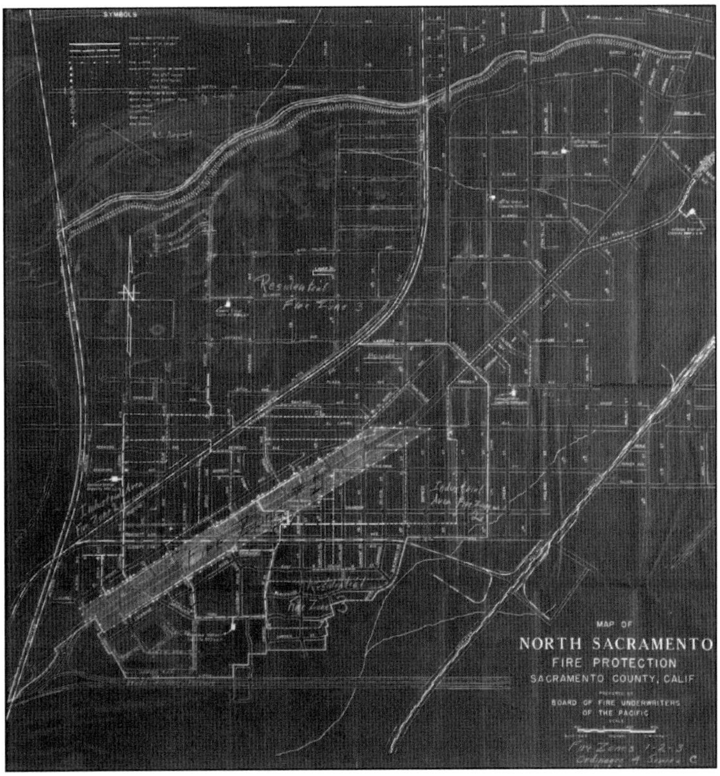

Prepared by the Board of Fire Underwriters of the Pacific, this fire-protection map of North Sacramento outlines the fire zones one, two, and three. Note the North Sacramento Airport in the upper left corner. This map was created in 1949. (SAMCC.)

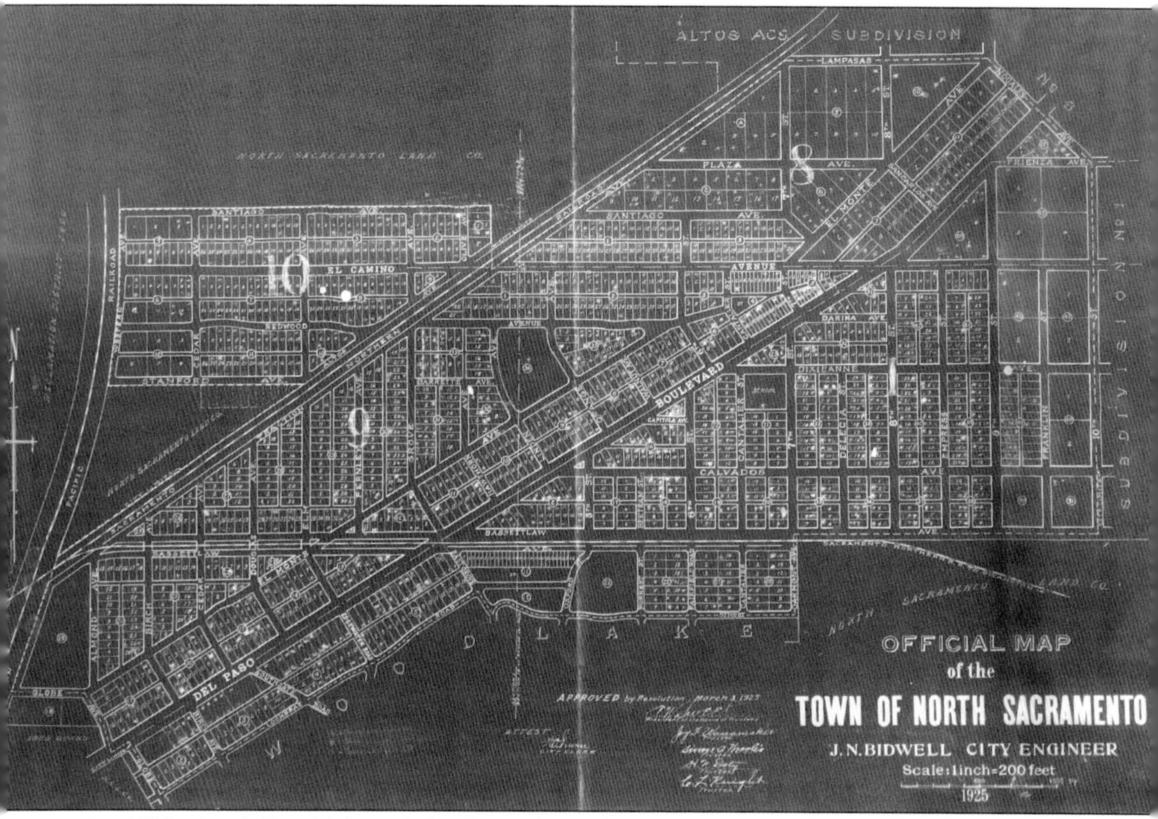

In 1925, the Official Map of the City of North Sacramento was drawn by city engineer J. N. Bidwell for the North Sacramento Board of Trustees, who included local Del Paso Boulevard businessmen A. W. Sweet, Simon Wroolie, and Joy Wannamaker. (Sacramento Room, Sacramento Public Library.)

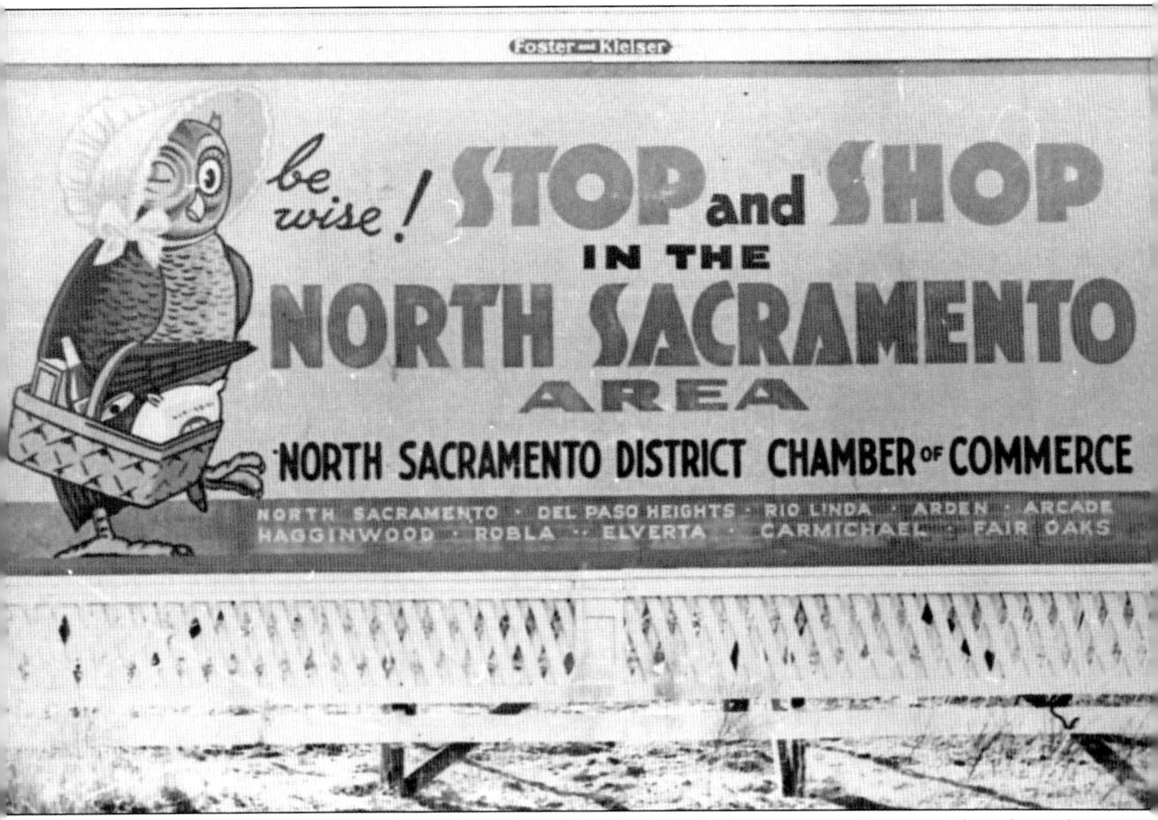

The wise owl on this 1950 billboard produced by the North Sacramento District Chamber of Commerce admonishes consumers to "be wise!" and shop the merchants of the North Sacramento area, which includes Del Paso Heights, Rio Linda, Arden, Arcade, Hagginwood, Robla, Elverta, Carmichael, and Fair Oaks. (SAMCC.)

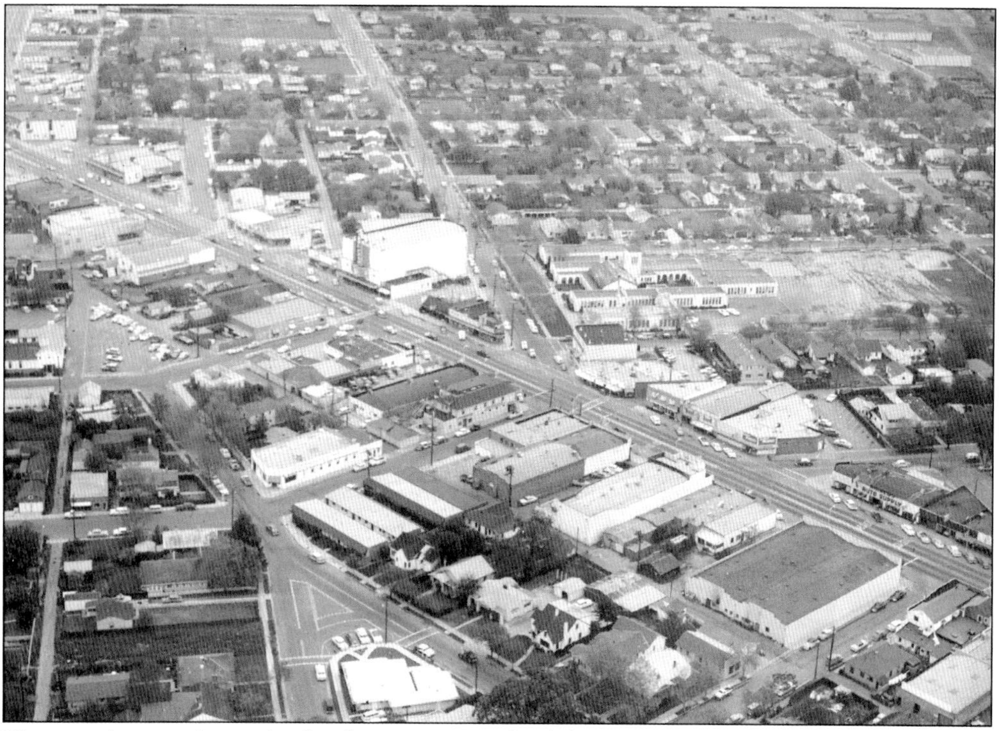

This aerial image shows the developing city north of the American River as it appeared in the mid-1950s, with the Grand Theatre near the center of the picture at Dixianne Avenue. (North Sacramento School District.)

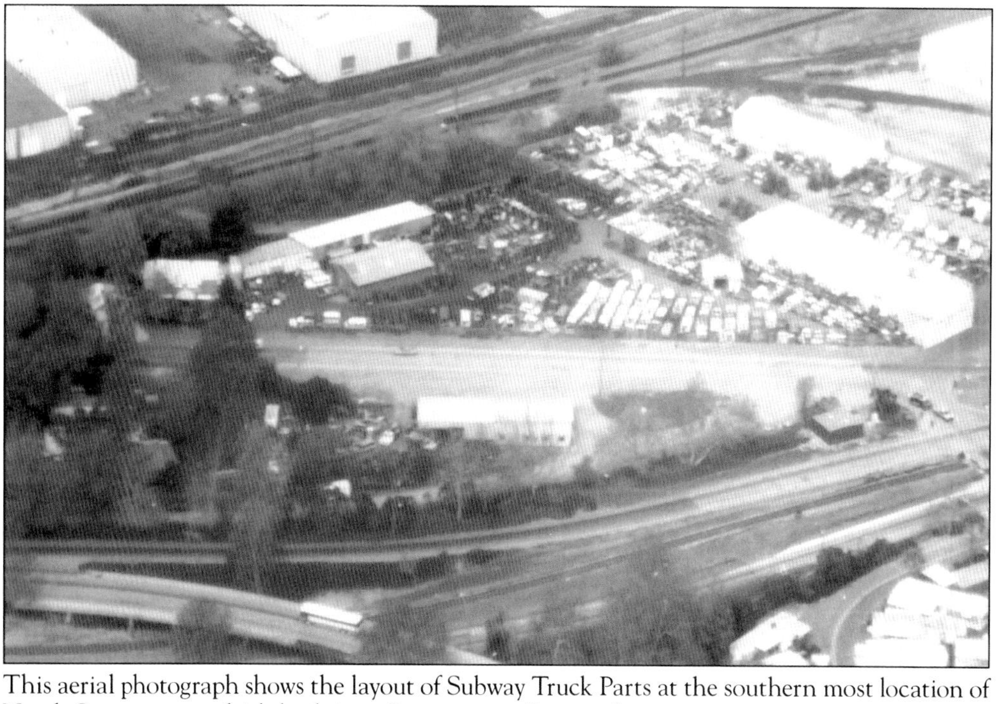

This aerial photograph shows the layout of Subway Truck Parts at the southern most location of North Sacramento, which leads into Sacramento. (Lauszus.)

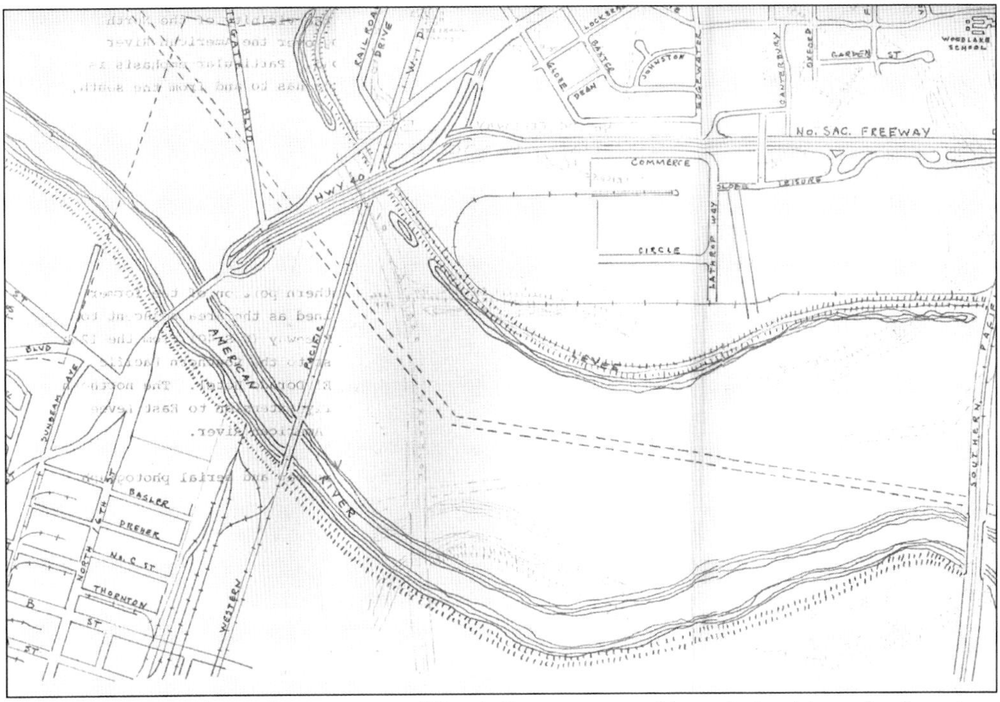

This map outlines the southern portion of North Sacramento and her relationship to the American River and Sacramento. (North Sacramento Land Company.)

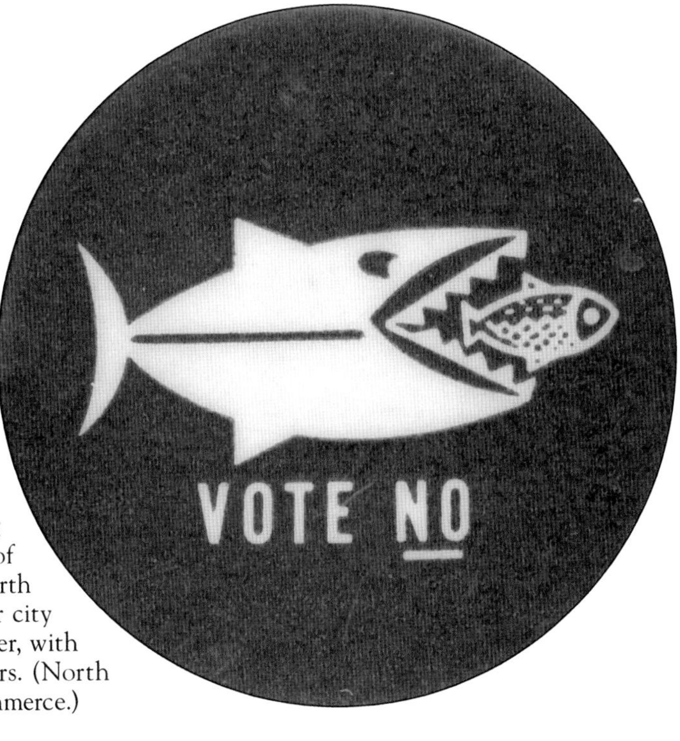

This campaign button urging North Sacramentans to "Vote No" on the merger depicts the big fish of the City of Sacramento swallowing the small fish of the City of North Sacramento. Some North Sacramentans believed their city would benefit from the merger, with such perks as no water meters. (North Sacramento Chamber of Commerce.)

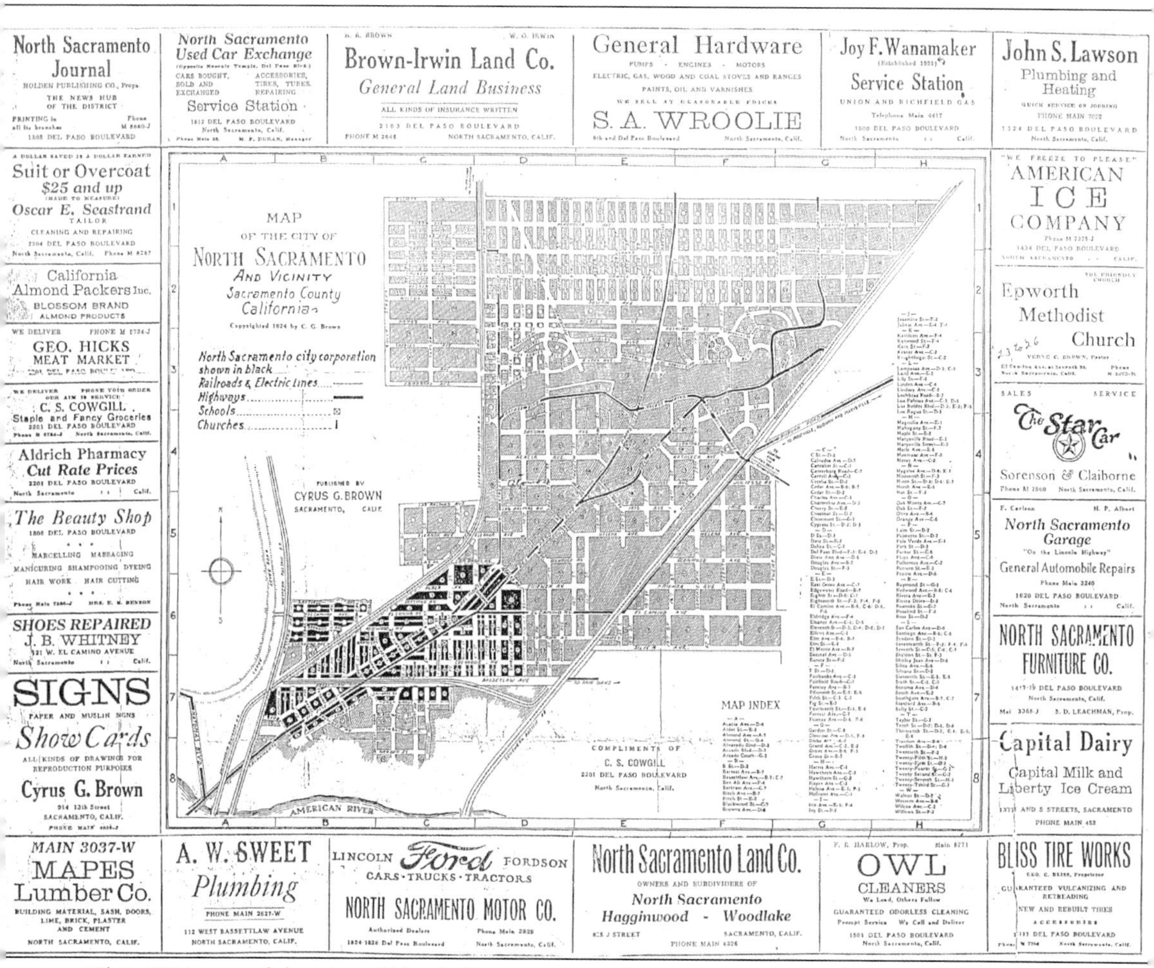

This 1924 map of the city of North Sacramento and vicinity was created as an aid for travelers by Cyrus Cowgill Staple and Francy Groceries located on 2201 Del Paso Boulevard. The map is framed with the various business on the boulevard. Del Paso Boulevard was a leg on the international highway known as the Lincoln Highway, and this complimentary map oriented motorists traveling between points north and south on the Lincoln Highway as well as being an inducement to stop and "fill 'er up" at one of the many service stations on the boulevard. (Rancho Del Paso Historical Society.)

Three

INFRASTRUCTURES

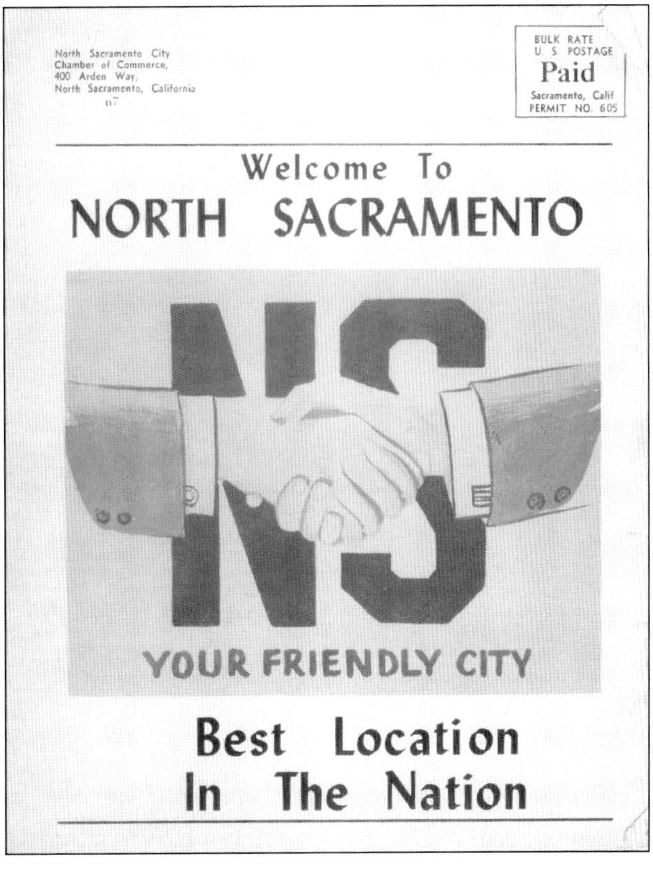

The North Sacramento City Chamber of Commerce published a monthly newsletter. The January 1959 edition featured Norte Del Rio High School and the North Sacramento Police Department. The back cover depicted a white handshake offered to those newcomers the city deemed "desirable." Redlining occurred in small towns like North Sacramento in the years before civil rights legislation where discrimination was covertly practiced. Wendell Echols remembers, "There were places [on Del Paso Boulevard] you knew you were welcomed and places you knew you were not." (Rancho Del Paso Historical Society.)

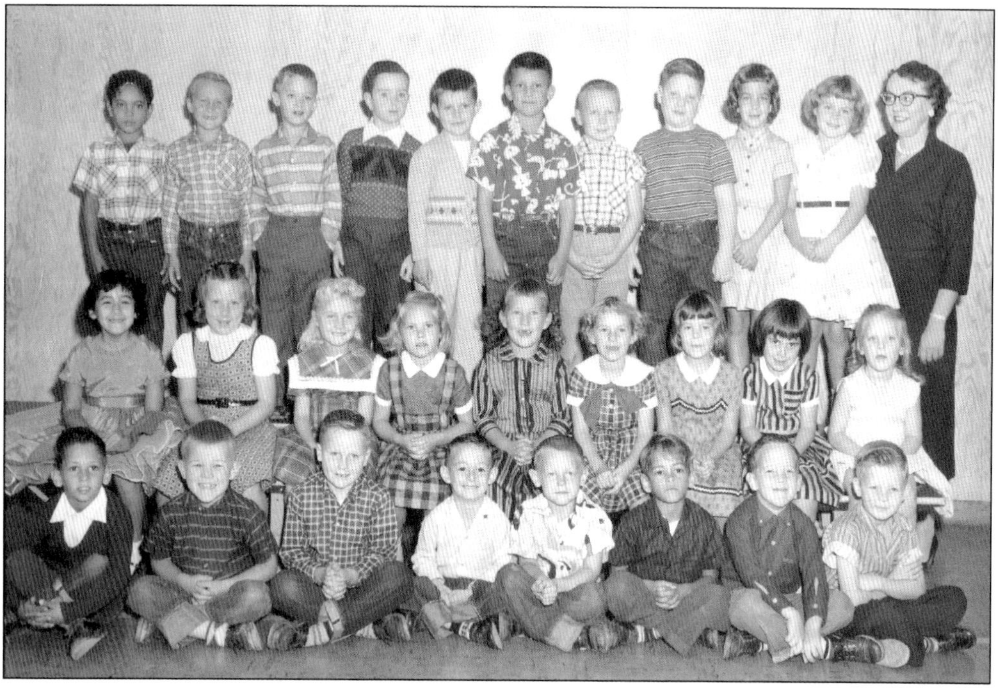

At Woodlake School in the 1950s, Jo Alice Erickson (Nastal), second row third from left, and Robert Slobe, third row center, of North Sacramento Land Company join the other students for the annual school photograph. (Erickson-Nastal.)

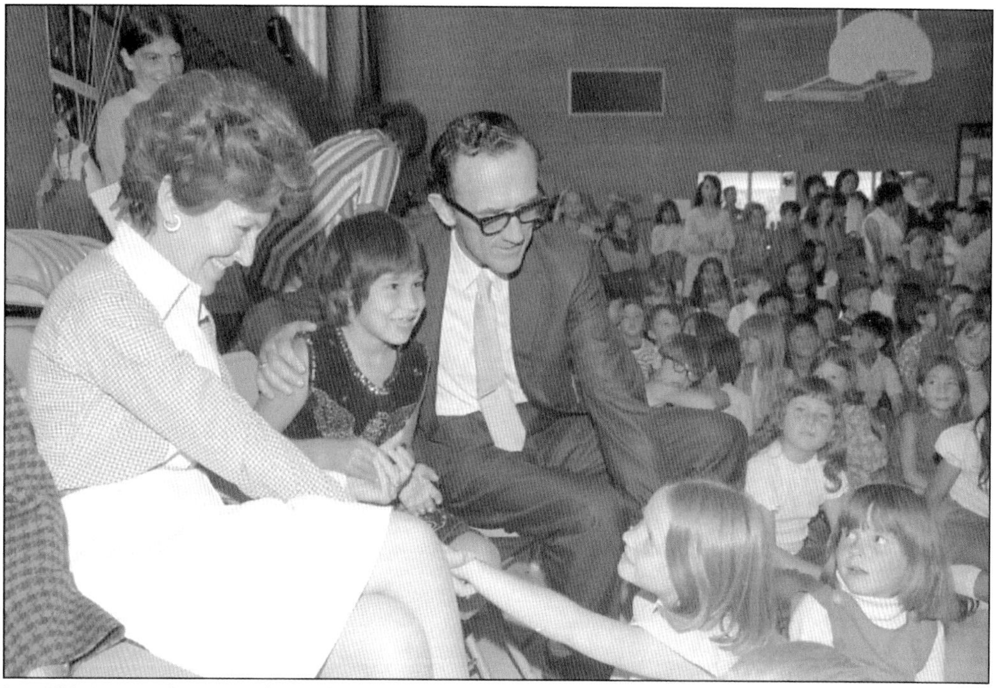

In 1973, Nancy Reagan, the wife of then governor and later president Ronald Reagan, honored the Alethea B. Smythe Elementary School with a visit to the school's Intercultural Day Program. (SAMCC.)

Nancy Reagan responds to students' questions on her visit to Alethea B. Smythe Elementary School on May 14, 1973. The Smythe school band performed for the first lady of California under the direction of James McClure. (SAMCC.)

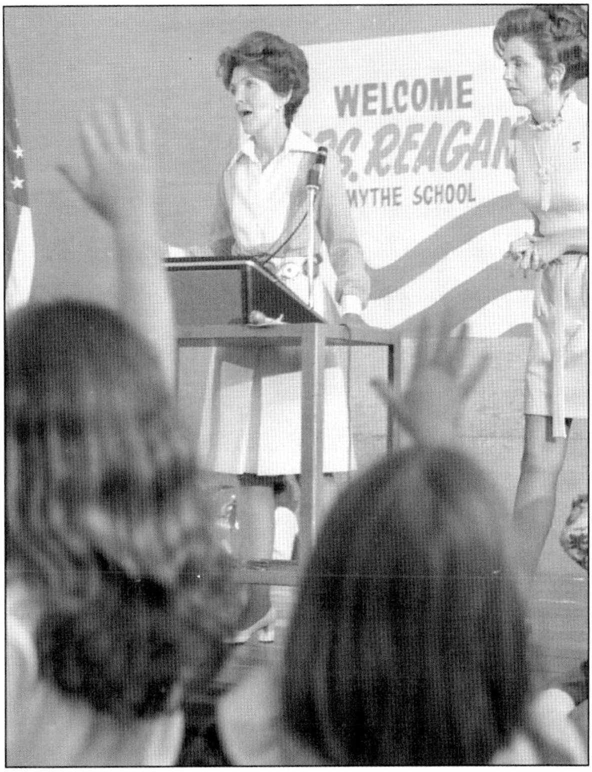

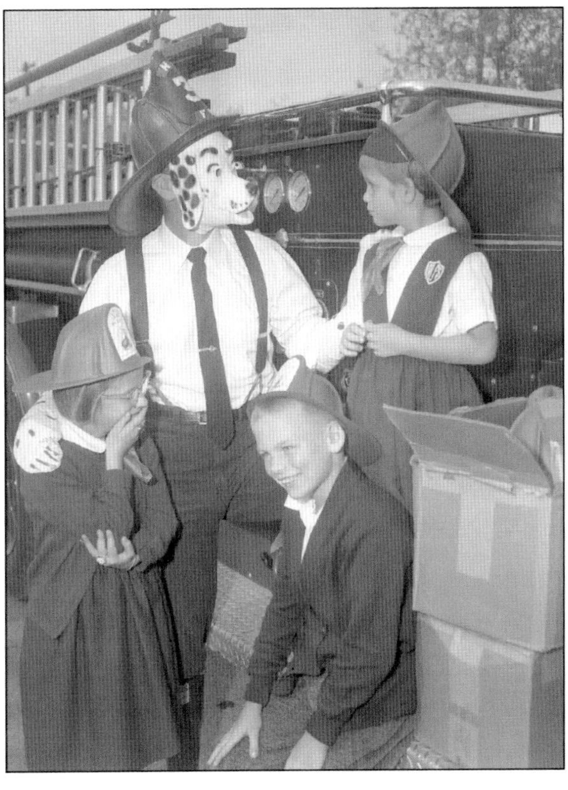

The North Sacramento "Dalmatian" firefighter visits Our Lady of Fatima School of St. Joseph's Parish in North Sacramento. The young students aren't buying the "dog" and recognize the firefighter behind the mask. (SAMCC.)

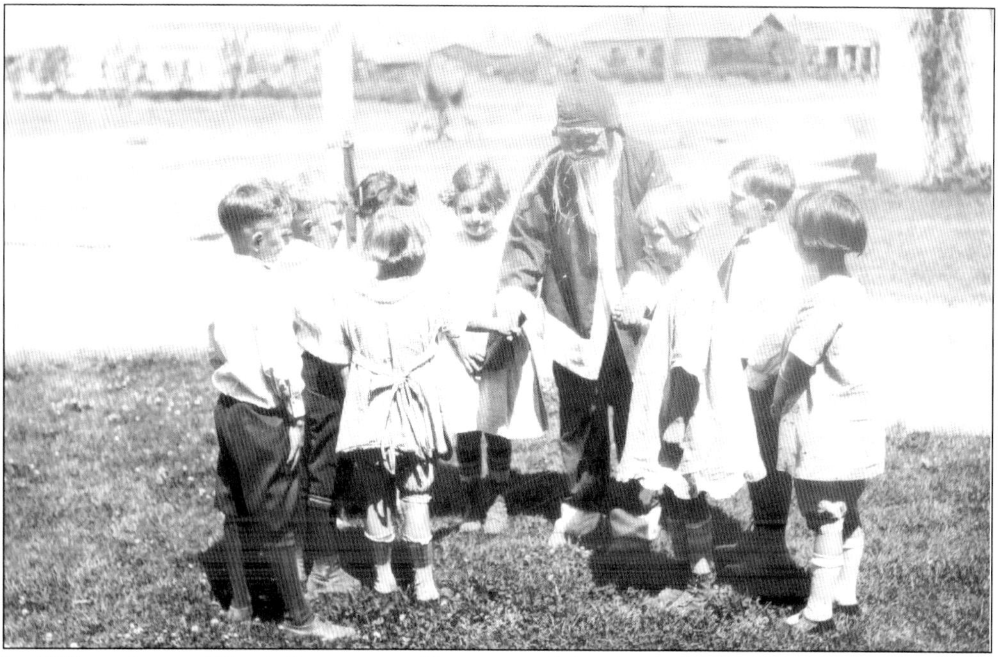

In 1920, students of North Sacramento Elementary School surround Santa Claus. As the first school in the newly formed school district, the area behind the school is undeveloped. (North Sacramento School District.)

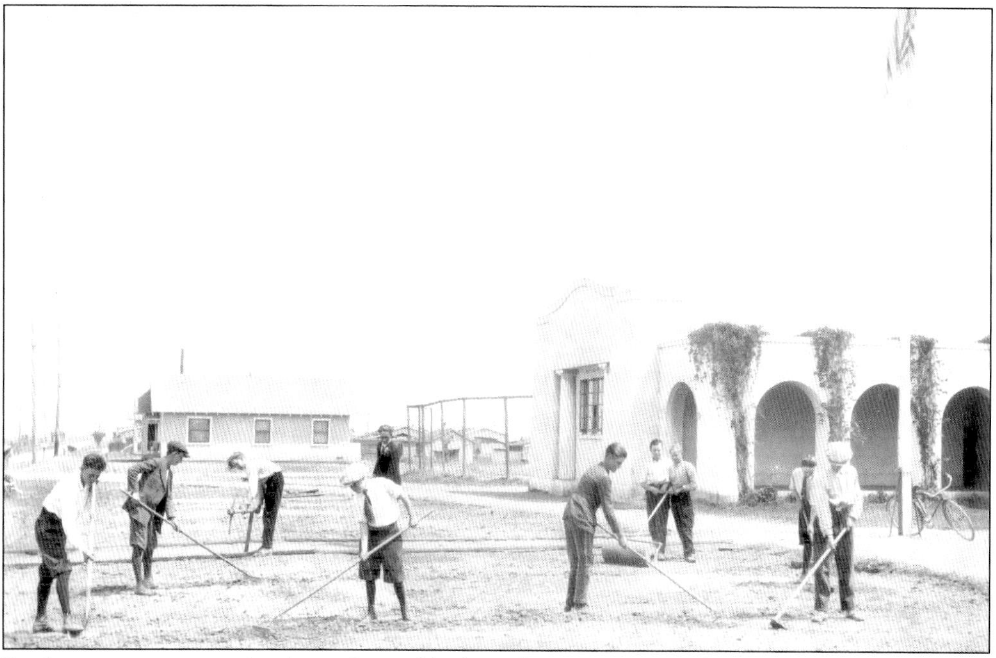

Students are put to task raking the soil before planting grass at the new North Sacramento Elementary School in 1920. Police chief Erskin Fish's family house is in the background. Born in 1913, Margaret Fish Smith, the chief's daughter, remembers as a child being able to see "clear to the American River from her front porch" at 213 Dixieanne Avenue. (North Sacramento School District.)

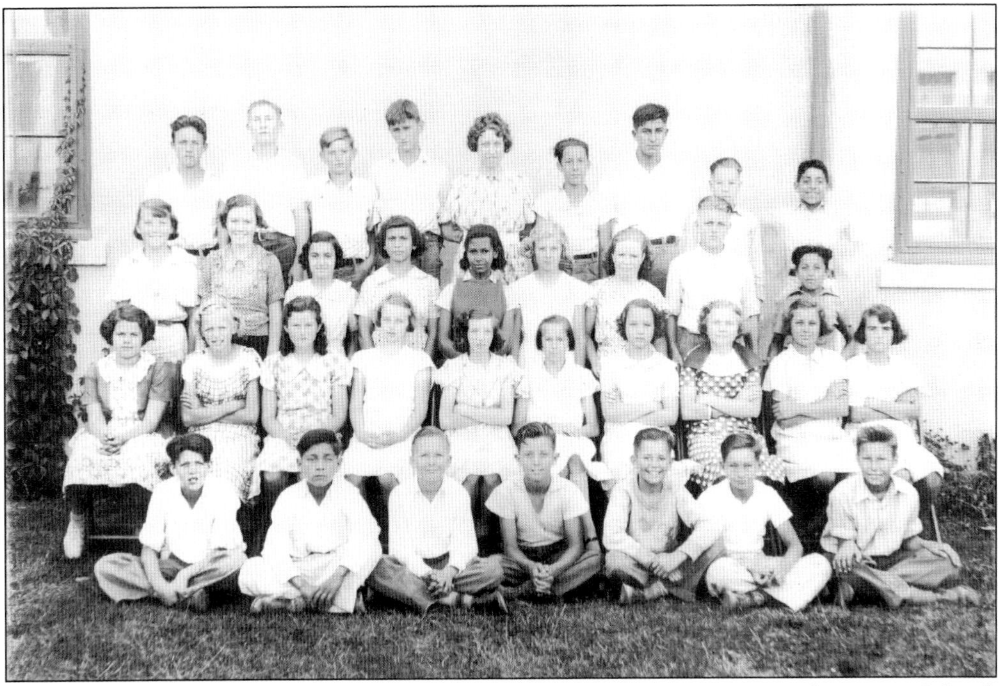

Lois Hansen Nickless remembers her sixth-grade class at North Sacramento Elementary School. In this c. 1930 photograph, from left to right are (first row) Jim Jimenez, Frank Jenning, Bob Gardner, Jack Johanh, Harlow White, Bob Gregg, James Mullick; (second row) Lorraine Miller, Helen Calloway, Ethel Green, Adella Bronsen, Dorothy Sabin, Jeanne Swallow, Laline Slippy, Lois Schneider, Lois Hansen [Nickless], Lois ?; (third row) Iris ?, Margaret Robertson, Dorothy Bousilman, Sara Girmona, Rosie Gonsalves, unidentified, Mary Fields, two unidentified; (fourth row) Jim Runyan, J. C. Duncan, Wallace Hammond, unidentified, Miss Reese [teacher], Bob Bland, John Blass, Lowell ?, and Ralph Baez.

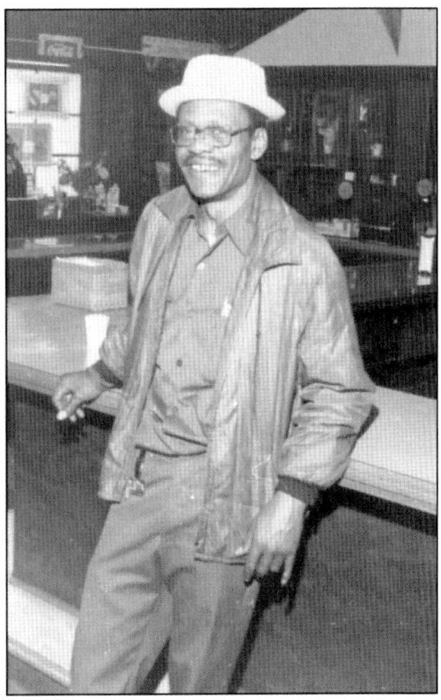

Here is influential North Sacramento resident Wendell Echols at work at Grant Union High School around 1980. (SAMCC.)

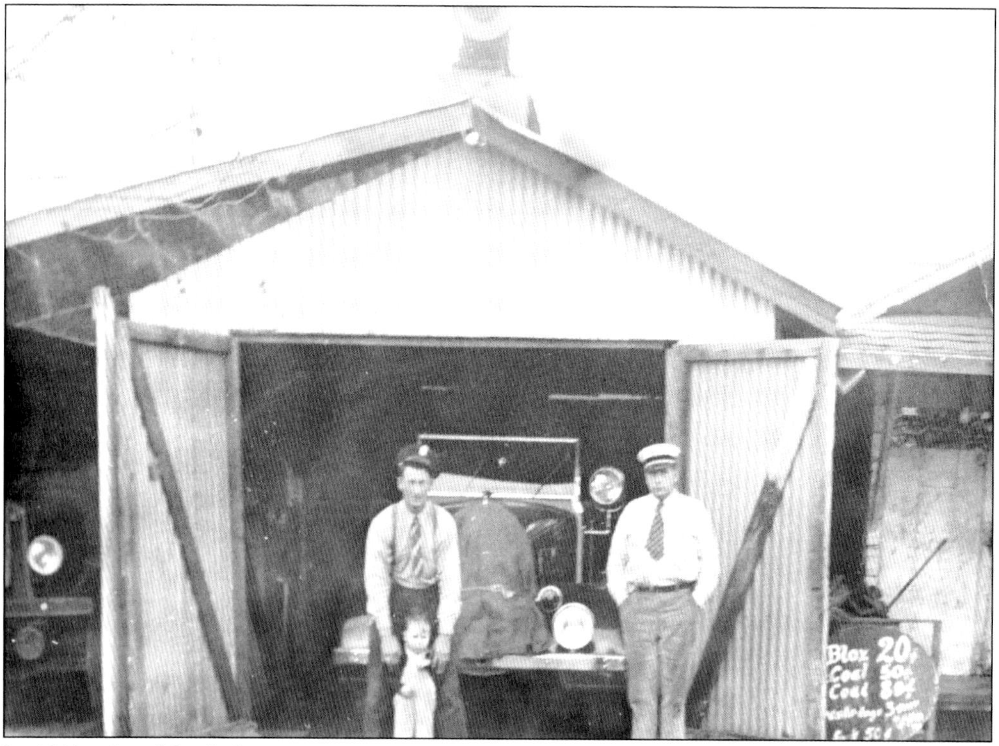

In 1910, when North Sacramento incorporated, a small cadre of volunteer firemen served the needs of the emerging city from their own garages, which housed the fire engines. Note the sign to the right hawking coal for 50¢. (Pioneer Mutual Hook and Ladder Society.)

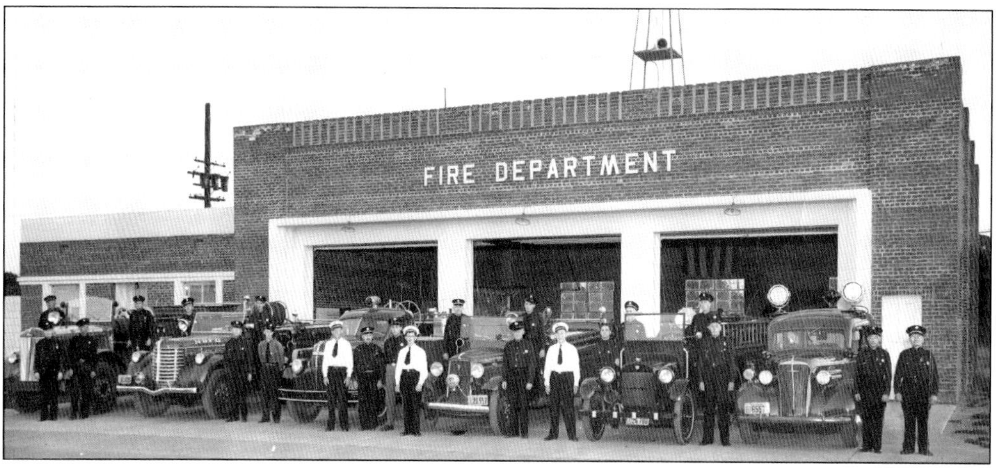

By 1950, not only had the number of firemen quadrupled, but the North Sacramento Fire Department had its own home, a paid fire chief, and two captains. Fire chief Louis Cassaglia is in the center in a white shirt under the letter F. Note the structure above the firehouse—a red light and siren that called the men to duty. The smaller structure on the left was the home of North Sacramento Police Department. A holding cell was located in the back of the firehouse. One North Sacramentan remembers playing hooky and eating ice cream in the "jail" while waiting for her parents to fetch her. (Pioneer Mutual Hook and Ladder Society.)

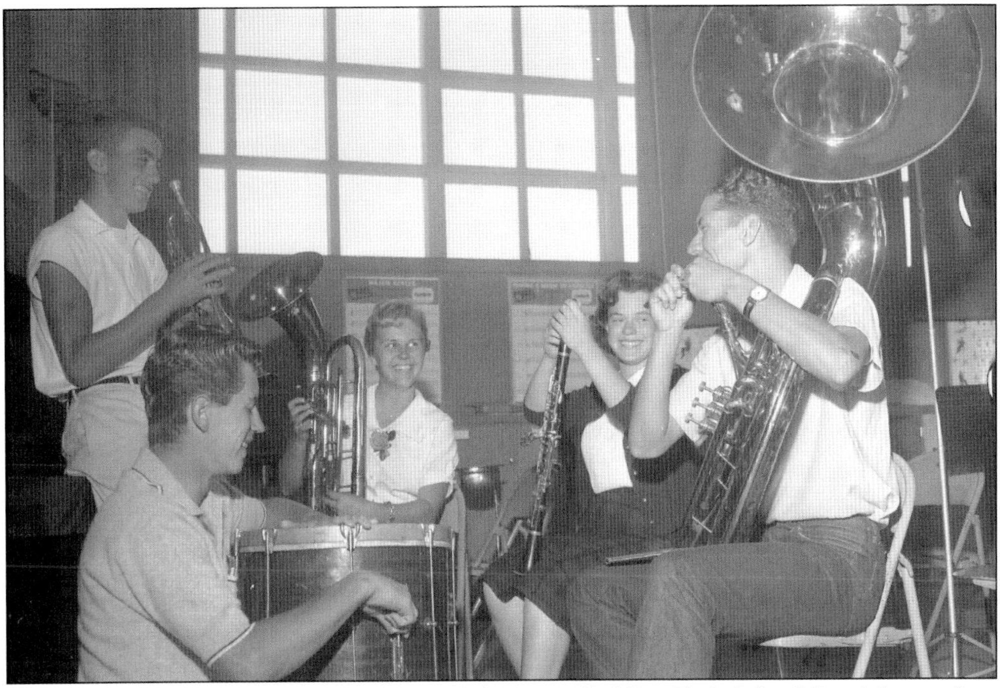

Photographer Neibaur captured the spirit of the Norte Del Rio High School Band during their practice in 1959. Before Norte Del Rio was built, North Sacramentans attended Grant Union High School; and before Grant was built, they attended Sacramento High School. (SAMCC.)

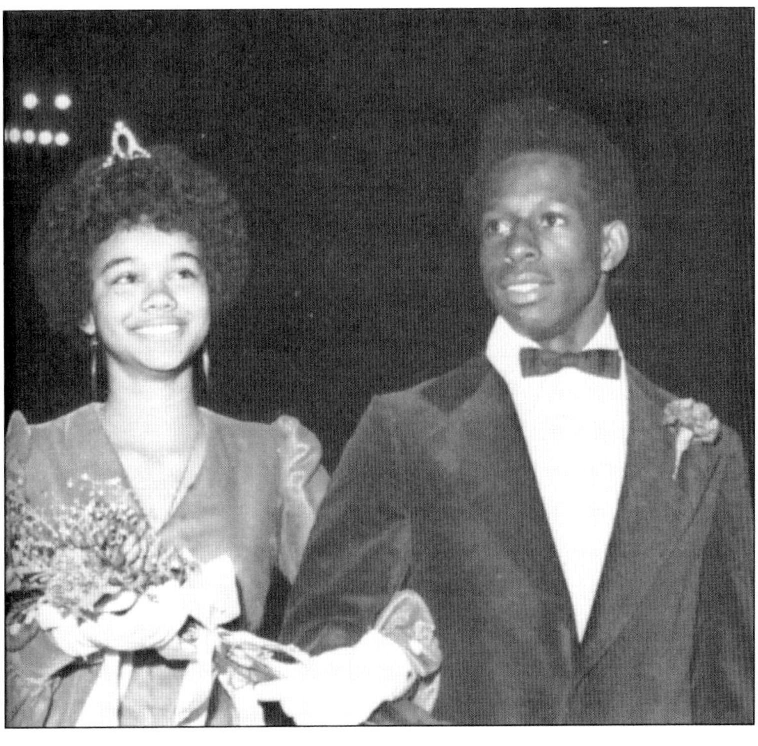

Junior varsity football hero and sophomore homecoming king Raymond Brewer takes the hand of his lovely homecoming queen at Norte Del Rio High School in 1972. (Grant Union High School Museum.)

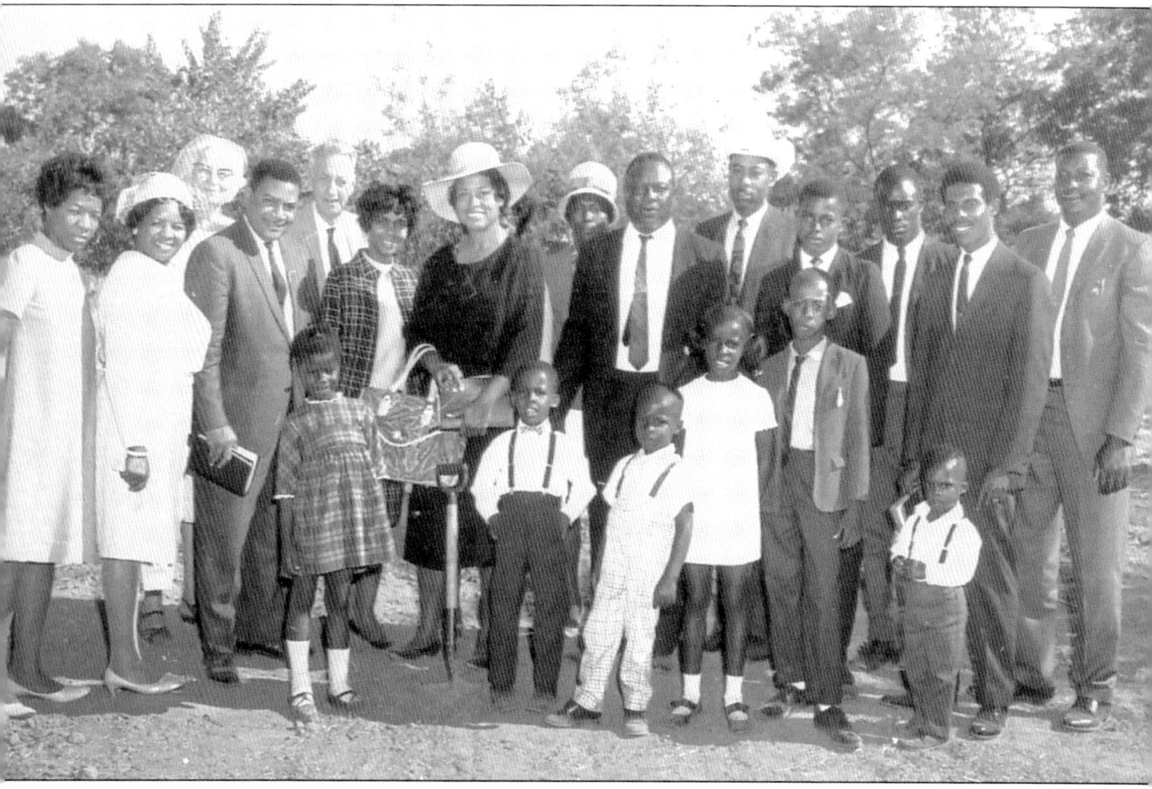

This moment was captured during the c. 1960 ground-breaking ceremony for the Mt. Moriah Baptist Church in the north area. (SAMCC.)

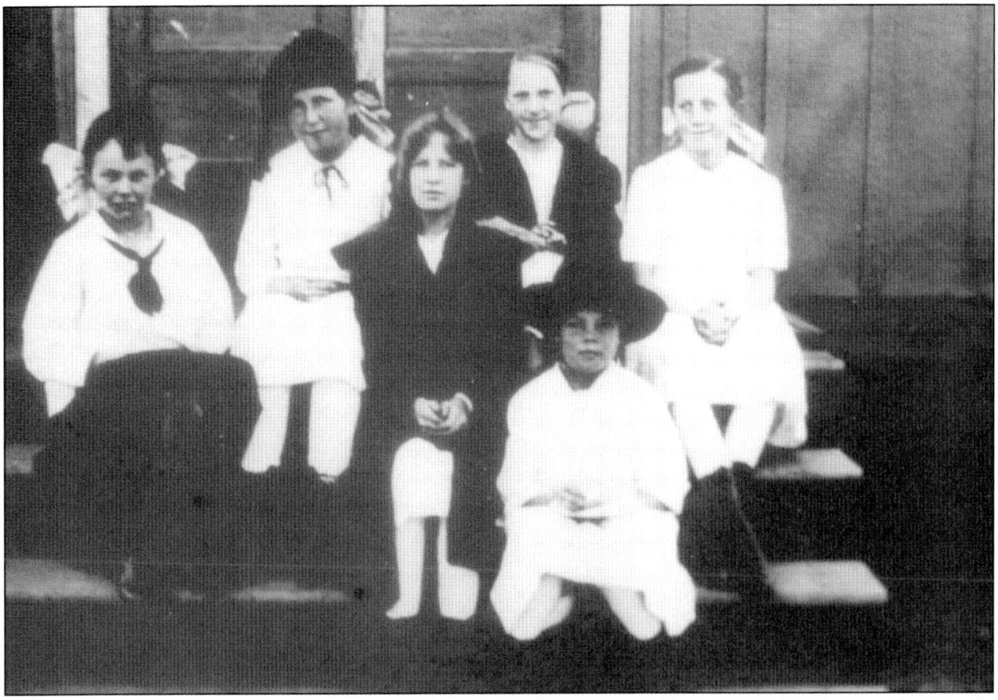

The 1918 Sunday school class sits outside the Epworth Social Hall on Cantalier Street. Originally known as Epworth Methodist Church in 1918, the congregation changed its name in 1950 to North Sacramento First Methodist Church and in 1952 to the current name, North Sacramento United Methodist Church. (North Sacramento United Methodist Church.)

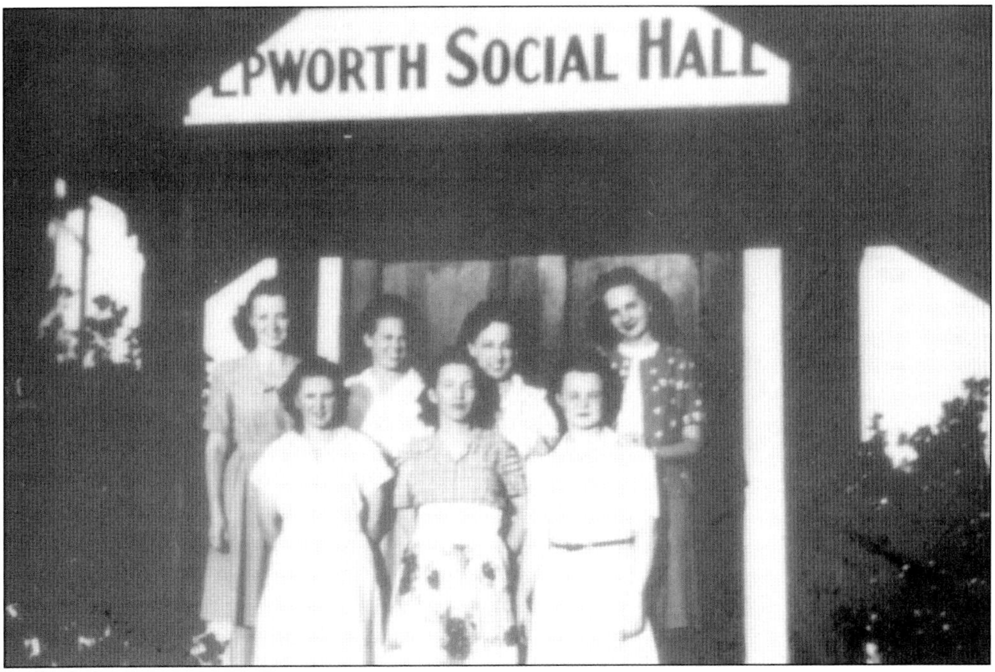

In 1949, a Sunday school class stands on Cantalier Street outside the Epworth Social Hall, which was added in 1926. (North Sacramento United Methodist Church.)

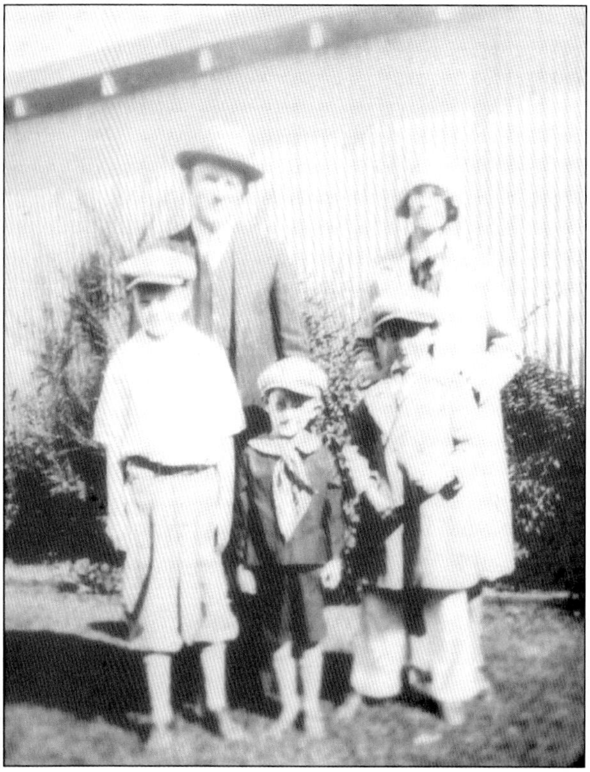

In 1929, Pastor Charles H. Stephens and family stand outside the social hall, which was added in 1926. (North Sacramento United Methodist Church.)

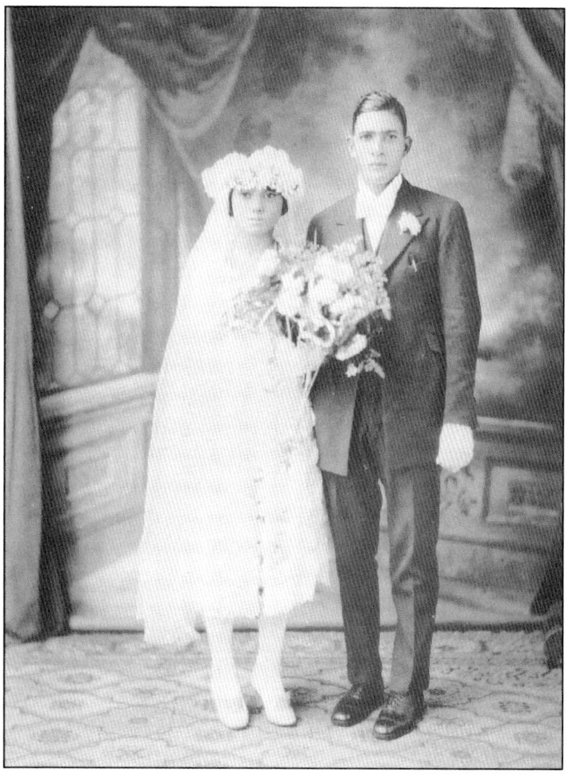

St. Joseph's Catholic Parish was established in 1924. On January 15, 1927, Mr. and Mrs. John DaVega wed in the first church of St. Joseph's Parish, a little stucco building at Linden Avenue and Del Paso Boulevard that later served as the parish hall. The present church located at 1717 El Monte Avenue in North Sacramento was completed in 1935. The parish school, Our Lady of Fatima Catholic School, opened in 1947. (St. Joseph's Parish.)

In 1949, the Epworth Community Church steeple was demolished in preparation for the new building. Epworth Methodist is renamed First Methodist Church. (North Sacramento United Methodist Church.)

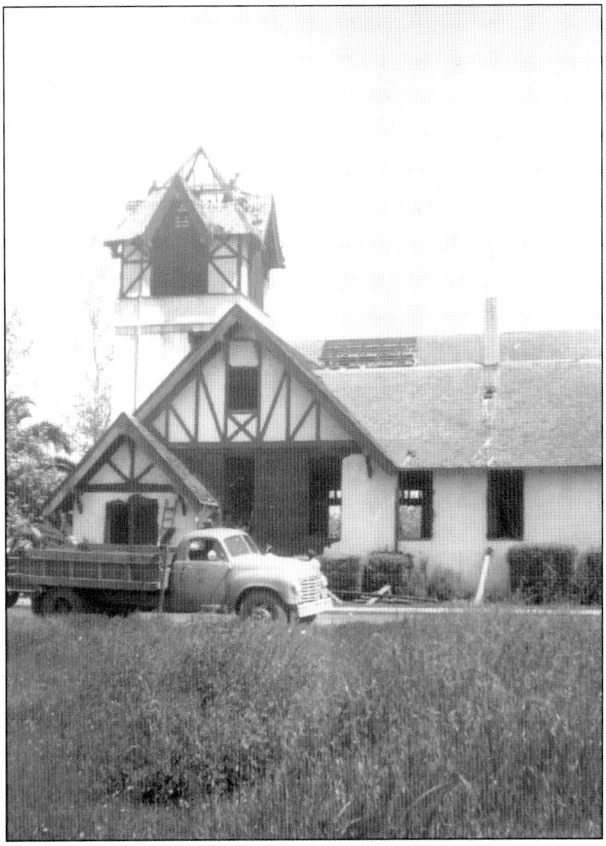

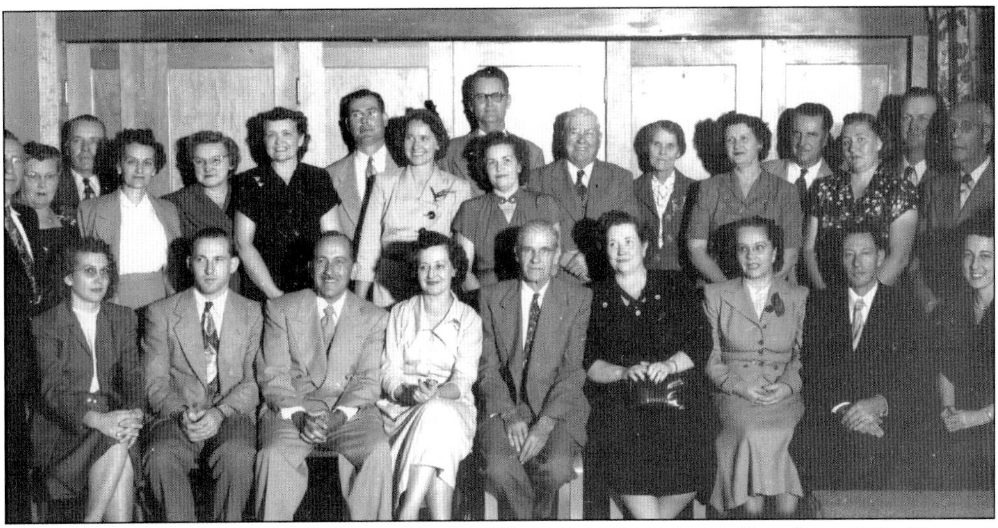

Members congregate inside the Social Hall of Epworth Community Church in 1949. Pictured from left to right are (first row) Dorothea Tribble, Don Tribble, Ed Lindley, Paula Lindley, Mr. Dukes, Daisy Brillhart, unidentified, Bob Hicks, and Thelma Hicks; (second row) six unidentifed congregants, Mr. Seely, Mrs. Doryce Seely, Rev. Don Fleming, unidentified, W. M. Burlingame, Mrs. Burlingame, Mrs. Devine, and four unidentified people. (Thelma Hicks, North Sacramento United Methodist Church.)

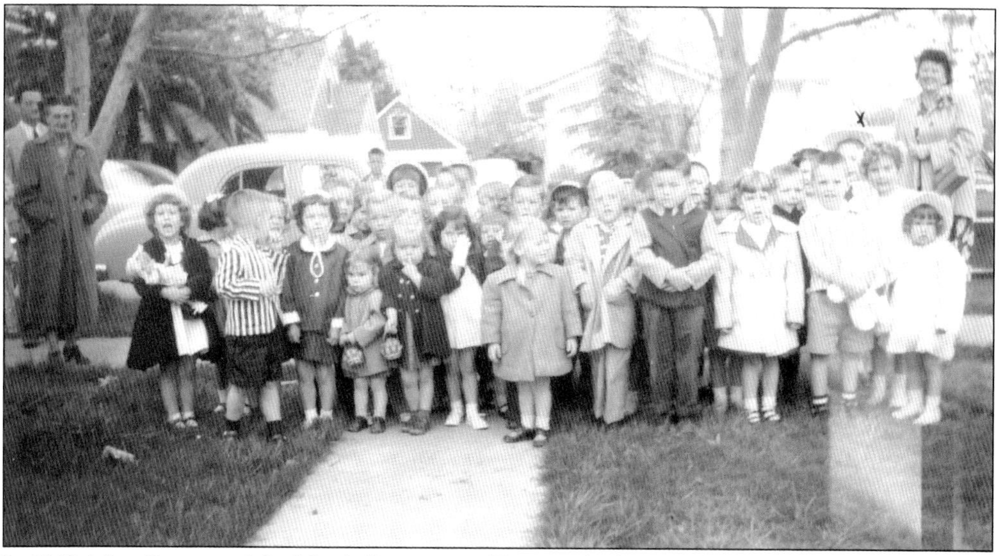

In 1949, Mary Sartar and the North Sacramento First Methodist Sunday School class stand outside a home in Woodlake. The church's name was Epworth Methodist. Today it is United Methodist. (North Sacramento United Methodist Church.)

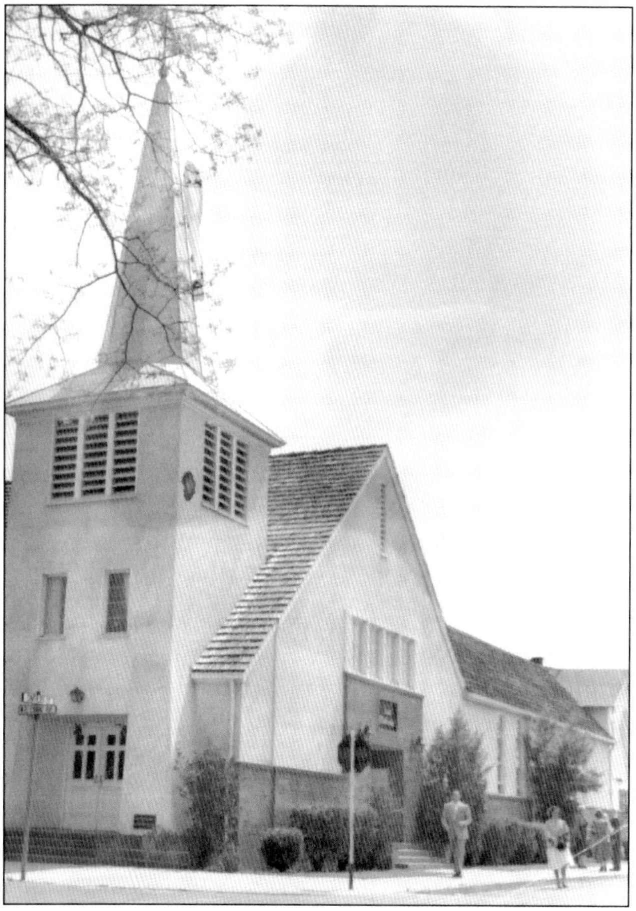

With architects Charles F. Dean and Ivan C. Satterlee, the Erickson Construction Company rebuilt the First Methodist Church of North Sacramento in 1954 on El Camino Avenue and Cantalier Street. (North Sacramento United Methodist Church.)

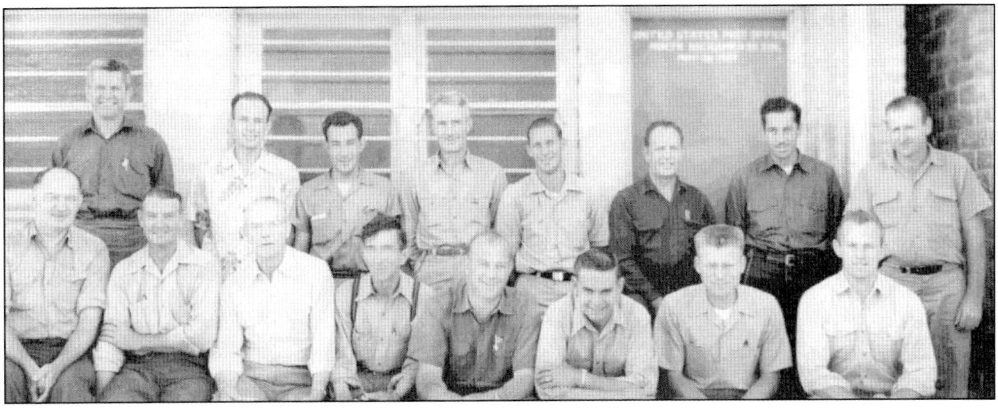

Volunteer fireman Pete (Emydius) Tellers joins his comrades as a postman at his paying job at the Royal Oaks U.S. Post Office in North Sacramento, the site of the old Essex Pencil Factory, on May 28, 1954. Pictured from left to right are (first row) Russell Hays, Manley Harris, Clarence Cushman, Percy Huff, Wayne Hansen, Bob McDonald, Pete Tellers, Jay Jensen; (second row) Woodrow Scott, Tom Valentine, Luis Guitenez, Lyle Buys, Art Griggs, Cecil Parks, Joe Petrie, and Ed Waszak. (Tellers.)

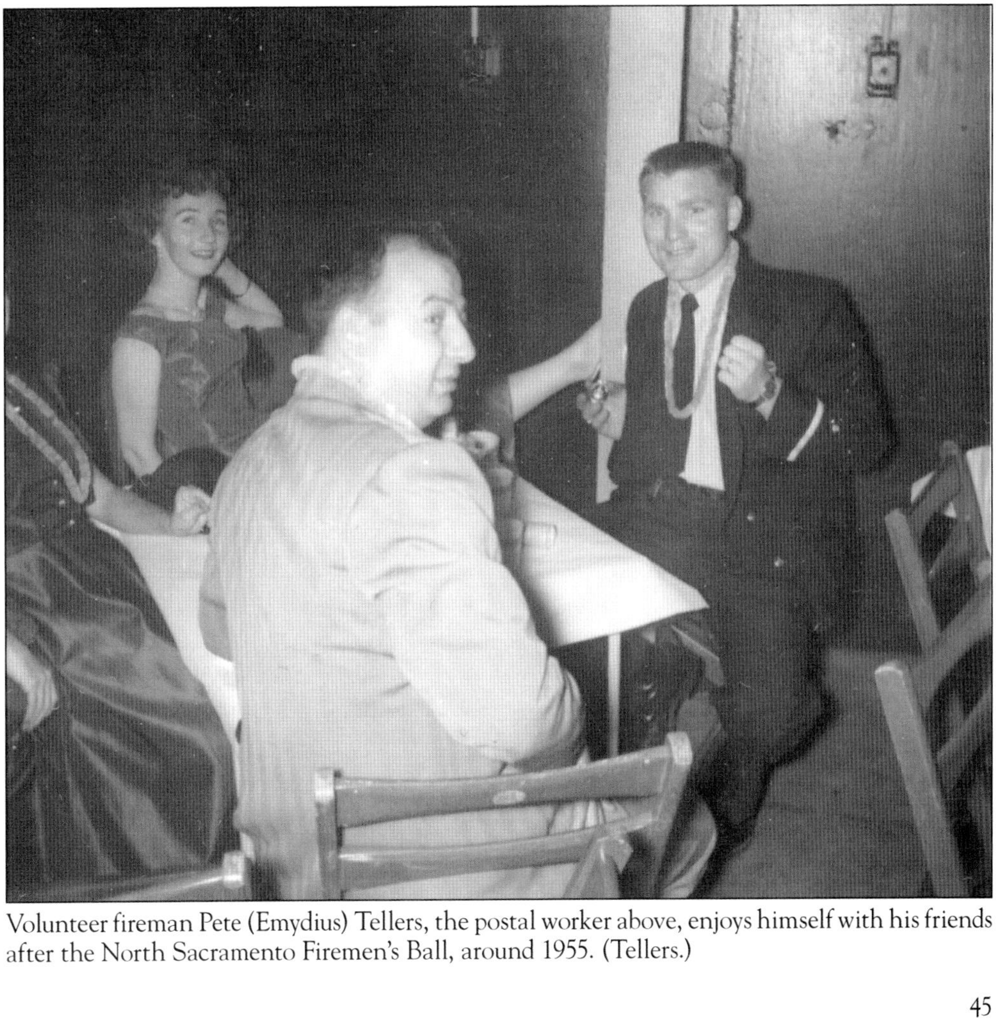

Volunteer fireman Pete (Emydius) Tellers, the postal worker above, enjoys himself with his friends after the North Sacramento Firemen's Ball, around 1955. (Tellers.)

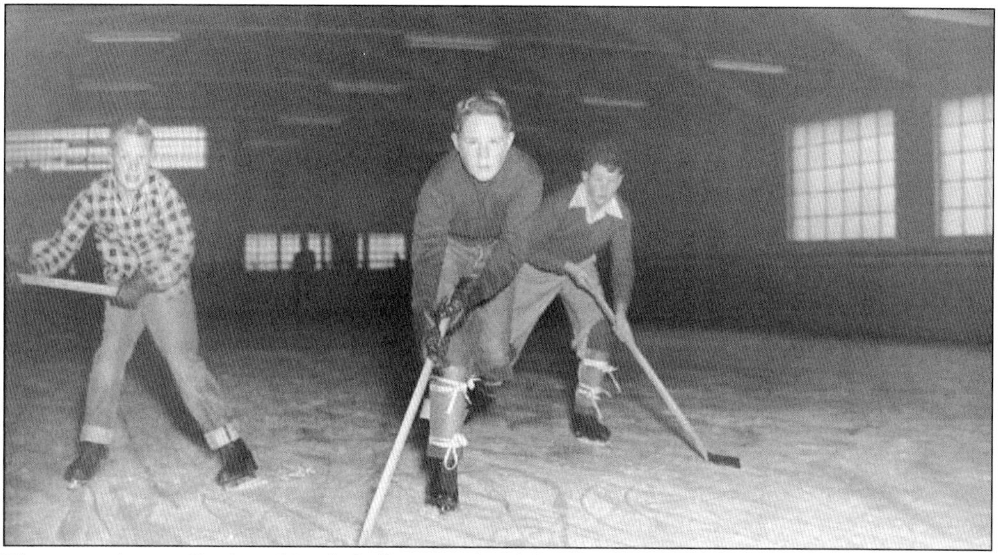

Three youths in a Stick and Puck drill session head for the goal at Iceland on Del Paso Boulevard in 1948. Iceland was nominated to be listed on the National Register of Historic Places. In March 2010, the location, which has seen the likes of Max Baer, Ronald Reagan, local weddings, countless ice hockey games and figure skating events over its 70 years of existence as a meeting spot in North Sacramento fell victim to a possible arson fire. Chris Lord, manager and owner of Iceland along with the Kerth family, states that North Sacramentans are rallying to rebuild the historic site beyond its past splendor. Perhaps the new Iceland will incorporate the fountain on the landmark "Iceland" pylon, as originally envisioned by architect Charles Dean in 1940. (Kerth.)

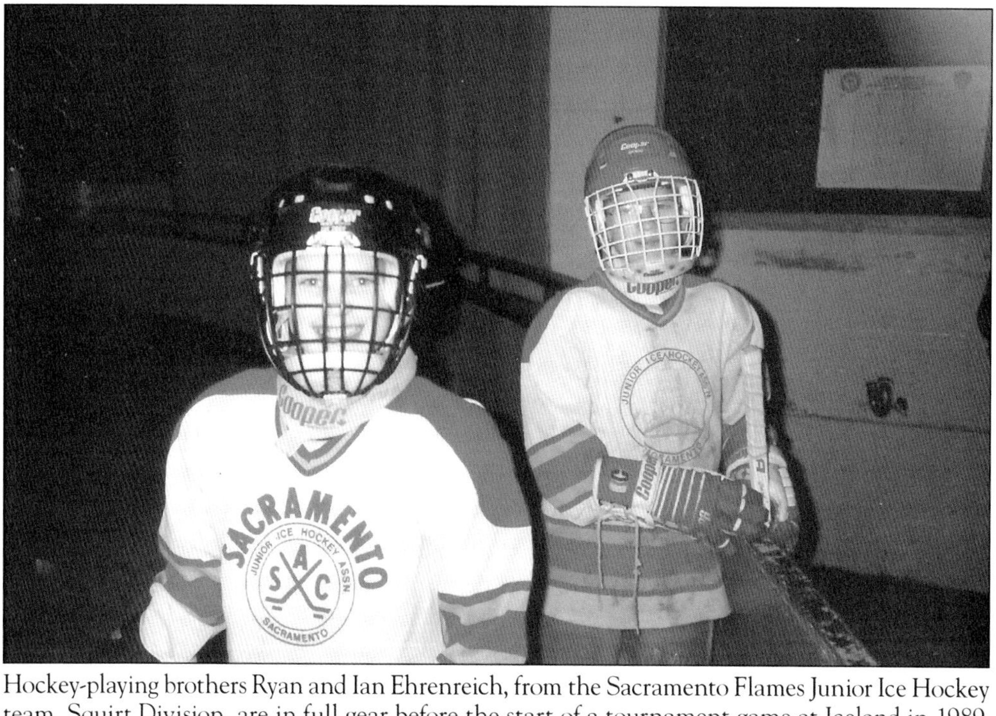

Hockey-playing brothers Ryan and Ian Ehrenreich, from the Sacramento Flames Junior Ice Hockey team, Squirt Division, are in full gear before the start of a tournament game at Iceland in 1989. (Ehrenreich-Risner.)

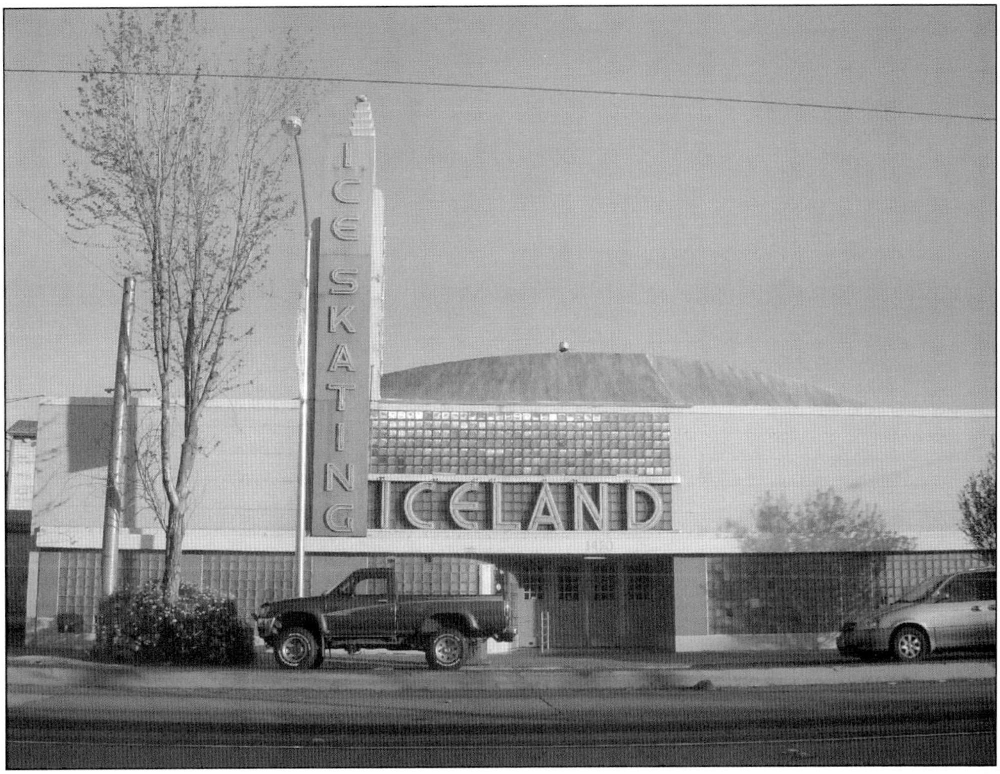

This 2008 photograph shows Iceland at 1430 Del Paso Boulevard before the tragic fire in March 2010. Over 500 North Sacramentans joined in the effort to clean up the debris after the fire, vowing to rebuild Iceland. Note the pylon with the words "Ice Skating" and the structure above, which was originally intended in 1940 by noted architect Charles Dean to be the fountain depicted below. (Ehrenreich-Risner.)

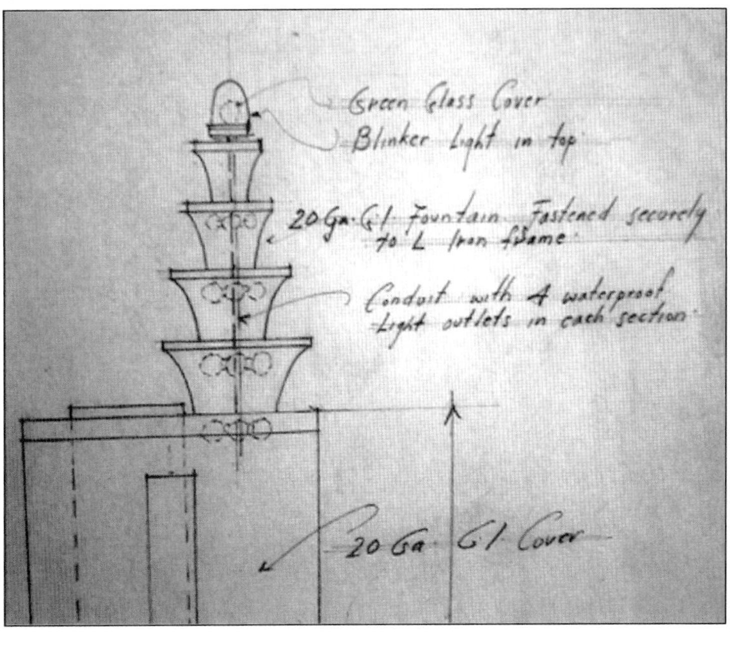

In 1939, Charles Dean of the firm Dean and Dean, who designed the Crest Theatre, included the three-tiered fountain to embellish the pylon atop Iceland. Due to limited finances, this extra feature was excluded from the final plan. (SAMCC.)

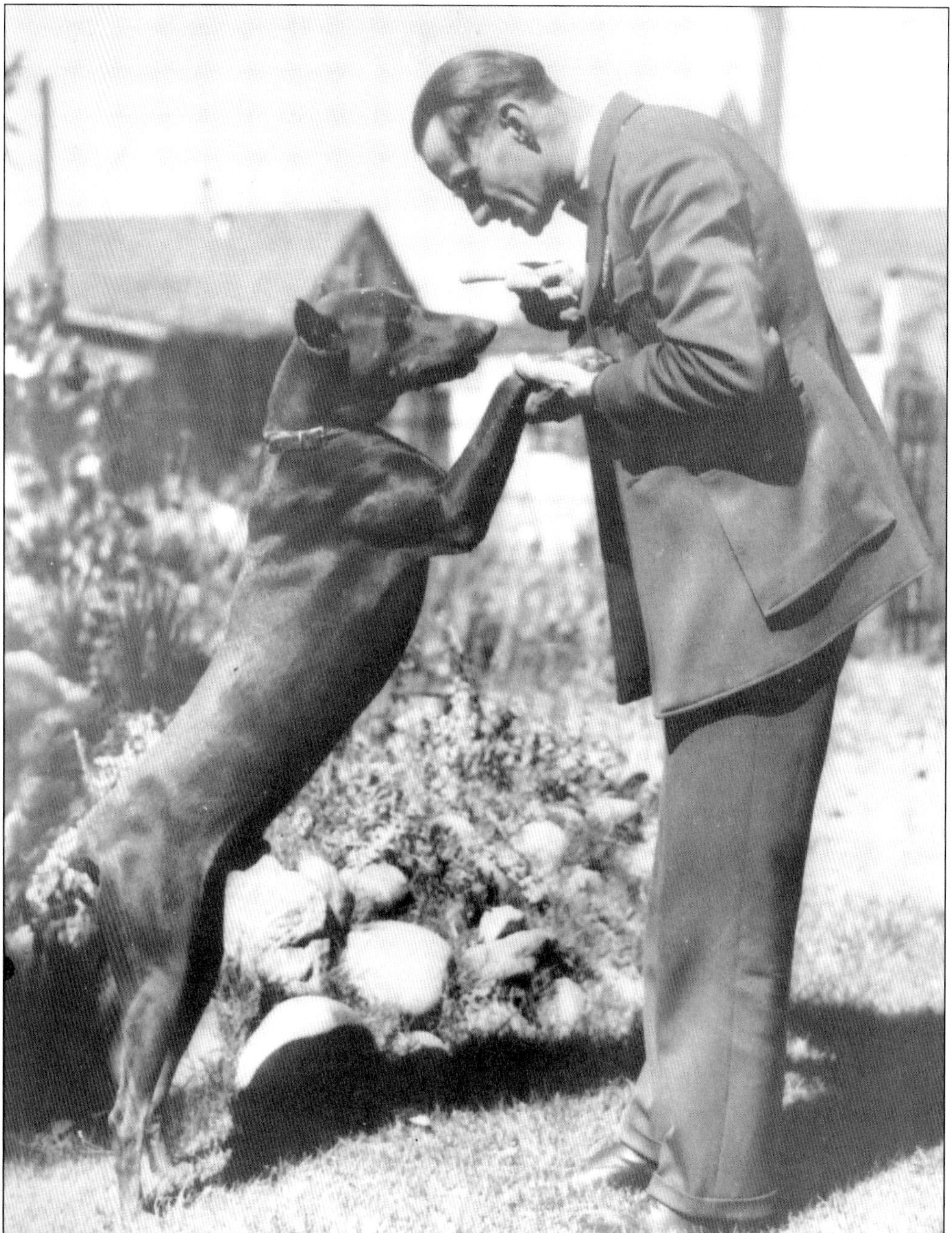

North Sacramento police chief Erskin George Fish give his dog, Pincho, a gentle but firm command outside the Fish home on Dixieanne Avenue. While on duty in 1935, Chief Fish was fatally shot by a robber. All the city's flags flew at half mast in his memory. Margaret, his daughter, was 22 at the time and about to deliver his first grandchild. Erskin and his wife, May Giffen, came from Red Bluff, California. He owned a Union Oil service station at Beaumont and Del Paso Boulevard and was recruited by the locals to serve as police chief, since he had worked as an engineer. A tree was planted in his honor, across from the police and fire department off Arden Way, and continues to be tended by the Woodlake Garden Club. (Fish Smith.)

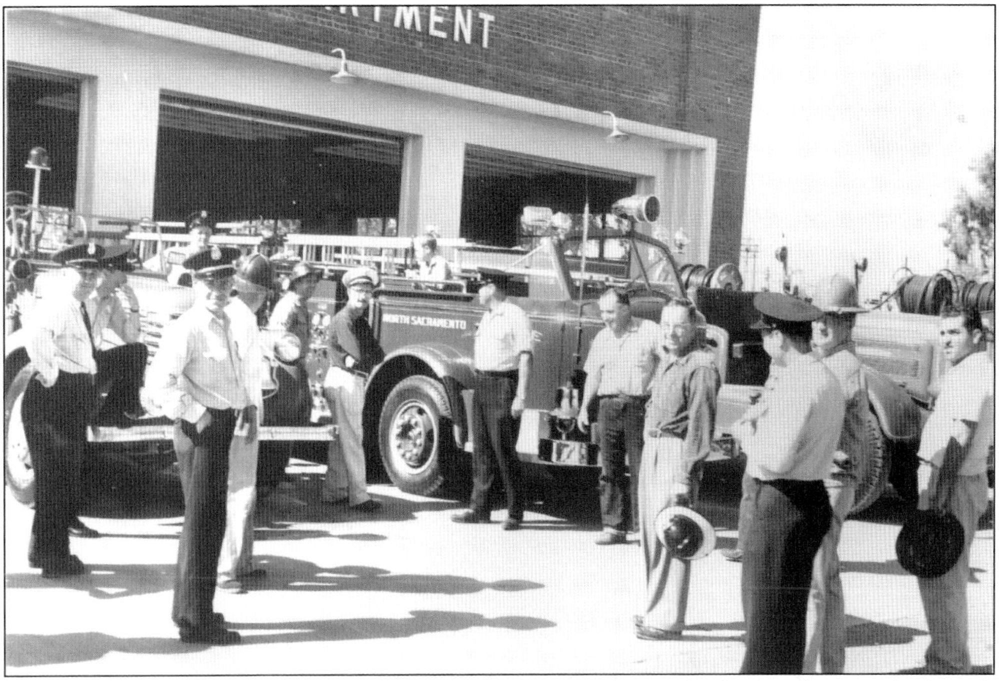

Chief Louis Cassaglia (center in the white cap); Mayor Olga Roth's husband, Capt. Fred Roth (with glasses and holding the fire helmet); and the rest of the North Sacramento firemen smile for the camera while sprucing up the fire engines on the weekly clean-up schedule. (Edward Gardiner Collection, Pioneer Mutual Hook and Ladder Society.)

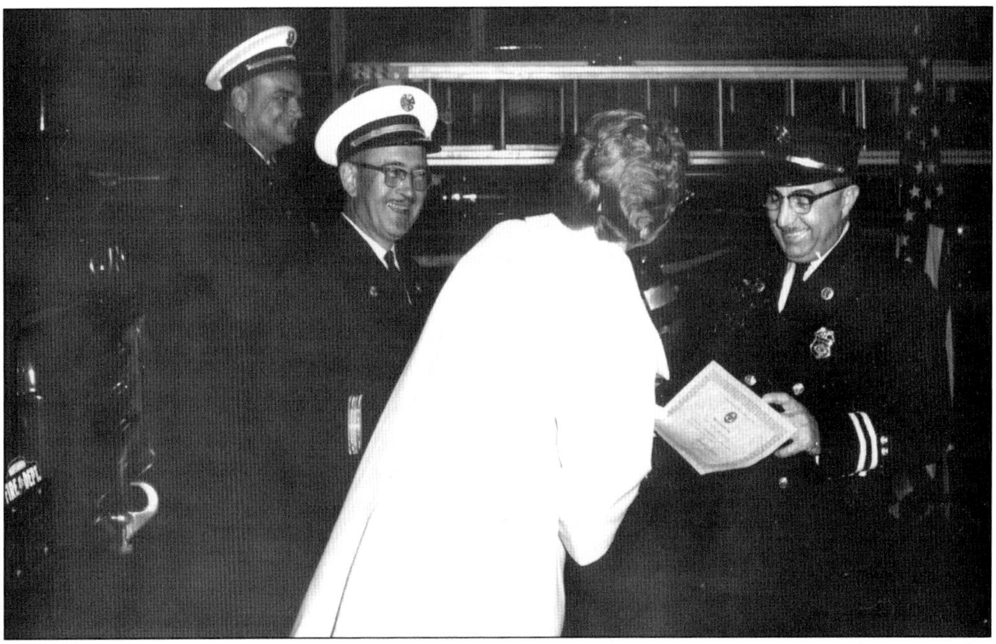

Capt. Fred Roth of the North Sacramento Fire Department was among 26 firemen who received certificates upon completion of a radiological training course around 1962. The woman presenting him the award is Mayor Roth's wife. Nearby are assistant chief Warren Jones and Louis Cassaglia, chief. (Roth.)

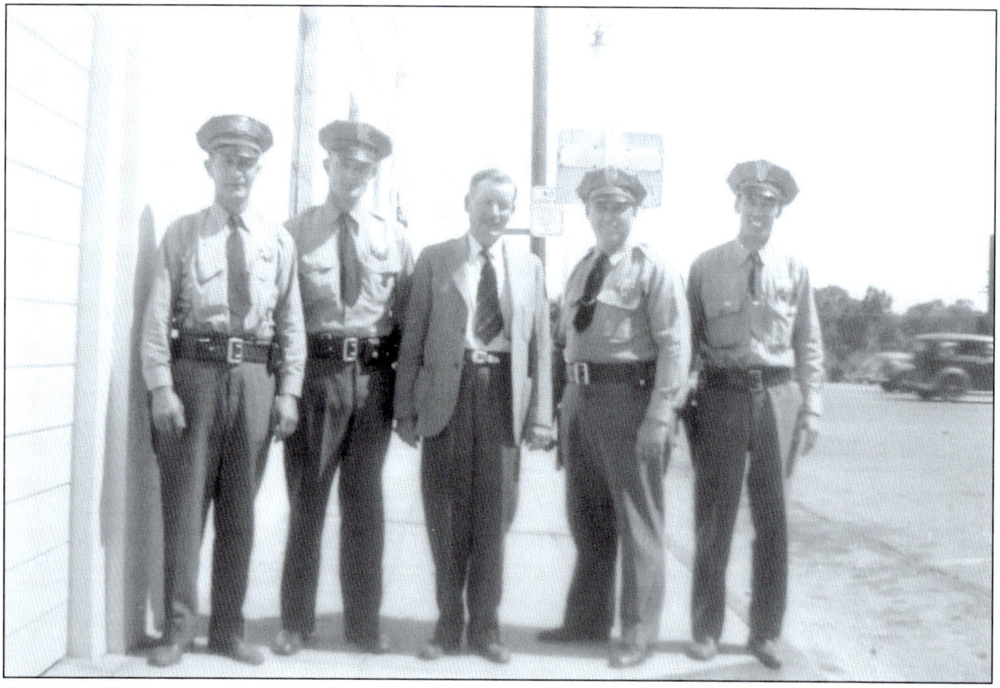

A young Percy Gassaway stands at the far right next to police chief Bill Wilson and North Sacramento police officers on Del Paso Boulevard around 1945. (Erickson-Nastal.)

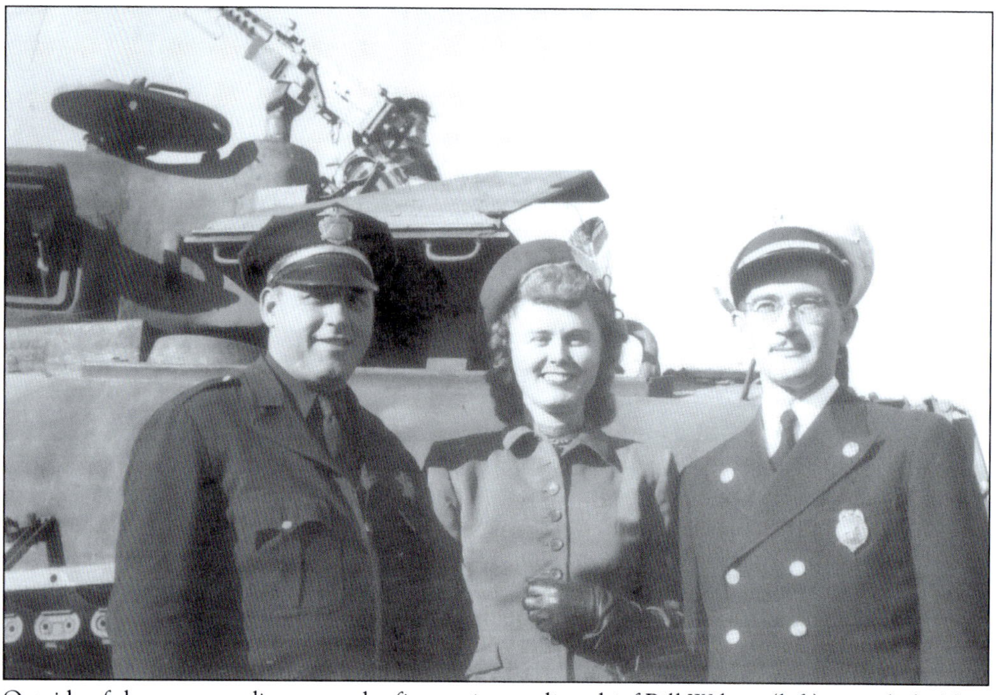

Outside of the armory adjacent to the fire station, police chief Bill Wilson (left), city clerk Alice Johnson (center), and fire chief Louis Cassaglia pose for the camera. (Erickson-Nastal.)

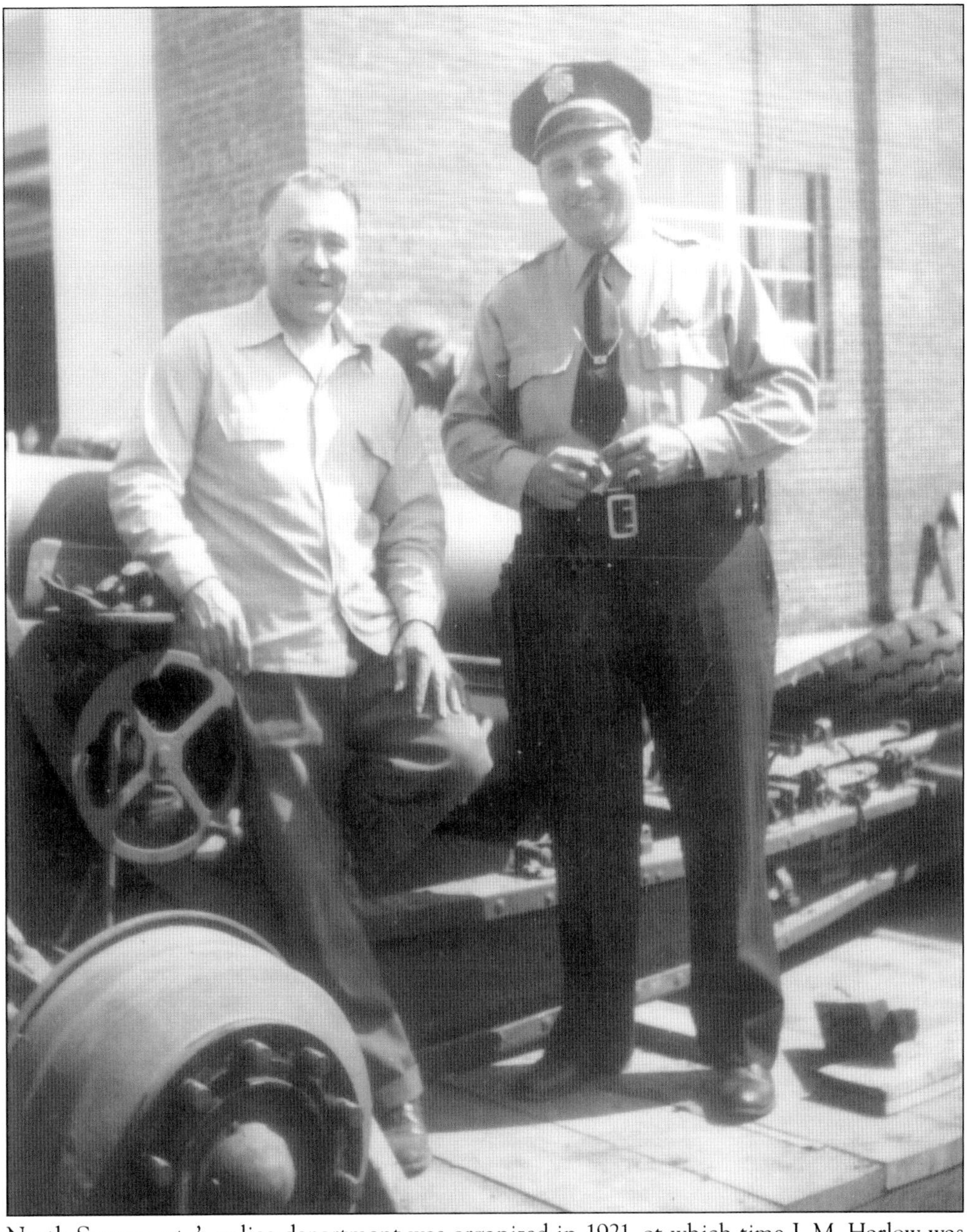

North Sacramento's police department was organized in 1921, at which time J. M. Harlow was appointed town marshall. The North Sacramento Police Department remained a one-man department until 1935, when Chief Erskin G. Fish was shot on August 11 in the line of duty. His assistant, William F. Wilson, became police chief, and soon Percy Gassaway was appointed to the force as patrolman. The department was initially at 1501 Del Paso Boulevard at the location of the current Wells Fargo Bank. In 1949, the NSPD moved adjacent to the fire house on Arden Way (formerly Bassetlaw), which held a one-man cell. On January 2, 1953, Gassaway and officer Francis M. (Jack) Rhea answered a call. Officer Rhea was fatally shot in the head during a running gun battle with a bandit. A plaque in Woodlake Park commemorates both his and Erskin Fish's sacrifice. (Erickson-Nastal.)

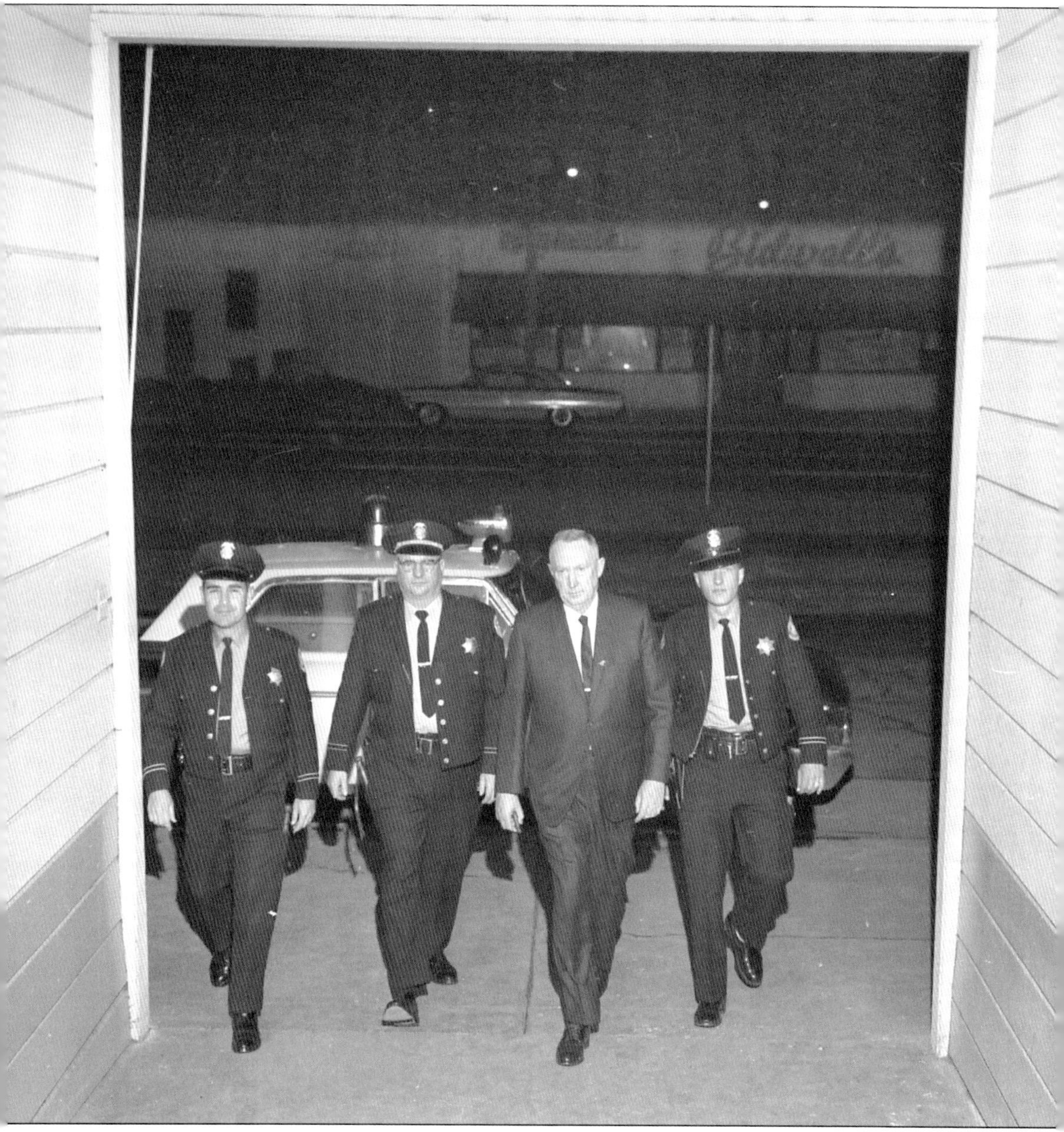

On December 31, 1964, at 11:59 p.m., the City of Sacramento took over the City of North Sacramento after a contentious fight including several elections and a court battle. The North Sacramento Chamber of Commerce remains a robust entity, and redevelopment of the city continues. (SAMCC.)

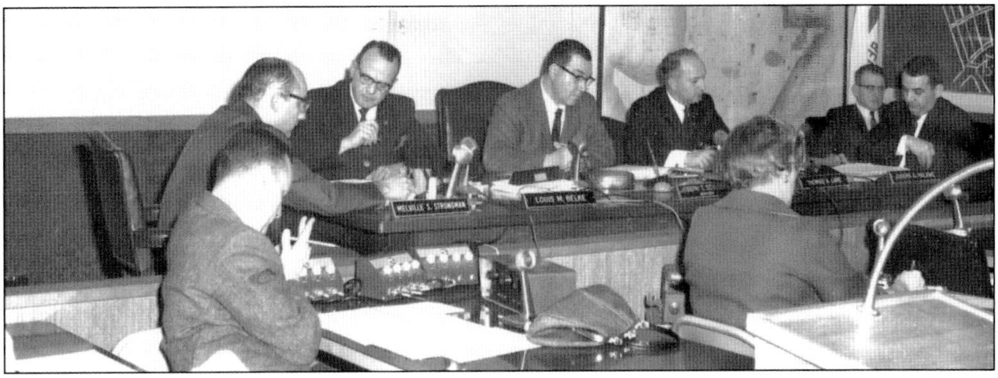

The North Sacramento City Council held its last regular meeting on December 28, 1964, before merging with the City of Sacramento. Pictured clockwise starting from the bottom left on the dais are councilman Melville S. Strongman, councilman Louis Belke, Mayor Joseph T. Schlegel, councilman Thomas A. Lane, unidentified man in the back, councilman Joseph G. Halawe, and city clerk Wilma Briggs (at the top table). When she was nine, Susan Strongman-Drake, daughter of Councilman Strongman, remembers thinking that "my dad was going to jail (he had put his "affairs" in order so that he could be absent for a period of time) because the city council was ordered by the court to vote for the annexation. It was a heated debate; my dad voted against the annexation but, ultimately, the proposal was passed by one vote (Louis Belke, who had been against the annexation and was expected to vote against annexation, changed his vote at the last minute). It was an emotionally charged evening that I remember like it was yesterday. And it followed a contentious election including a recount of the ballots (because the vote was so close), threats, accusations of all sorts . . . anyway, it was an interesting time." (Halawe.)

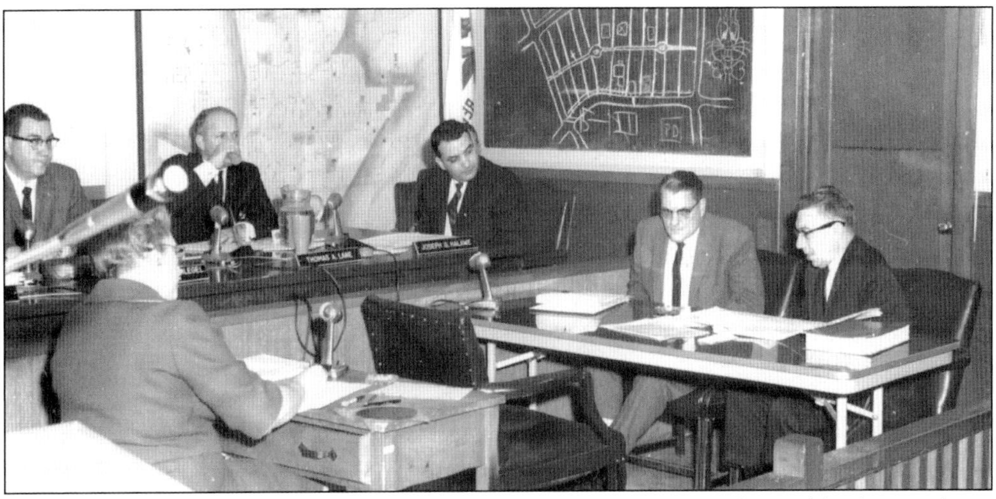

In attendance, pictured clockwise, are city clerk Wilma Briggs, Mayor Joseph T. Schlegel, councilman Thomas A. Lane, councilman Joseph G. Halawe, city attorney Raymond McClure, and city manager William H. Cunningham. In favor of the merger, Mayor Schlegel stated, "The civil war is over. Let's get down and work to make this a better community." Wilma Briggs, city clerk, opposed the merger. "We are proud, whether we were for or against the merger, that there is a lack of apathy among our citizens." A final resolution was adopted requesting the City of Sacramento to accept and preserve as a permanent memorial the badges of police chief Erskin G. Fish (killed August 11, 1935) and officer Jack Rhea (killed January 3, 1954). An obituary was written by the Committee for the City of North Sacramento, which read, "A lady died on August 19 at approximately 10:30 a.m.," when the final votes for the contested merger were counted. (Halawe.)

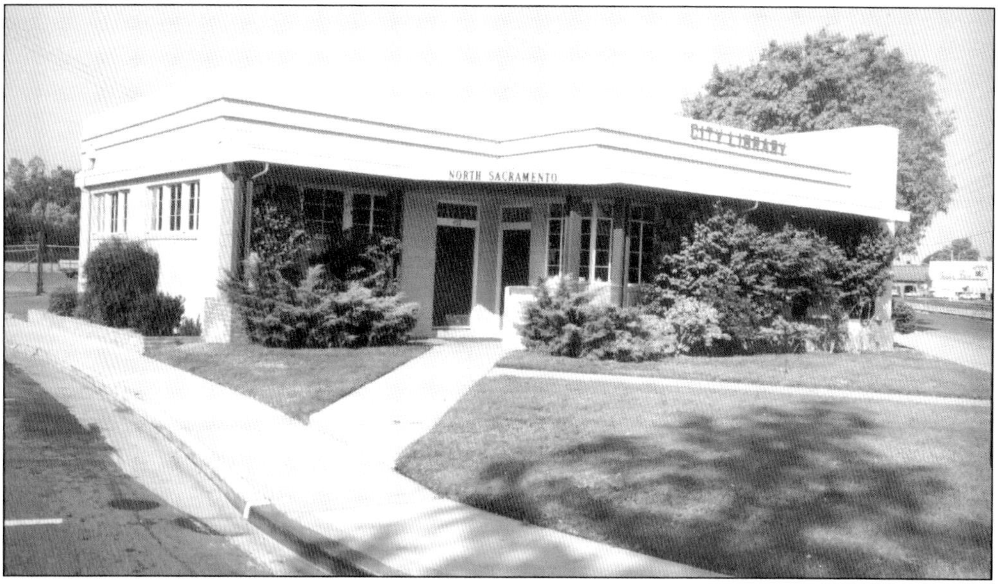

The first North Sacramento Library was called the Woodlake Free Public Library and was located in the back of Aldrich Pharmacy at 2001 Del Paso Boulevard. After the city acquired a new building, the facility, now named the North Sacramento City Library, moved to 492 Arden Way, adjacent to the police and fire departments. (Sacramento Room, Sacramento Public Library.)

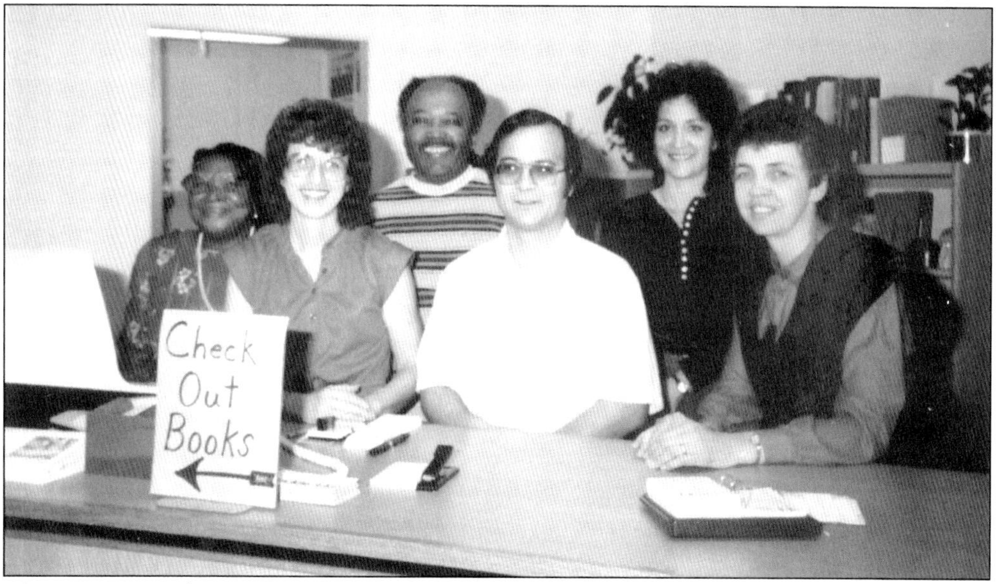

The current North Sacramento–Hagginwood Library (NSA) opened in 1987 at 2109 Del Paso Boulevard. The new 4,000-square-foot building provided room for an additional 30,000 books. Branch manager Mary Ann Stanek (far right) was pleased that the new spaced allowed for children's programming. The new branch is in an existing building owned by the Cook family and was completely renovated to meet the library's specifications. Dale Cook of Cook's Ace Hardware pays for all maintenance of the building. Councilman Grantland Johnson said NSA patrons would not travel to the new Natomas Library. He suggested instead combining North Sacramento and Hagginwood branches into one branch in North Sacramento. Grantland's proposal passed 3-1. (Sacramento Room, Sacramento Public Library.)

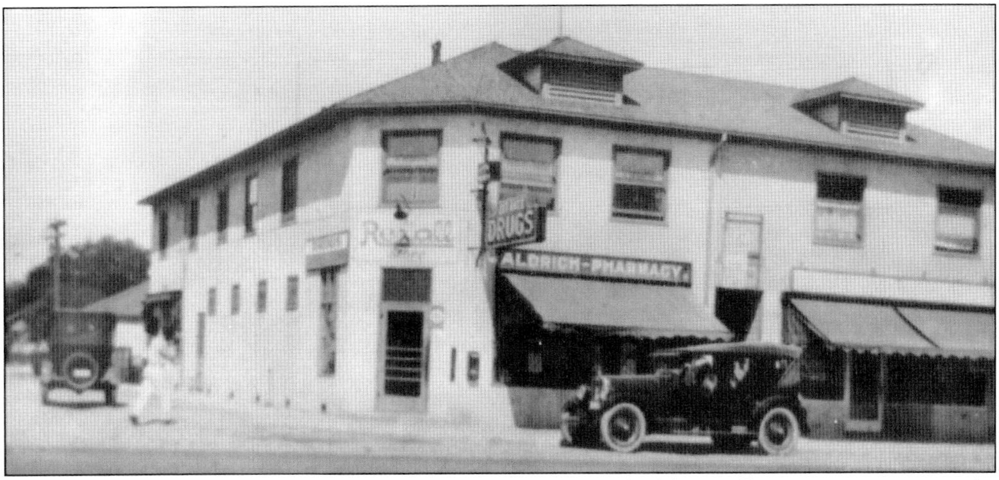

The rear of Aldrich Pharmacy at Del Paso Boulevard served additionally as a temporary site for the North Sacramento Fire Department and the Woodlake Free Public Library in the early 1920s. Above Aldrich Pharmacy is the Masonic lodge, which was built specifically on the second floor, as Masonic meetings may not be held on the ground floor. (SAMCC.)

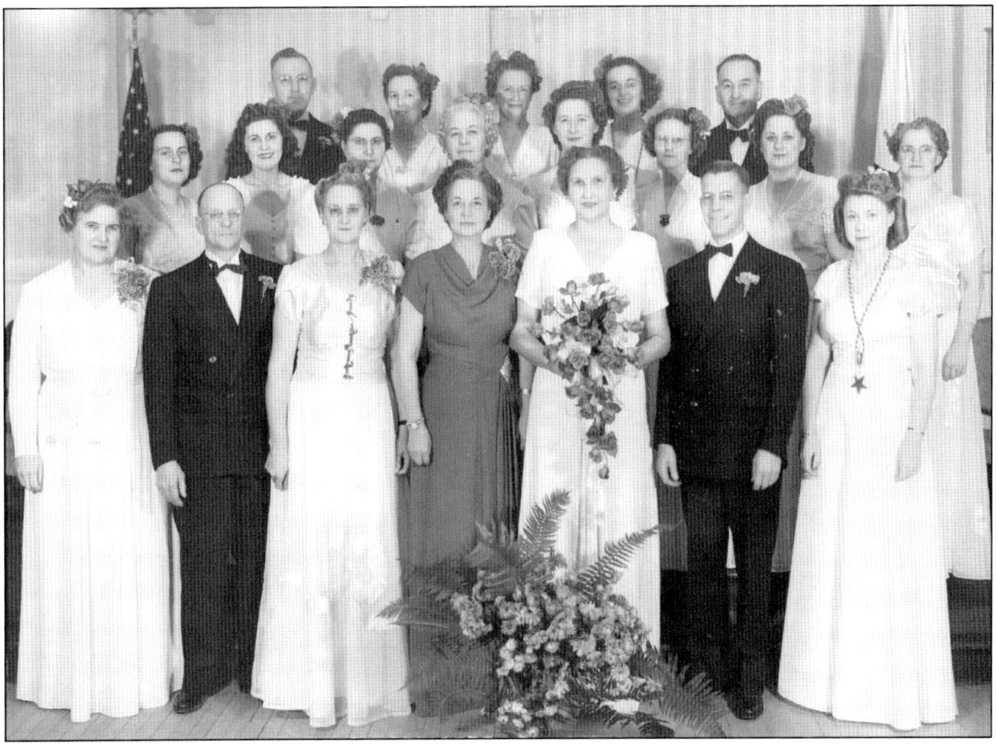

Members of the Order of the Eastern Star, El Camino Chapter, pose in 1944 in the Masonic lodge on Del Paso Boulevard. Pictured from left to right are (first row) Elwood Miller, Lovina Hansen (mother of Lois Hansen Nickless), unidentified, Betty Simpkins (with roses), Ed Tyhurst, Jeanette (last name unidentified); (second row) Eva Kerth (Iceland), Gladys Ruppin, unidentified, Haddy Vanderford, Kathyline Wilson, Mrs. Tyhurst, Lois Hansen (Nickless), Ida Mellinger; (third row) unidentified, Evelyn Tonnemaker, Rachel Lombard (of Lombard Funeral Home), Margie Lee (third grade teacher), and Dick Mellinger. (Hansen-Nickless.)

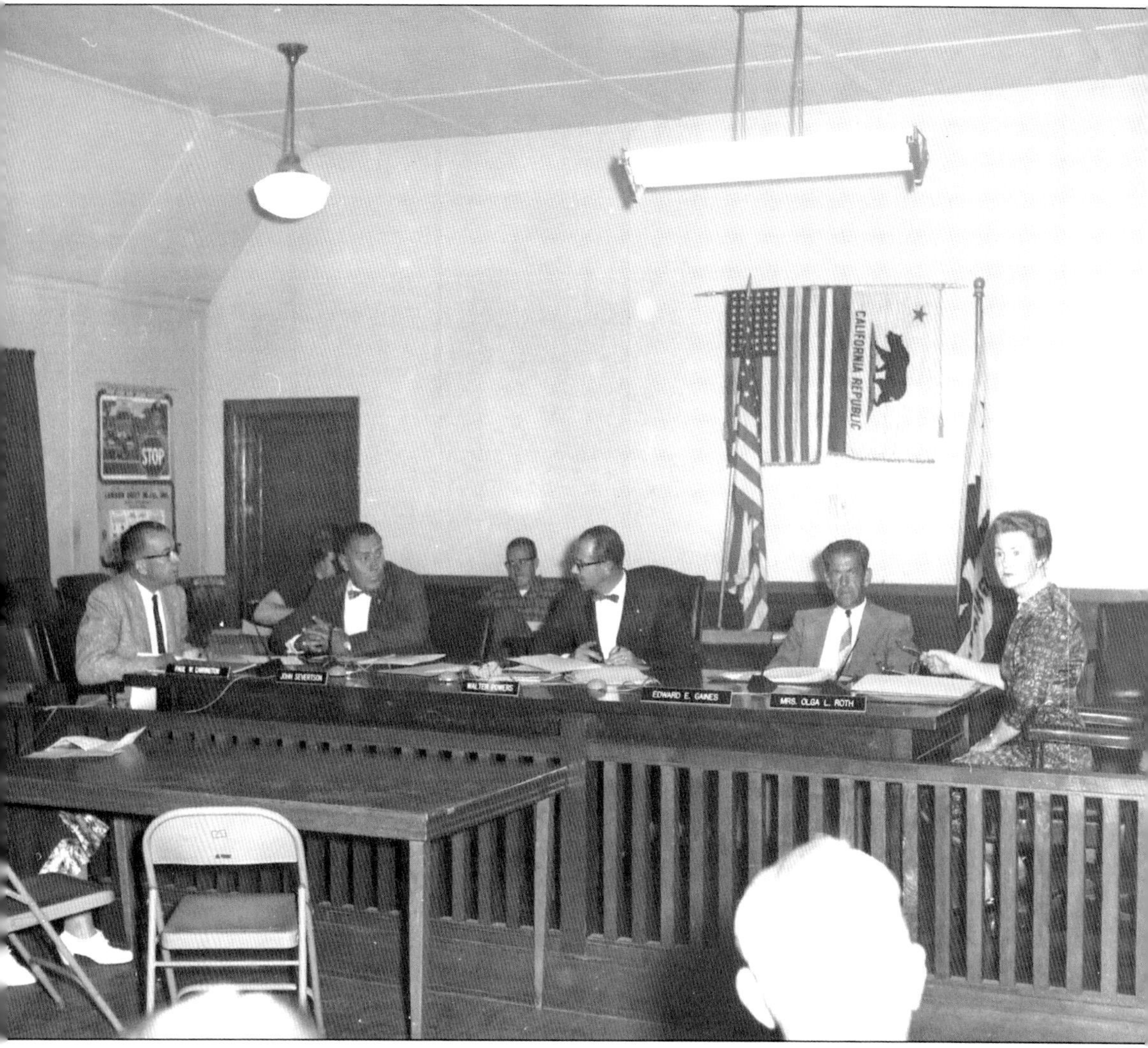

The North Sacramento City Council held its first meeting after the elections in 1960. Note the "Mrs." on Olga Roth's nameplate. She was the first councilwoman and later the first and only female mayor of the North Sacramento. Pictured clockwise are councilman Paul W. Carrington, councilman John Severtson, Mayor Walter Powers, councilman Edward E. Gaines, and councilman Olga L. Roth. North Sacramentans placed their ballots in the box at the Woodlake polling location in the Roth's refurbished garage. (Roth.)

Four

Transportation and Water

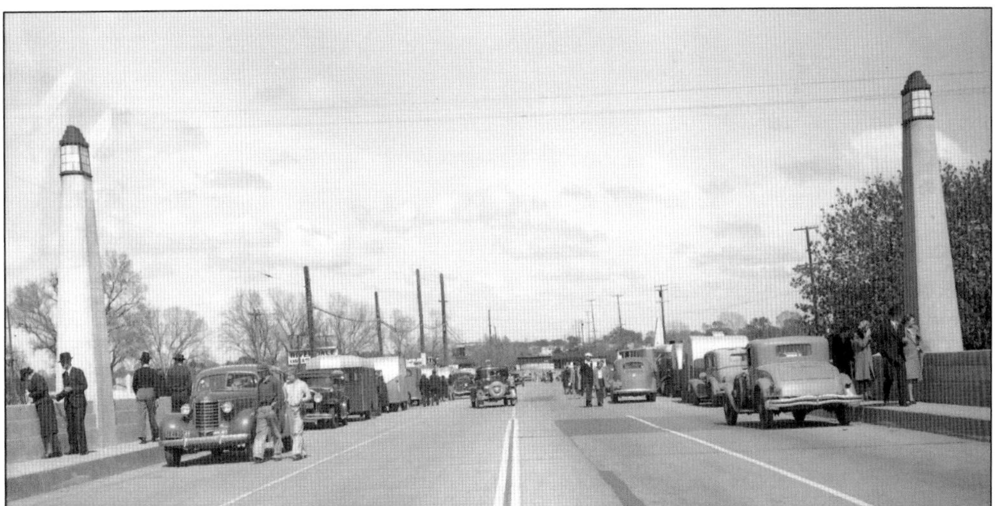

This photograph from March 31, 1936, shows the original Sixteenth Street Bridge with the architectural poles that are now torn down. North Sacramentans look over the bridge as the waters rise. The water dropped 3 feet overnight. (SAMCC.)

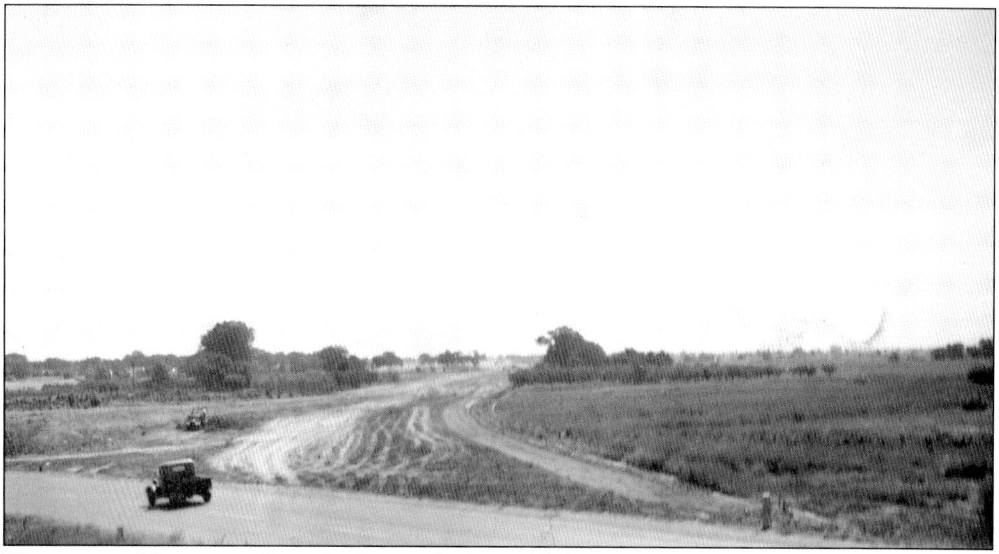

This image of the proposed new highway, which would eliminate going through North Sacramento and come out at the Ben Ali station, passed by Swanston Packing Company grounds around 1940. (SAMCC.)

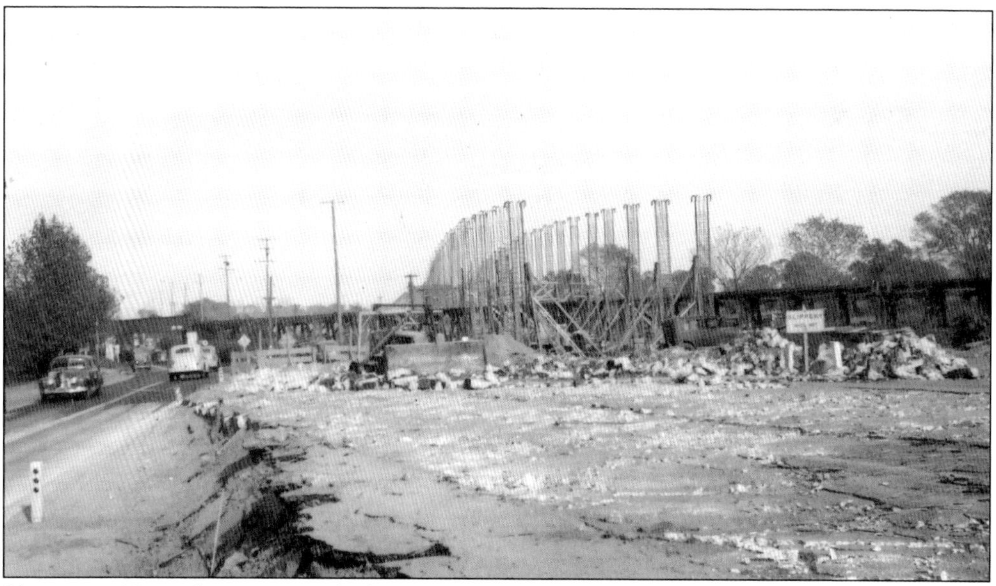

Shown on November 14, 1941, looking northeast toward North Sacramento is the new state overpass to North Sacramento, Highway 160. (SAMCC.)

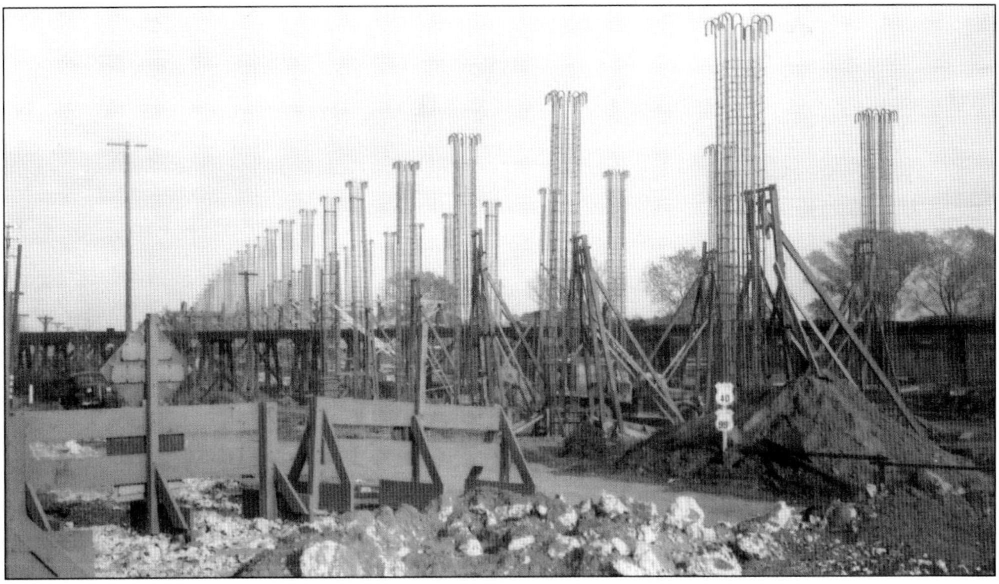

This image is a close-up of the overpass toward North Sacramento on November 14, 1941. (SAMCC.)

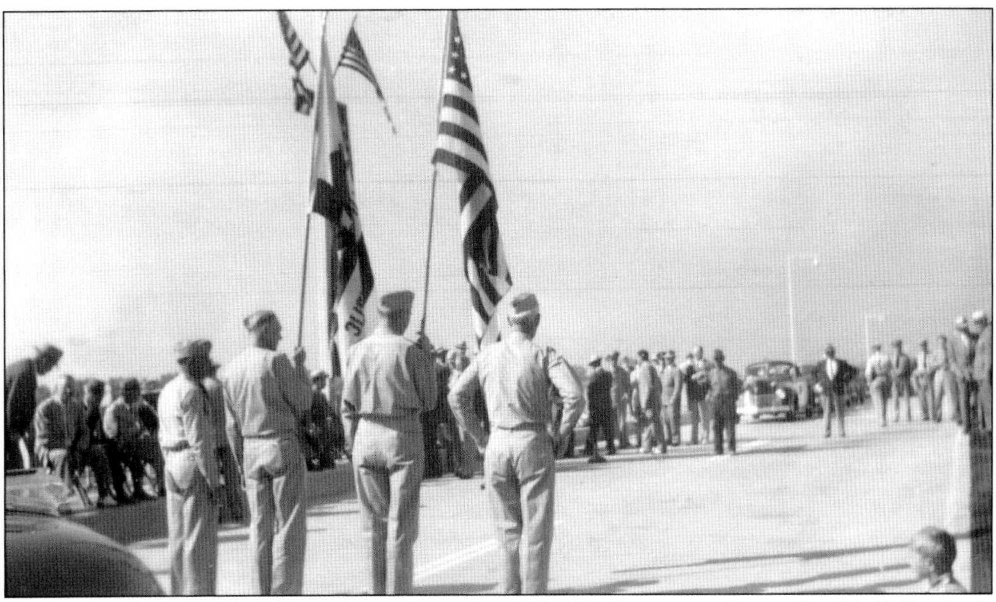

Pictured here is the dedication of the viaduct to North Sacramento on September 14, 1942, which included an appearance by the color guard. (SAMCC.)

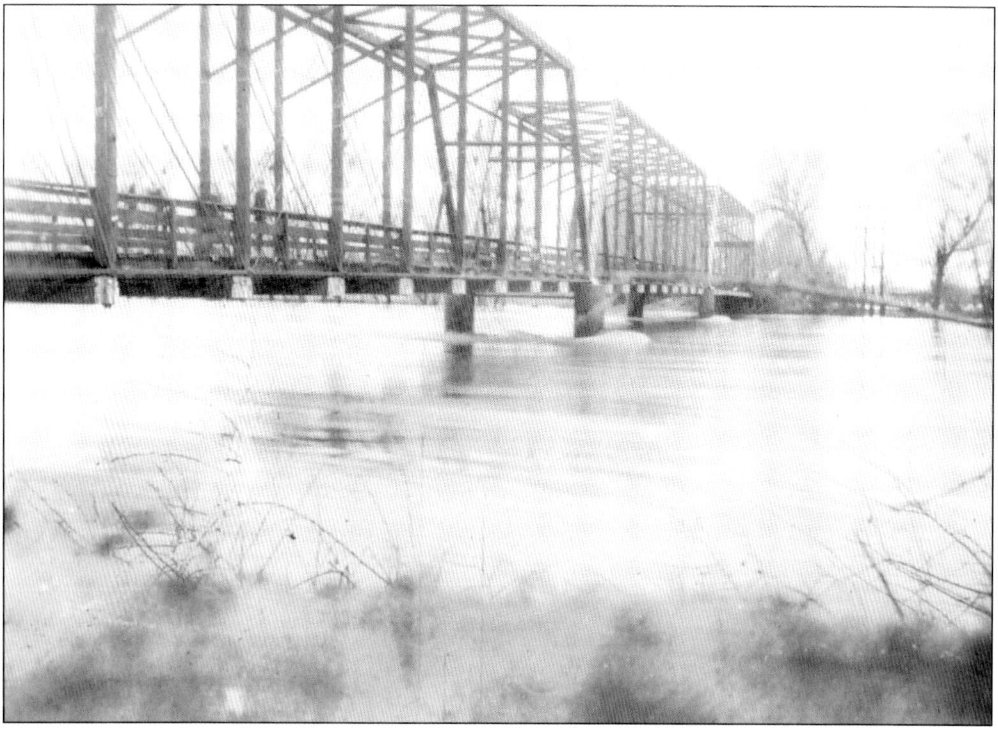

Joe Gross, an acquaintance of Hepting, took this photograph on January 1, 1914, of the old county bridge at Twelfth Street crossing over the American River. (SAMCC.)

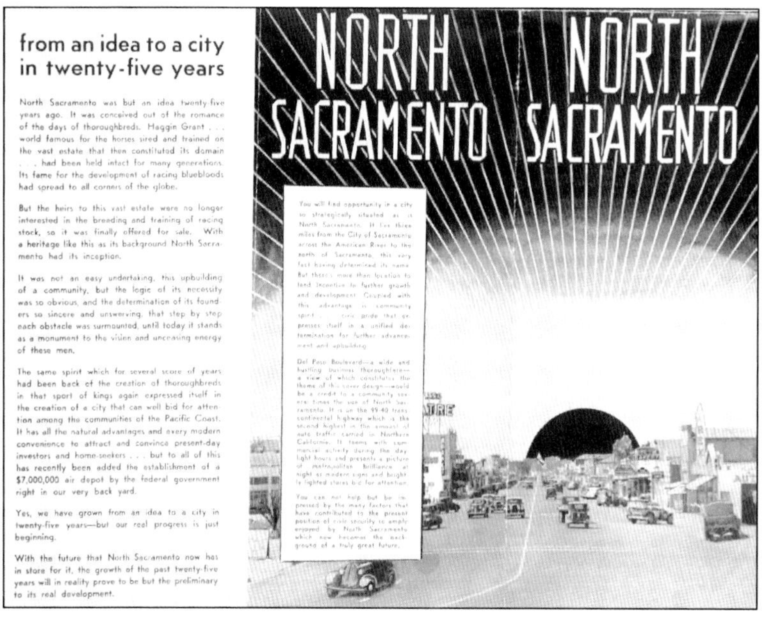

from an idea to a city in twenty-five years

North Sacramento was but an idea twenty-five years ago. It was conceived out of the romance of the days of thoroughbreds. Haggin Grant . . . world famous for the horses sired and trained on the vast estate that then constituted its domain . . . had been held intact for many generations. Its fame for the development of racing bluebloods had spread to all corners of the globe.

But the heirs to this vast estate were no longer interested in the breeding and training of racing stock, so it was finally offered for sale. With a heritage like this as its background North Sacramento had its inception.

It was not an easy undertaking, this upbuilding of a community, but the logic of its necessity was so obvious, and the determination of its founders so sincere and unswerving, that step by step each obstacle was surmounted, until today it stands as a monument to the vision and unceasing energy of these men.

The same spirit which for several score of years had been back of the creation of thoroughbreds in that sport of kings again expressed itself in the creation of a city that can well bid for attention among the communities of the Pacific Coast. It has all the natural advantages and every modern convenience to attract and convince present-day investors and home-seekers . . . but to all of this has recently been added the establishment of a $7,000,000 air depot by the federal government right in our very back yard.

Yes, we have grown from an idea to a city in twenty-five years—but our real progress is just beginning.

With the future that North Sacramento now has in store for it, the growth of the past twenty-five years will in reality prove to be but the preliminary to its real development.

NORTH SACRAMENTO

NORTH SACRAMENTO

You will find opportunity in a city so strategically situated as is North Sacramento. It lies three miles from the City of Sacramento across the American River to the north of Sacramento, this very fact having determined its name. But there's more than location to lend incentive to further growth and development. Coupled with this advantage is community spirit . . . civic pride that expresses itself in a unified determination for further advancement and upbuilding.

Del Paso Boulevard—a wide and hustling business thoroughfare—a view of which constitutes the theme of this cover design—would be a credit to a community several times the size of North Sacramento. It is on the 99-40 transcontinental highway which is the second highest in the amount of auto traffic carried in Northern California. It teems with commercial activity during the daylight hours and presents a picture of metropolitan brilliance at night as modern signs and brightly lighted stores bid for attention.

You can not help but be impressed by the many factors that have contributed to the present position of civic security so amply enjoyed by North Sacramento which now becomes the background of a truly great future.

This 1935 brochure advertising the metropolis of North Sacramento highlights the many motorists and businesses along the Del Paso leg of the Lincoln Highway. With the 1950 building of Highway 160, locally known as North Sac Bypass, traffic diminished and businesses suffered. (Sacramento Room, Sacramento Public Library.)

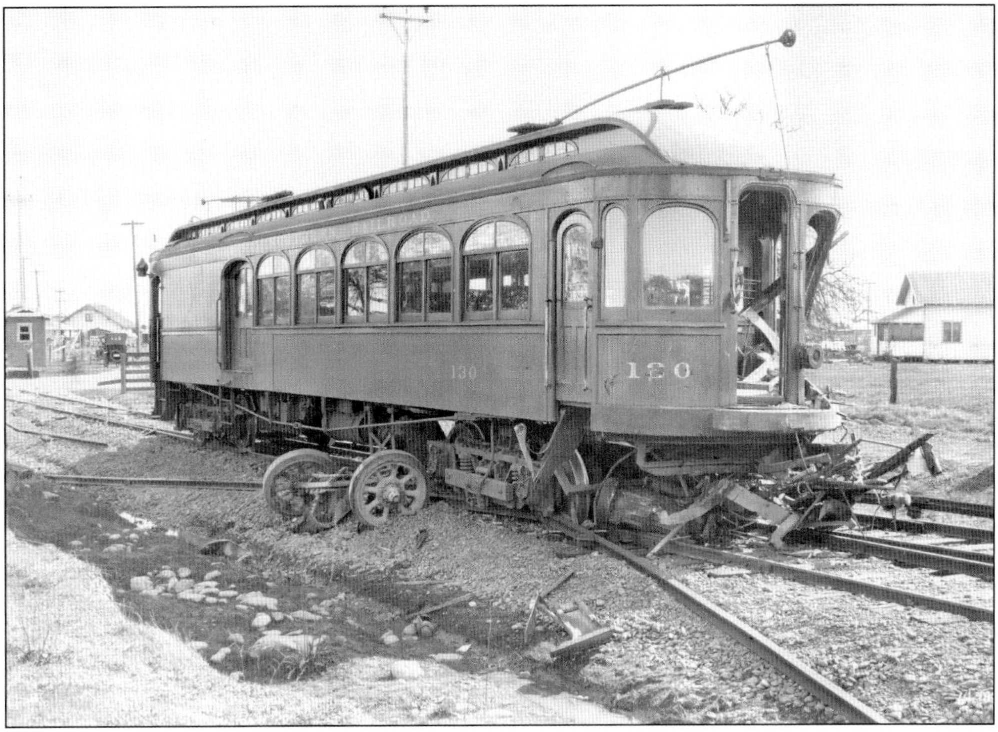

Derailments were not uncommon. The No. 130 Sacramento Northern Railroad electric car derailed at the North Sacramento Depot pictured below. Note the upper third rail on the right that North Sacramentans fought for years to have removed. (SAMCC.)

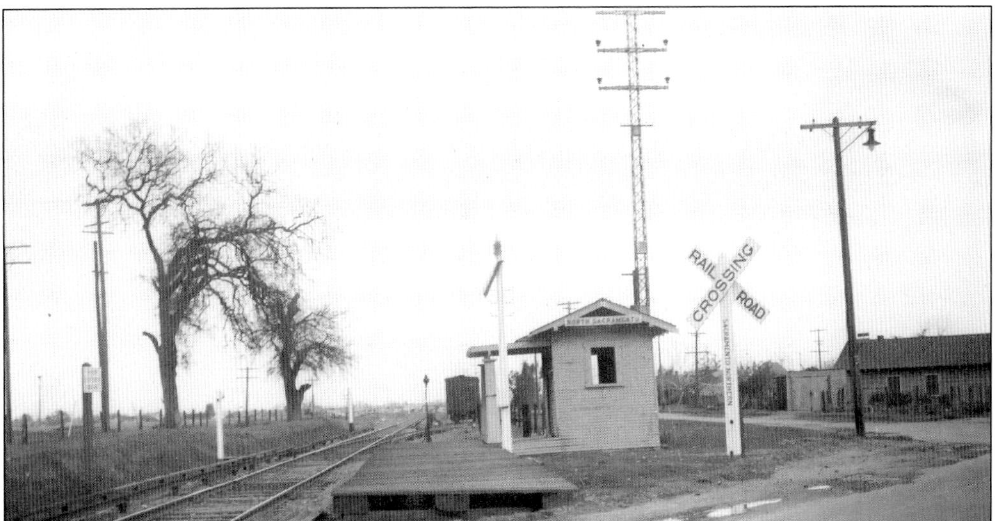

The City of North Sacramento warranted its own train depot along Traction Boulevard. Note the raised third rail above the left ground rail. A "hot" rail, the iron carried an electrical charge that caused two child fatalities before it was finally removed. Margaret Fish Smith, Lois Hansen Nickless, and Bob Kent remember their parents scaring the daylights out of them with warnings to "stay away from the third rail." Cook's Hardware came in their trucks to the depot to pick up the latest General Electric Laundromat off the train car. (SAMCC.)

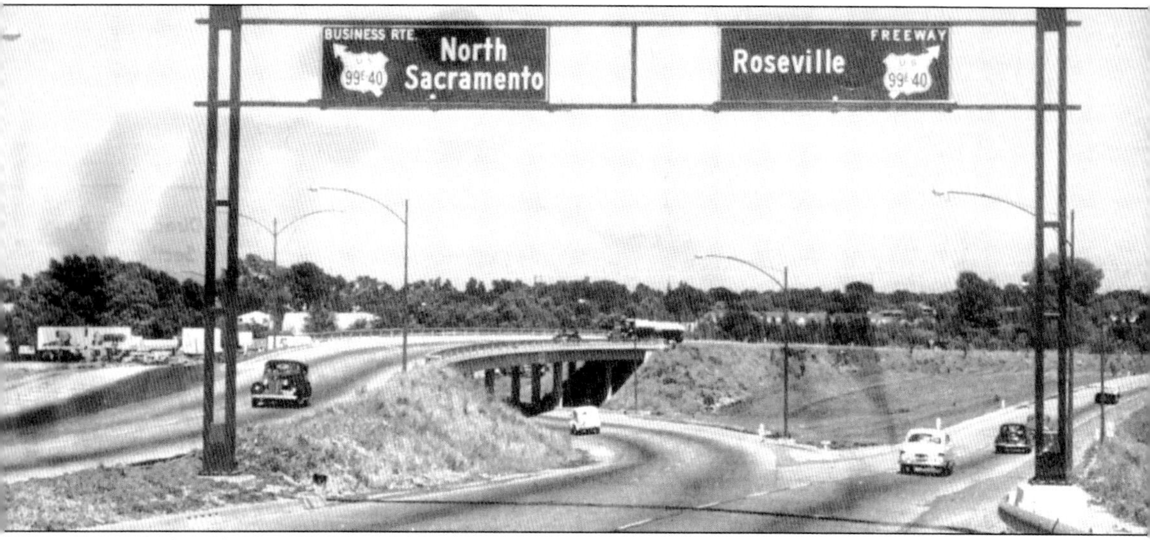

Featured in this c. 1942 photograph is the overhead sign bridge on North Sacramento Freeway.

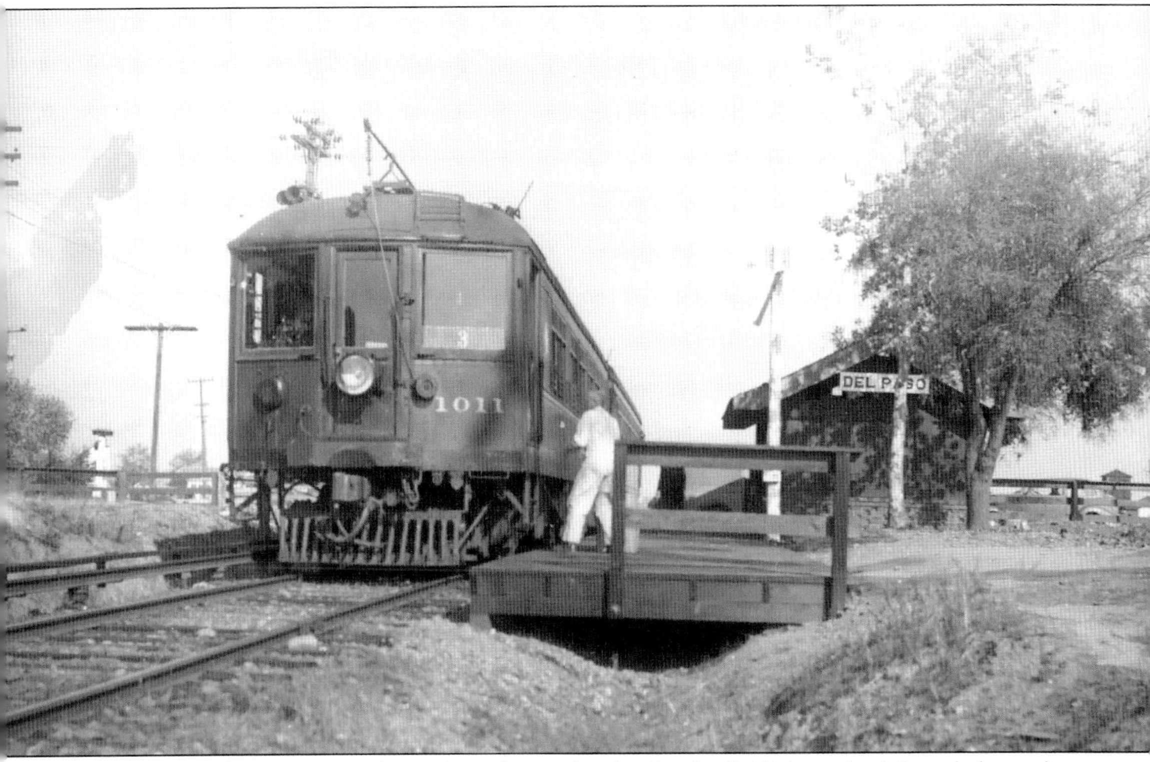

Del Paso Heights Station is shown here. Note the third rail, which is to the left and above the ground rails. The third rail caused havoc with its live electricity and had two fatalities. The longest interurban line in the world, 300 miles of track from Chico to Oakland with ferry connection to San Francisco was electrically powered, with an electrified third rail contacted by a shoe from the engine giving swift and sure movement. In Sacramento, not North Sacramento, the power was derived from the overhead line and trolley. In 1935, North Sacramento asked the line to remove the third rail, but due to cost the railroad said no. In 1945, the railroad commission outlawed all third rails. The railroad company was originally named Northern Electric Railway Company in 1907, then Sacramento Railroad Company in 1918, then Sacramento Northern Railway Company in 1921. Rightaways are still at Rio Linda Boulevard and Traction Avenue Swanston spur at the intersection of Arden Way and the SP tracks. North Sacramento Land Company indemnified Sacramento Northern against loss. (SAMCC.)

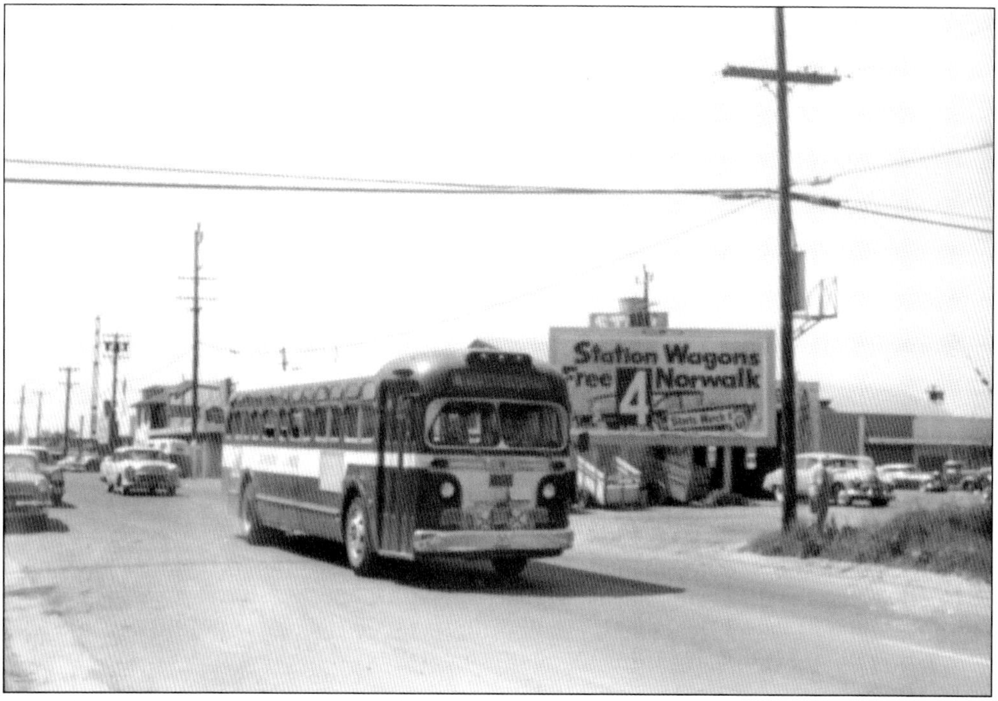

This photograph was taken on April 26, 1957, of Gibson Lines No. 5102 along Grand Avenue and Rio Linda Boulevard in North Sacramento. (SAMCC.)

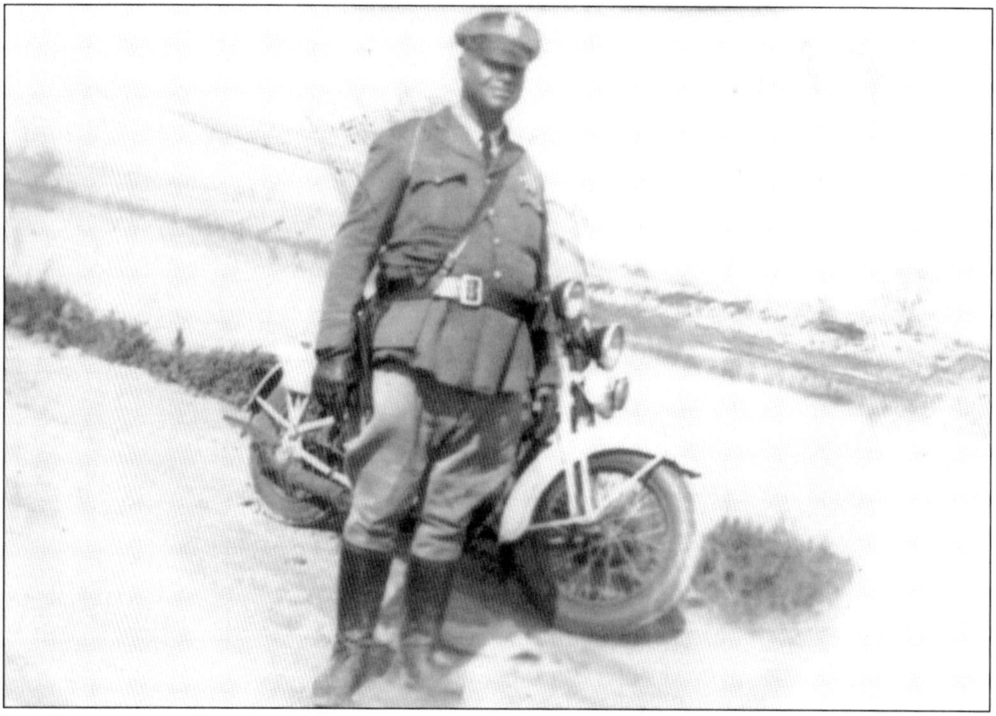
In 1931, a police officer stands by his motorcycle on the levee in North Sacramento. (Risse.)

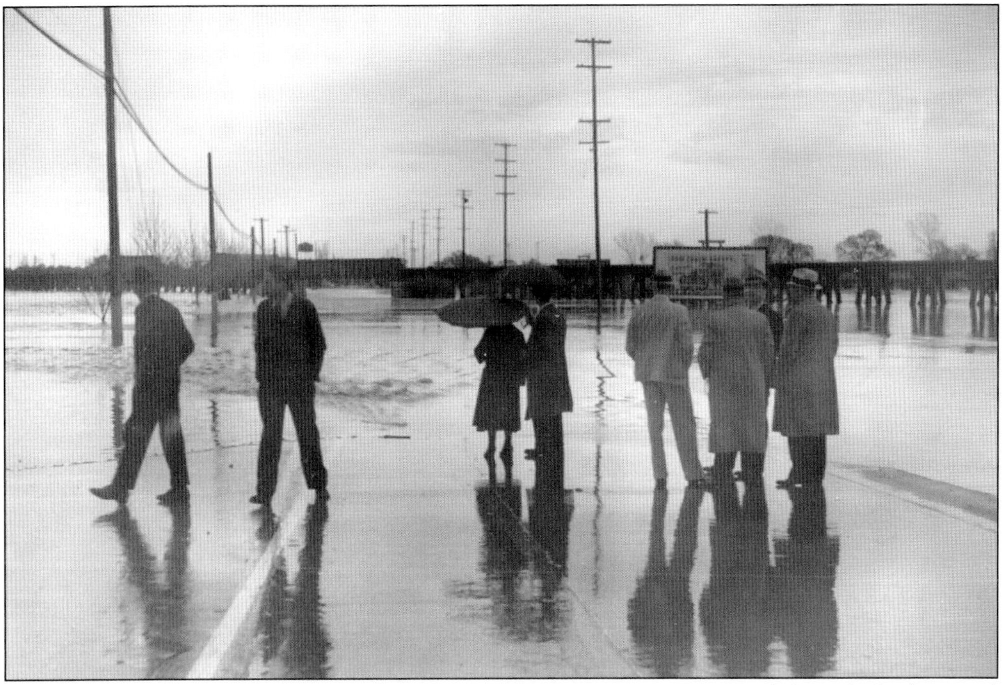

This image depicts the flood of 1927 in North Sacramento. Note at center left in the background the water tower of Liberty Iron Works. Margaret Fish Smith remembers it was always a big event when the area flooded and people would gather to watch the tide rise. "It was great fun." (Sacramento Room, Sacramento Public Library.)

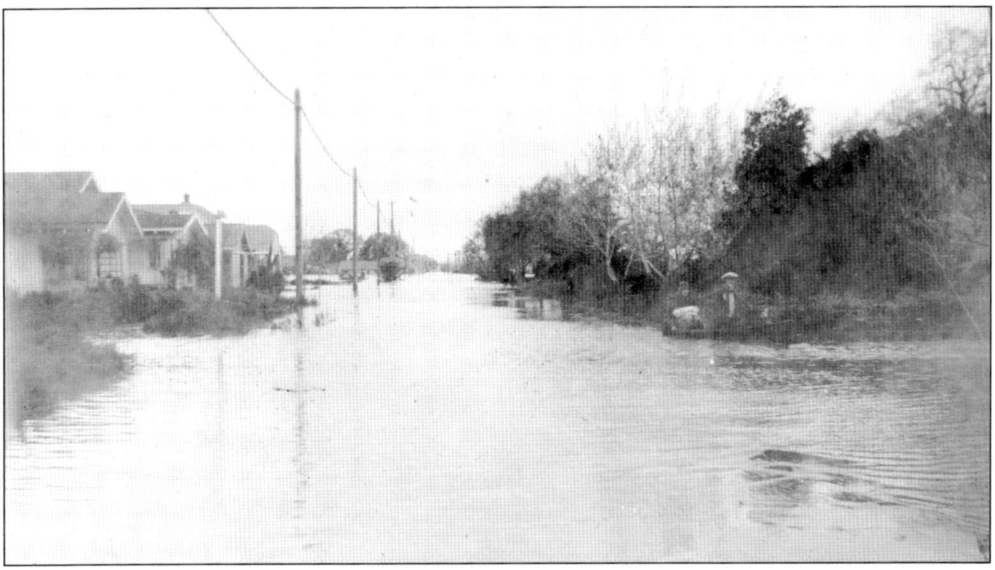

This Roth family album photograph shows El Monte Avenue, looking toward Sacramento from Gibson Corner during the major flood of March 26, 1928. Note the boat at the right. Volunteers in boats rescued families from homes and took them to the safety of high ground on Del Paso Boulevard to join other rescued families and their horses and cows. (Roth.)

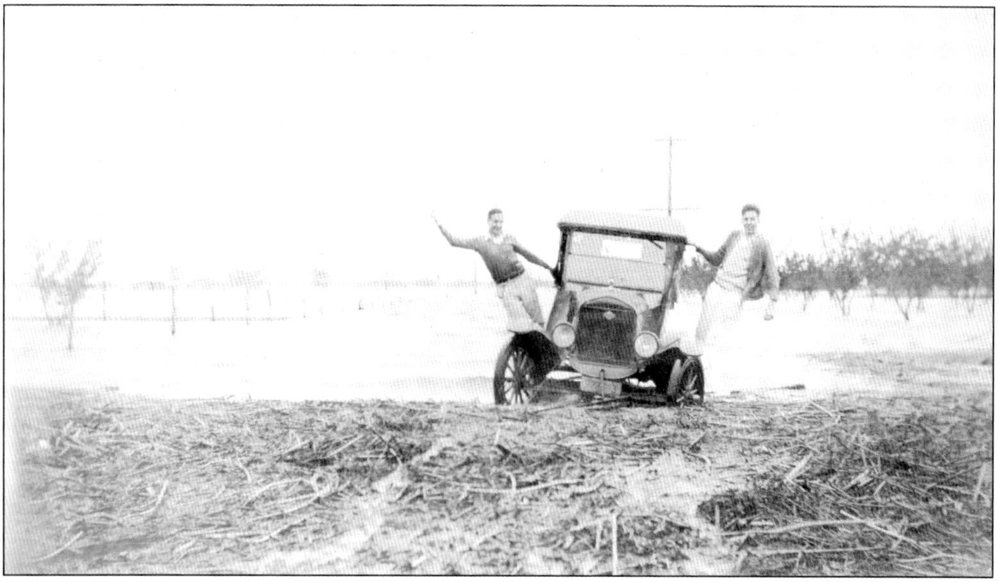

Two young men enjoy themselves during the March 26, 1928, flood north of North Sacramento in Del Paso Heights. (Roth.)

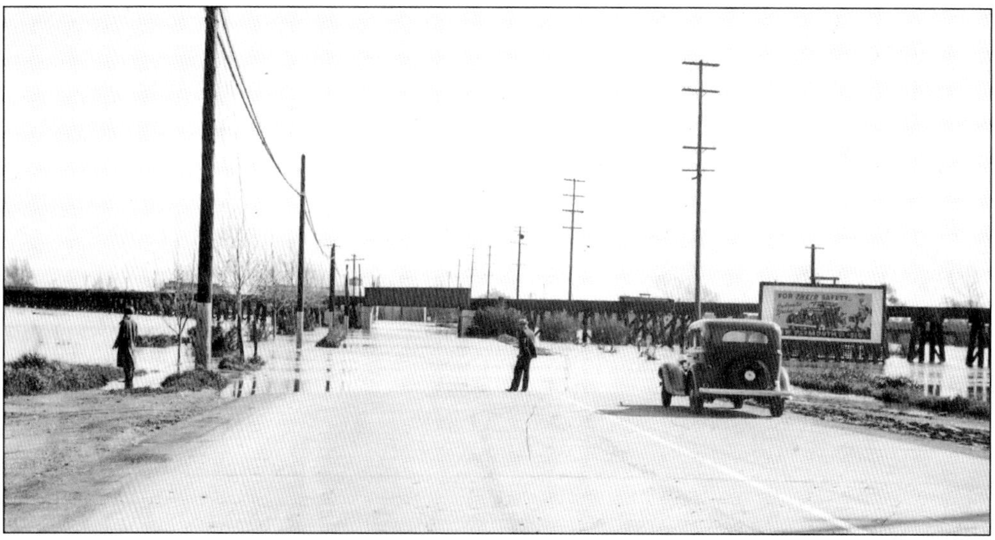

This image shows the highway to North Sacramento on April 22, 1935. Eugene Hepting was a native Sacramentan who was prompted by historian Caroline Wentzel to start a photograph collection, which he did between 1930 and 1960. In the center of the photograph are the floodgates on Del Paso Boulevard (formerly old U.S. 40) that were closed for several days during the annual rainy season to catch the overflow from the nearby American River, necessitating crowded detour routes for commuters. These floodgates were installed after the horrendous flood of 1928, depicted above. (SAMCC-Hepting.)

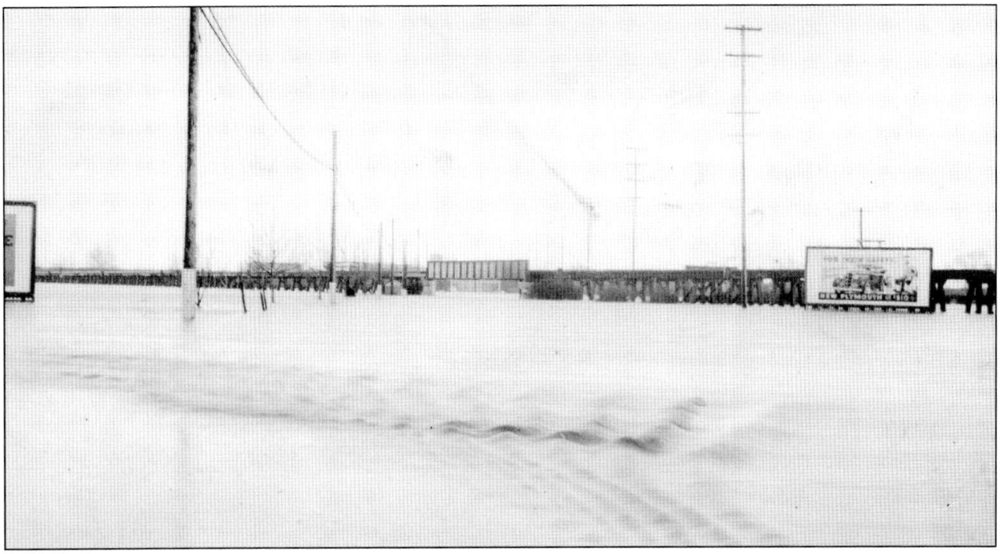

Eugene Hepting, a native Sacramentan who was prompted by historian Caroline Wentzel to start a photograph collection, took this photograph of Highway 12 south of Del Paso Boulevard, looking toward North Sacramento on April 22, 1935. The flood is higher than in the previous image. Note that the billboard is almost underwater. (SAMCC-Hepting.)

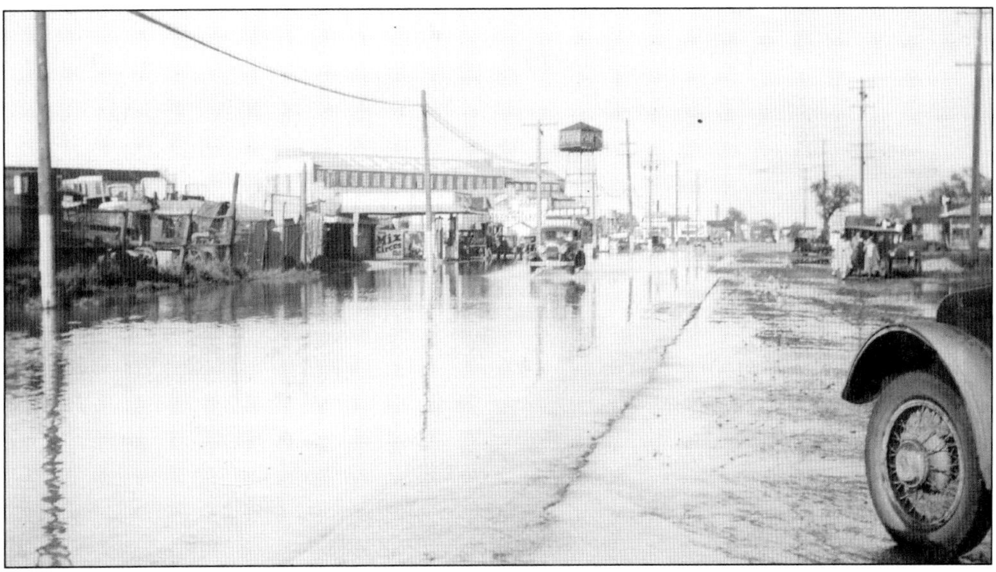

This image looks north while cars travel south on Del Paso Boulevard and water from the American River spills over the levee on April 22, 1935. Liberty Iron Works is now an auto and tractor parts enterprise. Note the "auto parts" water tower below it; on the far left is Subway Parts, which exists today. (SAMCC.)

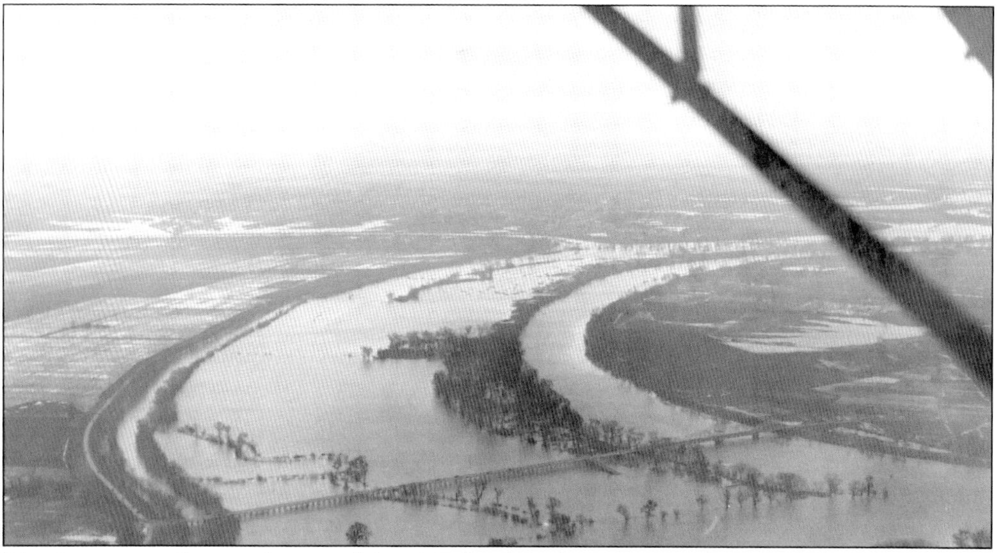

This *Sacramento Bee* aerial image of the 1938 flood "looks east across the Sacramento River toward the mouth of the American River. North Sacramento is in the background." (SAMCC.)

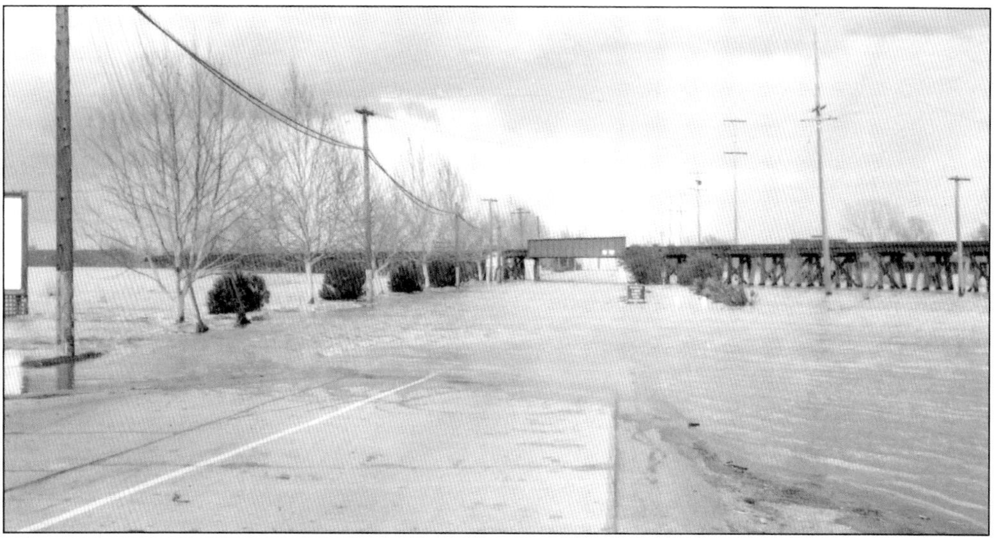

Highways 40 and 99 to North Sacramento are pictured here at the first high water on February 28, 1940. (SAMCC.)

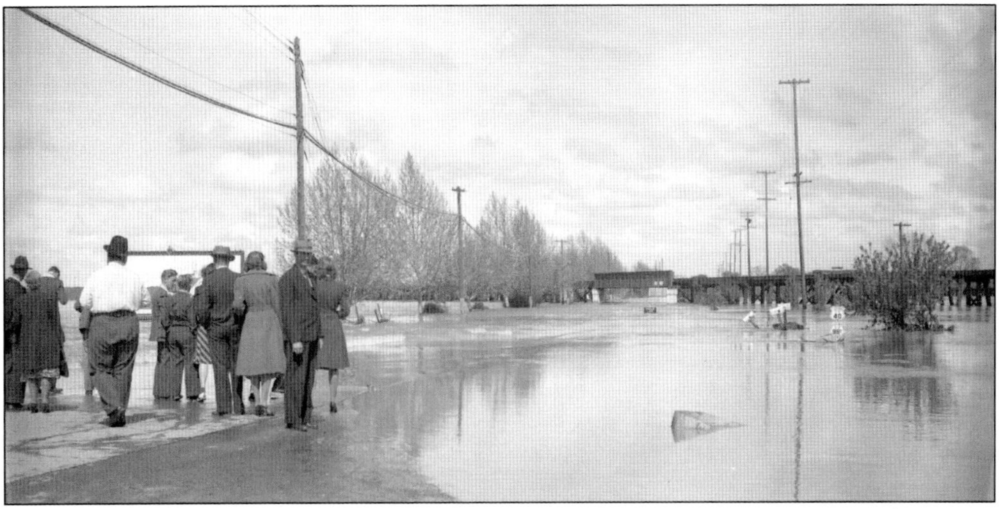

A few minutes later, as the water continues to rise, North Sacramentans congregate with cameras to note the March 31, 1940, flood. Looking toward us is the photographer, Eugene Hepting, who had the forethought to photograph and label the images. Additional Hepting images appear on pages 66–68. (SAMCC-Hepting.)

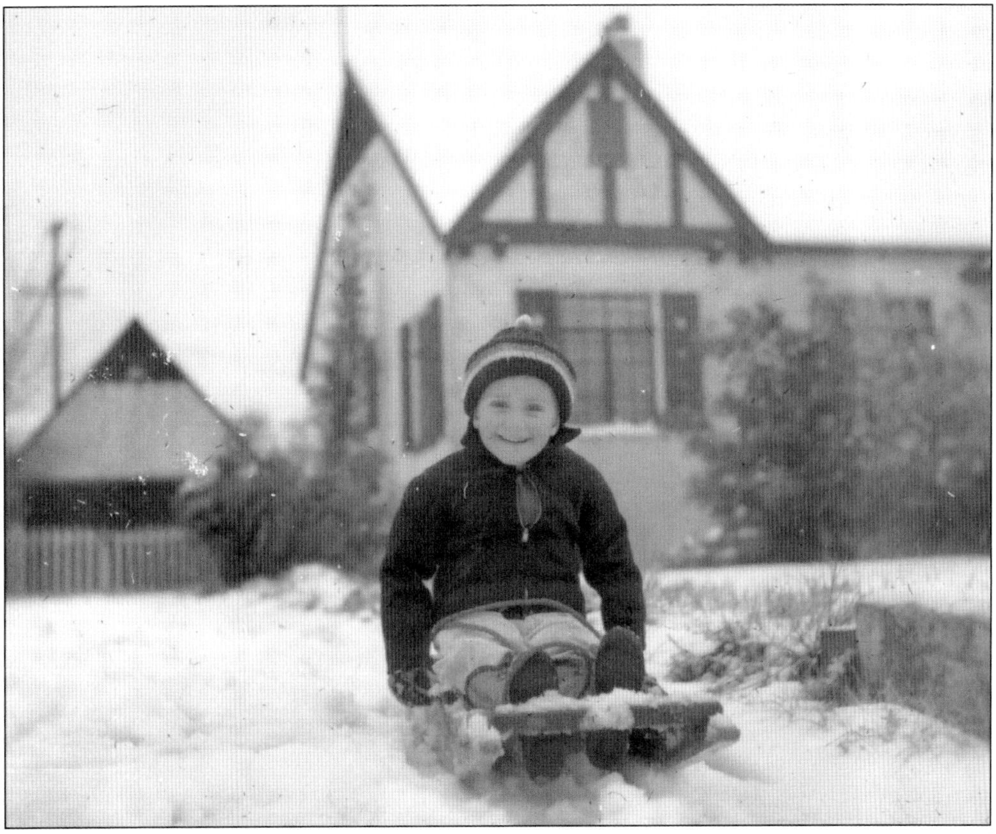

Snow! In North Sacramento on March 14, 1942, two inches of white stuff fell from the sky, and North Sacramentans, like Robert Roth of Woodlake, tore into their closets to find seldom-used snow gear. (Roth.)

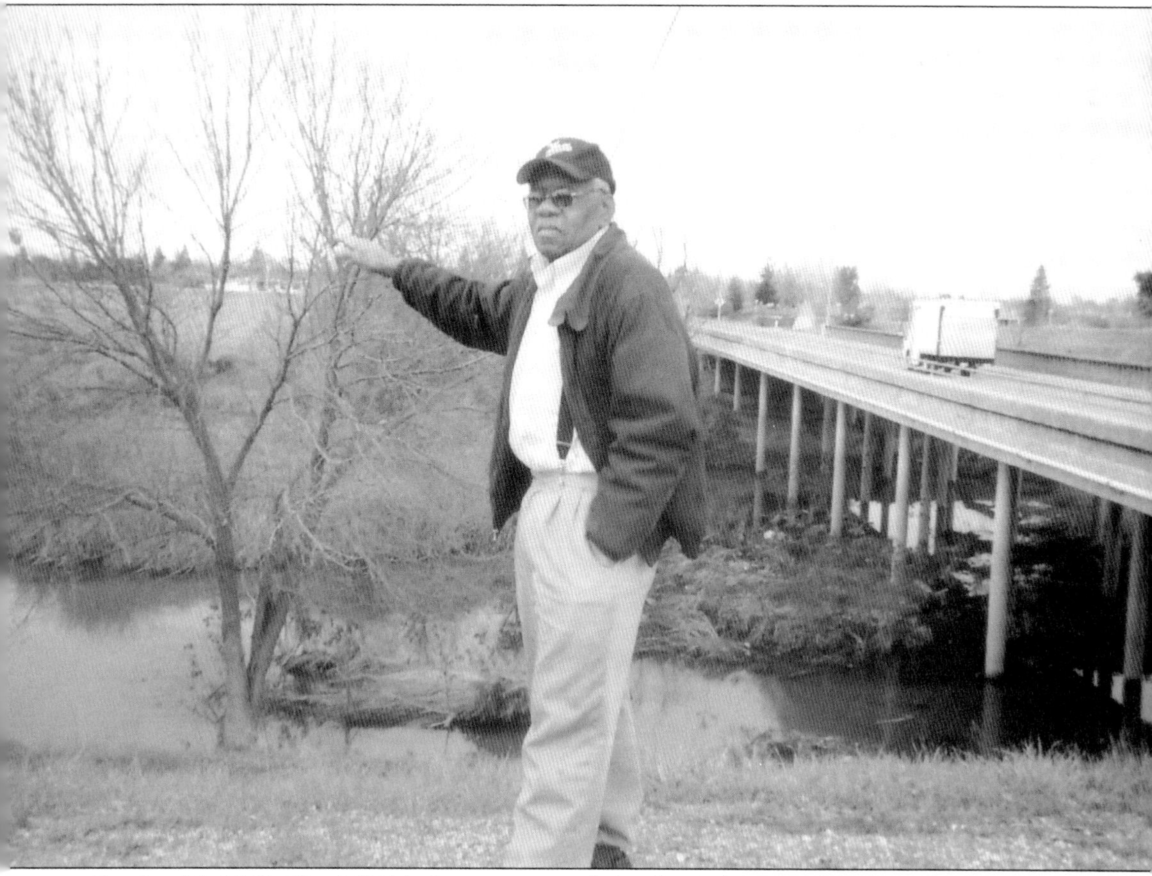

On April 2, 2009, Wendell Echols points toward the flooded area and sump in the Strawberry Manor dispute. The February 18, 1986, collapse of a sandbag dike that city workers built, where the Rio Linda Bridge cuts through the Arcade Creek levee during the storm, caused flooding in the Strawberry Manor housing development. (Ehrenreich-Risner.)

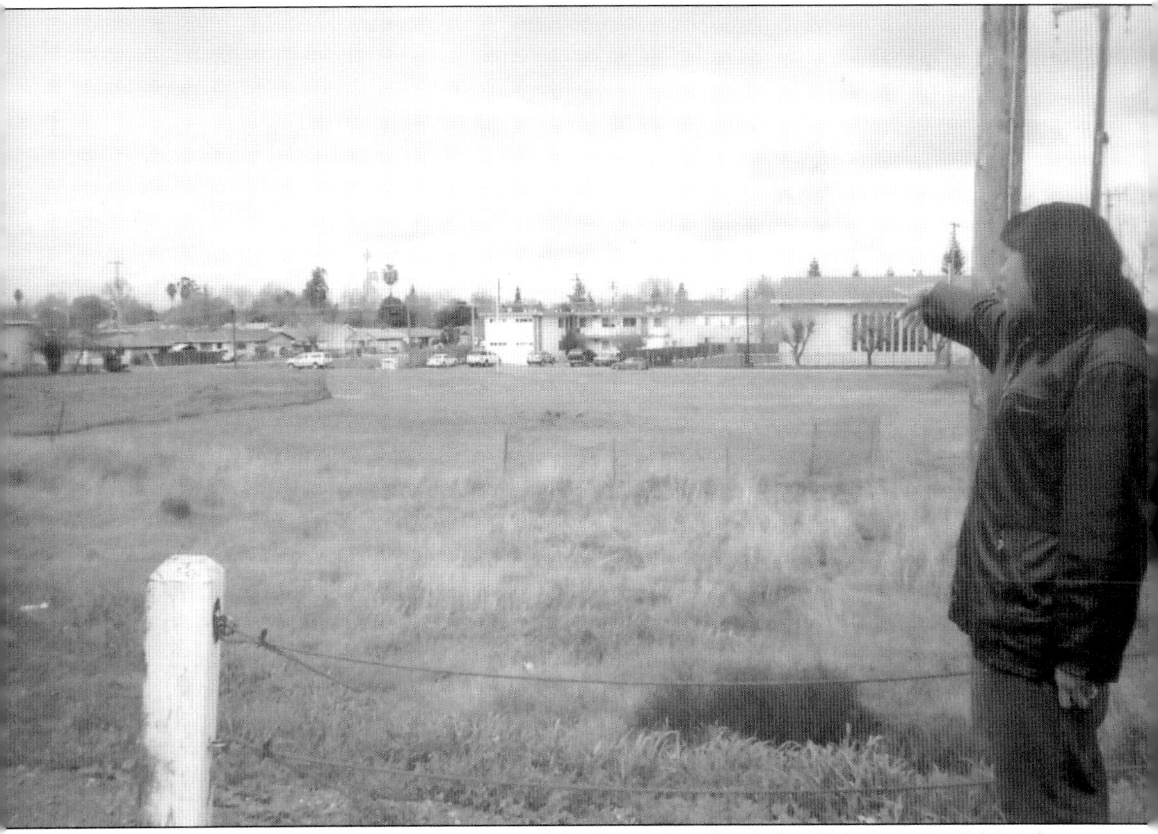

Edwina Minor remembers the area in her neighborhood that flooded on February 18, 1986. After 500 houses were submerged in 8 feet of water, citizens sued the city in what became known as the Strawberry Manor Dispute. Floodgates have since been installed. (Ehrenreich-Risner.)

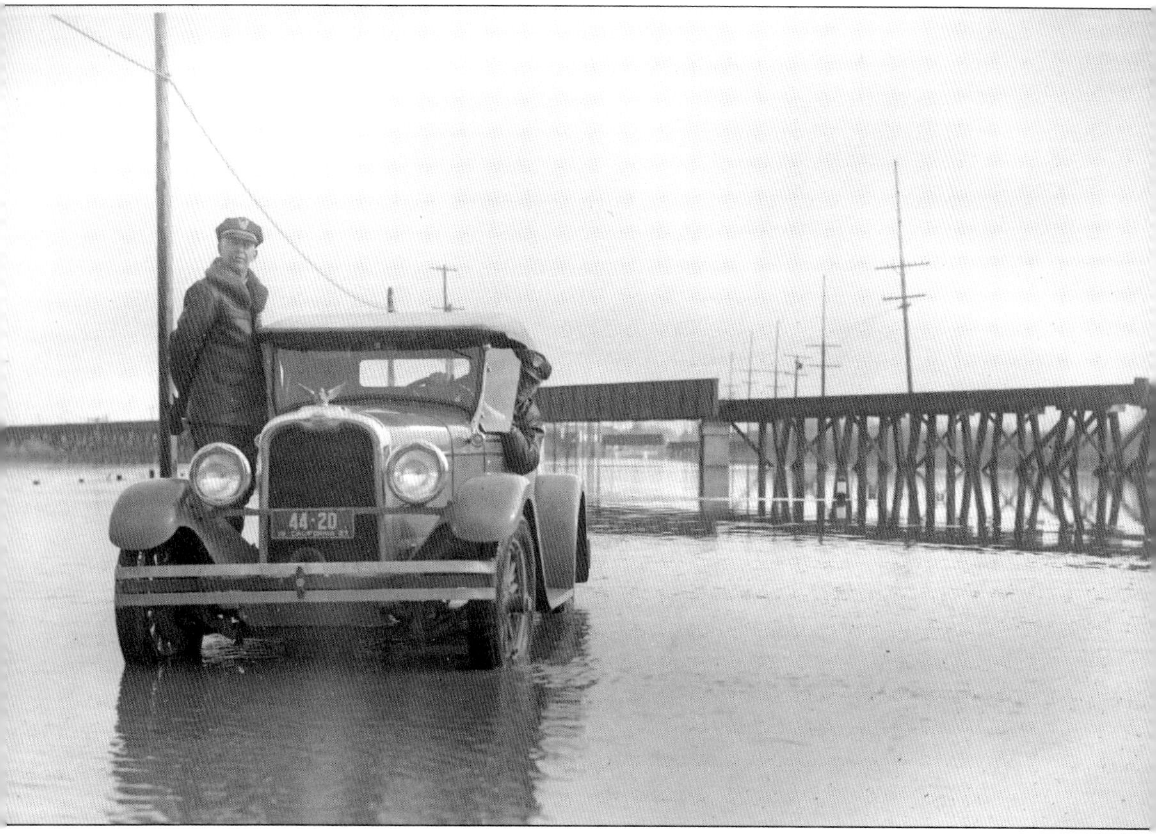

At the onset of the 1928 flood, North Sacramento police chief Erskin George Fish (behind the wheel) and Police Officer Bill Wilson (on the running board) patrol the city. When Chief Fish was fatally shot in the line of duty on August 11, 1935, flags were flown at half-mast. Wilson was appointed North Sacramento police chief and served for two decades. Margaret Fish Smith inscribed the following on the back of this photograph: "My father in the car, Bill Wilson standing. We all went to watch the flood come up Del Paso Boulevard. It stopped at about the old North Sacramento City Office building. M. F. Smith." (Fish Smith.)

Five

FAMILIES

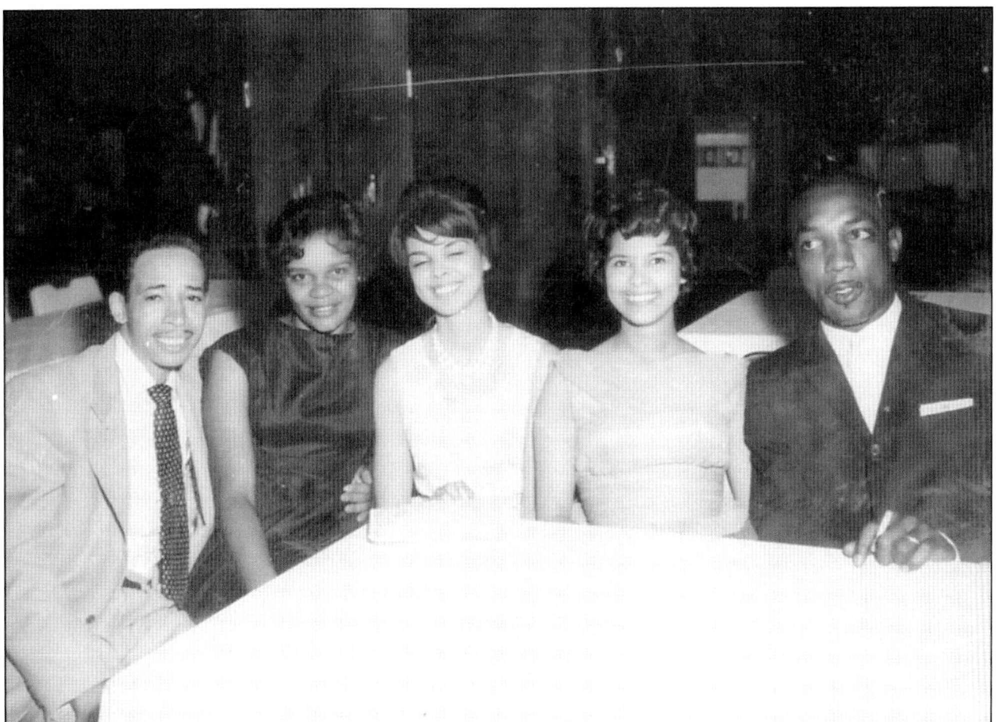

Posing for posterity around 1961, from left to right are Del Paso Heights residents Mr. and Mrs. Raper, Fran Barker, Barbara Hale, and an unidentified man. (SAMCC.)

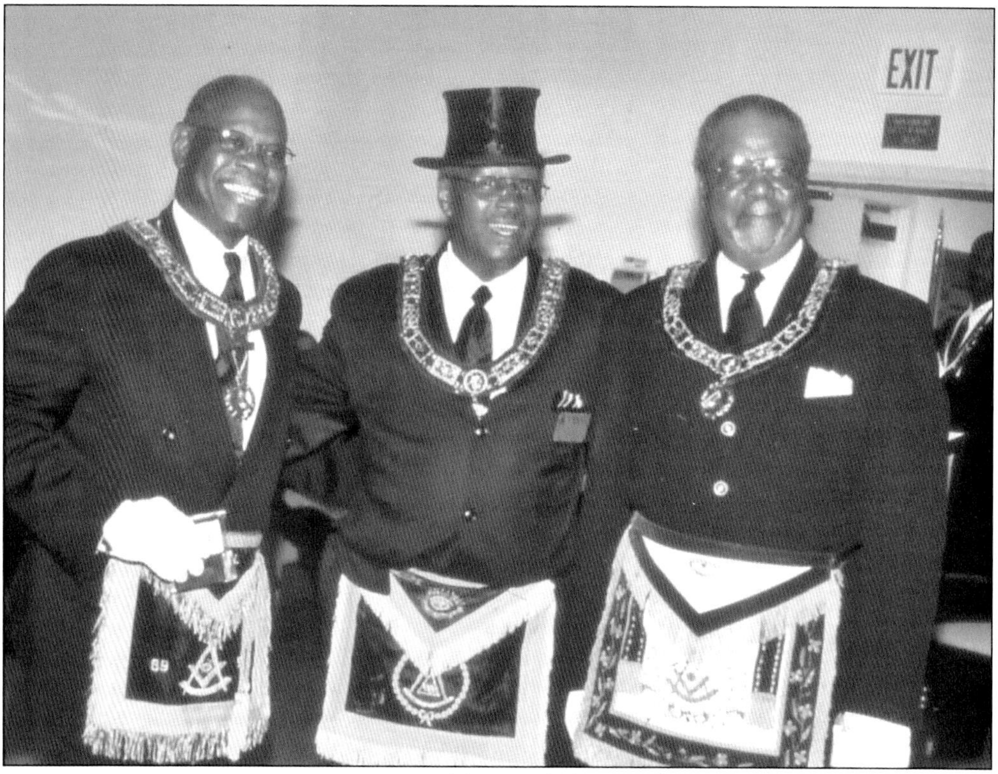

Masonic lodge members in Del Paso Heights celebrate. Pictured around 2001 are past grand master Martin L. Kennison (left), George Blue (center), and past grand master Arthur Jackson. (SAMCC.)

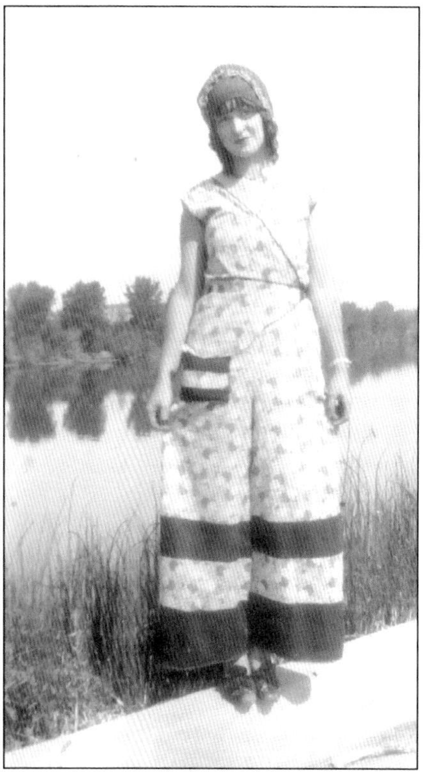

Embracing the culture of the gypsy migrants along the creeks in North Sacramento, Betty wears her gypsy garb and enjoys an outing on the American River with her second husband, Charlie Newth, in 1936. Born on January 18, 1904, Betty "Ollie" (Porticeo) Keeler Newth Bryan, thrice married, was a woman before her time. An entrepreneur, Betty ran two businesses before the age of 22 (Betty's Candyland at 1919 Del Paso Boulevard, then 2116 Del Paso Boulevard from 1927 to 1939, and finally at 2126 Del Paso Boulevard and Betty's Photo Studio at 1725 Del Paso Boulevard and then in North Sacramento Hotel). Margaret Fish Smith remembers that Betty was lovingly called Betty "Boop" (after the cartoon character) by the children who visited Betty's Candyland after school or on their way into the Del Paso Theatre. (Risse: Betty Bryan.)

In 1926, 22-year-old Betty "Boop" "Ollie" (Porticeo) Keeler Newth Bryan stands in front of the back house at 415 Santiago Avenue. Tim Risse bought Betty's house in August 2002. While treating wood under the house, Tim noticed a concrete structure that did not "make any sense." He took up the floorboards and discovered Betty's fallout shelter with her photographs and ephemera. A professional photographer, Betty catalogued her life in pictures. (Risse: Betty Bryan.)

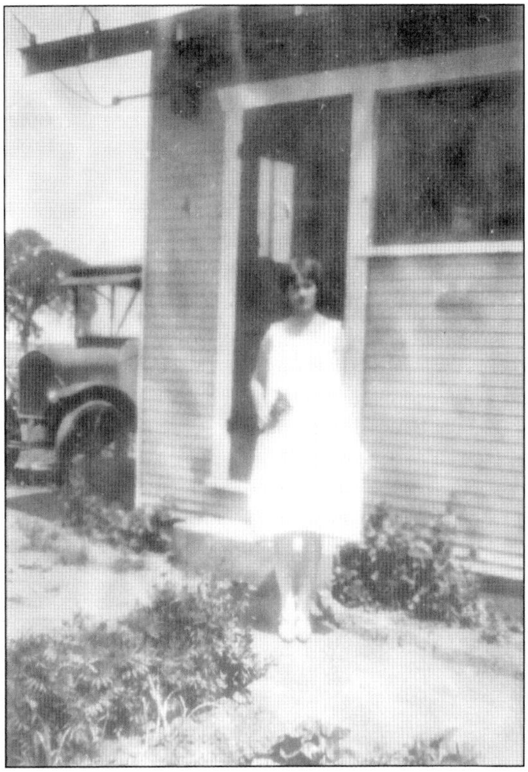

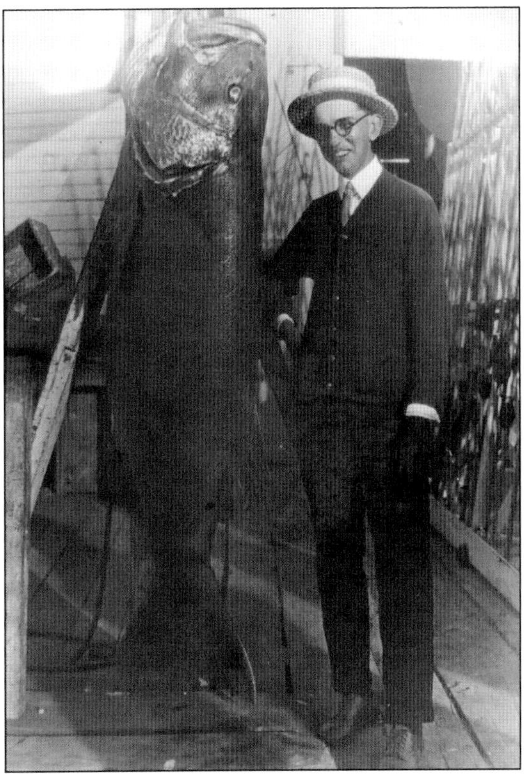

A young Charlie Newth, Betty's second husband, smiles beside the sturgeon caught probably in the American River around 1910. In 1926, 22-year-old Betty "Boop" "Ollie" Porticeo (Keeler Newth Bryan) stands in front of the back house at 415 Santiago Avenue. Tim Risse bought Betty's house in August of 2002. While treating wood under the house, Tim noticed a concrete structure that didn't "make any sense." He took up the floorboards and discovered Betty's fallout shelter with her photos and ephemera. A professional photographer, Betty catalogued her life in pictures. (Risse: Betty Bryan.)

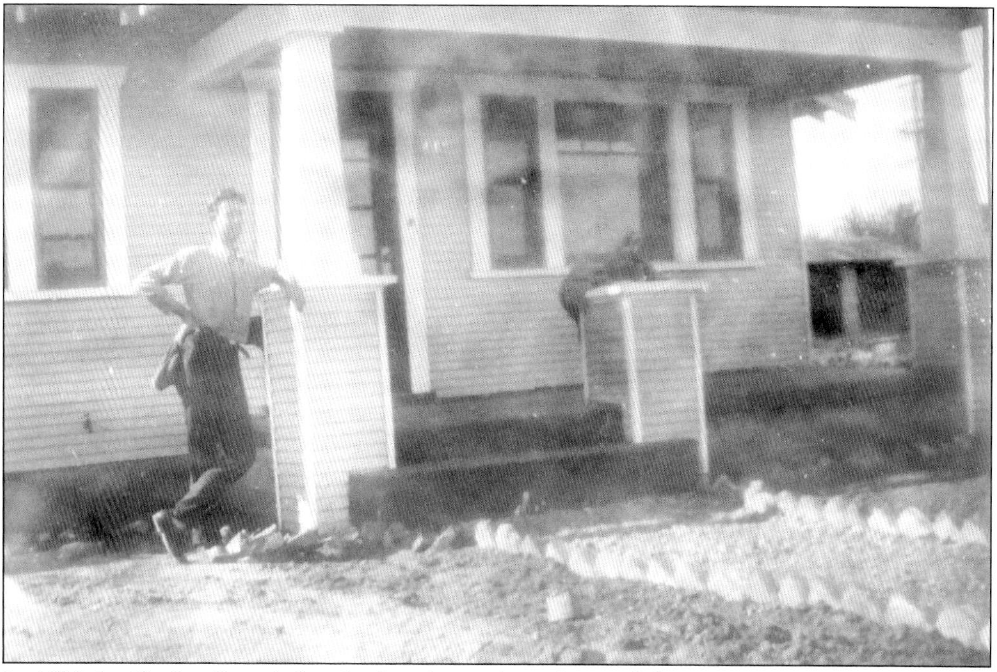

In 1926, Ira Keeler, Betty's first husband, stands in front of their new home at 415 Santiago Avenue in North Sacramento. The Sacramento directory lists Betty as Miss Betty Keeler in the New Theatre (Del Paso Theatre) Building at 2116 Del Paso Boulevard. After 1929, she is listed as Betty Newth (Charlie Newth was her second husband) at the Santiago address, then later as Mrs. Rae Roscoe Bryan. (Risse: Betty Bryan.)

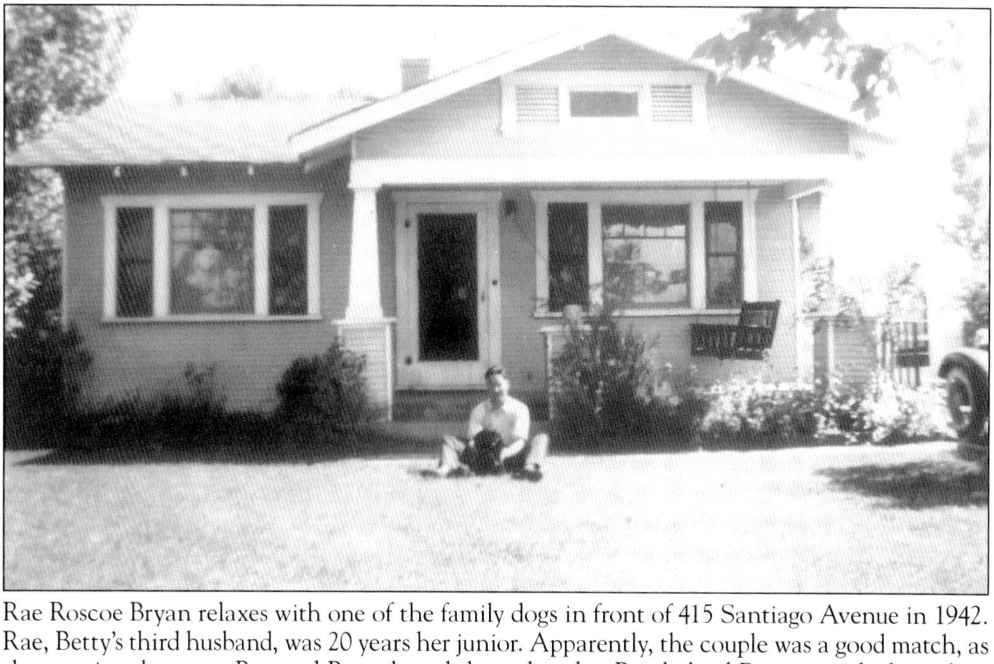

Rae Roscoe Bryan relaxes with one of the family dogs in front of 415 Santiago Avenue in 1942. Rae, Betty's third husband, was 20 years her junior. Apparently, the couple was a good match, as the marriage between Rae and Betty lasted three decades. Rae helped Betty care for her ailing mother. (Risse: Betty Bryan.)

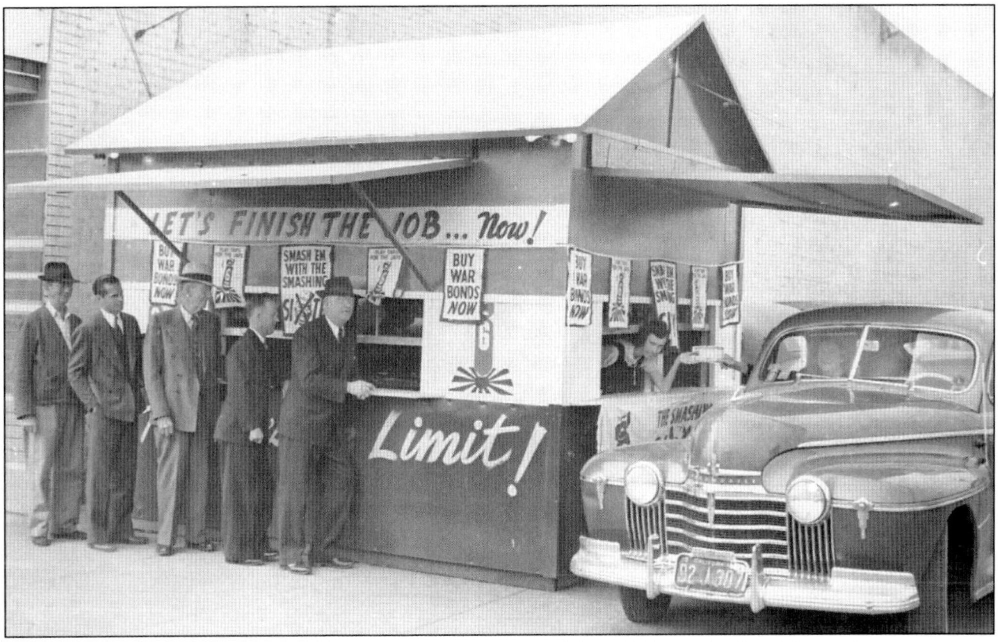

"Let's finish the job . . . now!" Virgil Chapman, second from left, and other North Sacramentans buy war bonds from a booth adjacent to the bowling alley on Del Paso Boulevard around 1942. Today at the juncture of Arden Way and Del Paso Boulevard, a sculpture of Virgil Chapman greets citizens with the inscription "It's a beautiful day. How can I help you?" As the owner of Chapman Real Estate, Virgil answered his office phone at 285 Arden Way (where Regal gas station now sits) with these words. (SAMCC.)

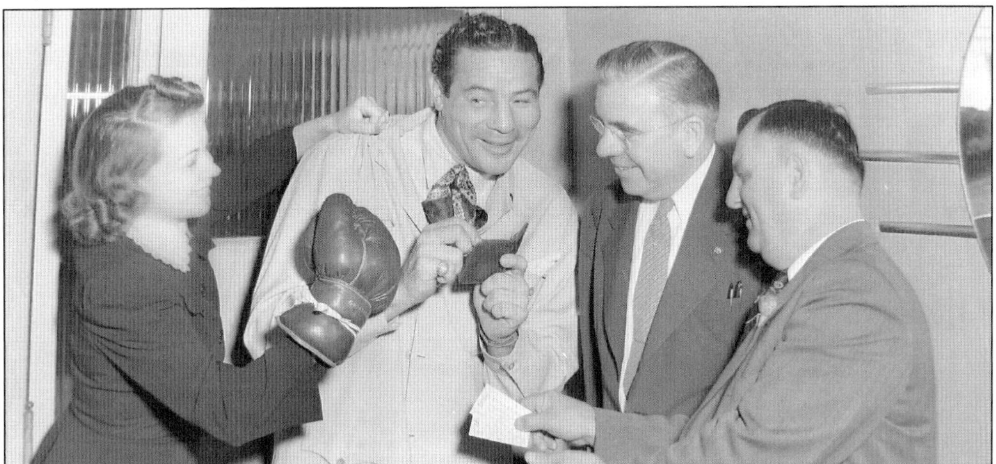

Max Baer joined in festivities at the opening of Iceland in 1940. The dressing room at Iceland is tiny, which required the use of a special lens that caused the photograph's distortion. Max trained in the 1920s at the open-air theater in North Sacramento, whose location is under debate. Jo Alice Erickson-Nastal remembers her uncle Harry Erickson saying he got into the ring with Baer and came out with a broken nose—and a story to tell his descendants, including Jo Alice. Jo believes the open-air theater was where Taber's Furniture is currently located, and Margaret Fish Smith remembers the sparring area as being adjacent to the theater that backed up onto Dixieanne Avenue going east. (SAMCC.)

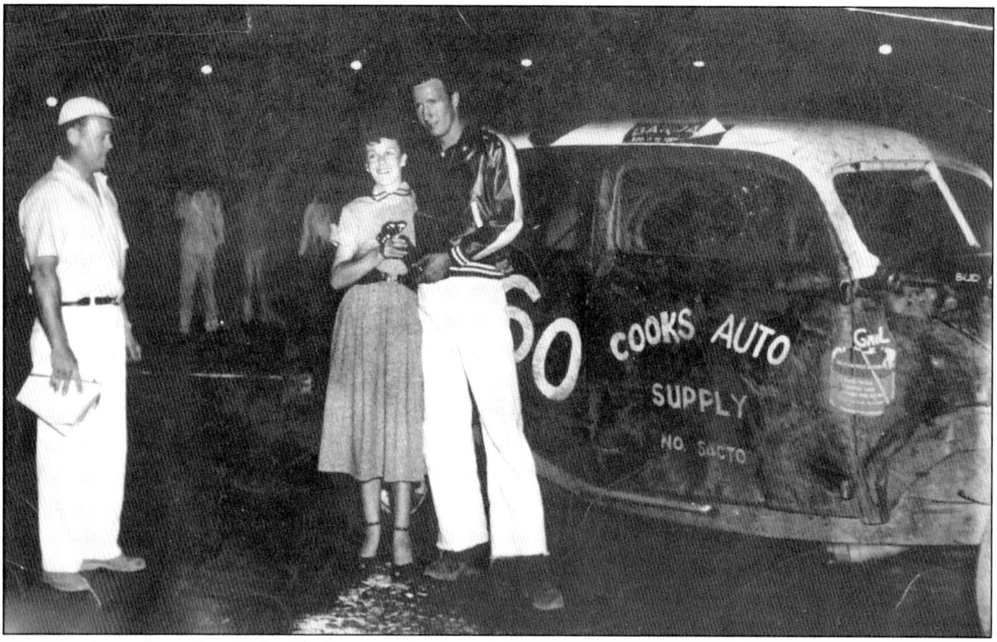

Cook's Auto Supply of North Sacramento sponsored car No. 60 at the Sacramento Raceway, pictured here around 1950. (Cook family.)

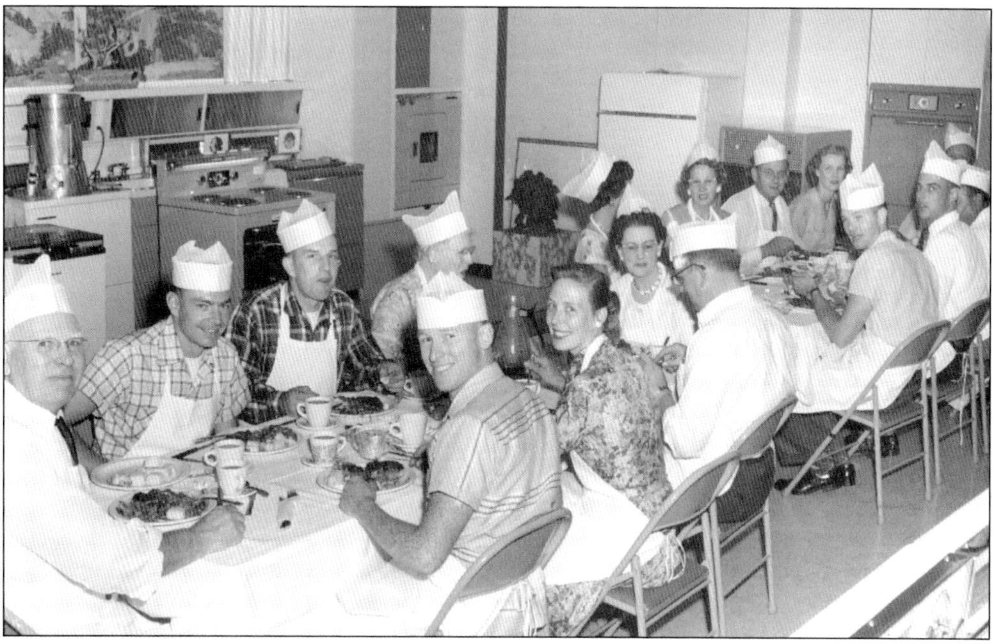

The Cooks and the employees of Cook's Auto Supply sit down for a company dinner provided compliments of General Electric. Roscoe Sr. sits at the head of the table (far left), on his left is Steve Cook, and to Roscoe's right are Dale Cook and Sophia Cook. Roscoe's wife, Susie Cook, is at the end of the table. (Cook family.)

Growing up, Lois Hansen (Nickless) remembers playing softball with her chums in Woodlake Park. Lamb's Furniture sponsored the 1941 girls' softball team. From left to right are (first row) Betty Hartan, Margaret Anin, Eillen Green, Bernice Johnson; (second row) coach Max Hartle, Arlene Matson, unidentified, Lucille Armstrong, Lois Hansen, and an unidentified Marilyn Monroe look-alike. (Hansen-Nickless.)

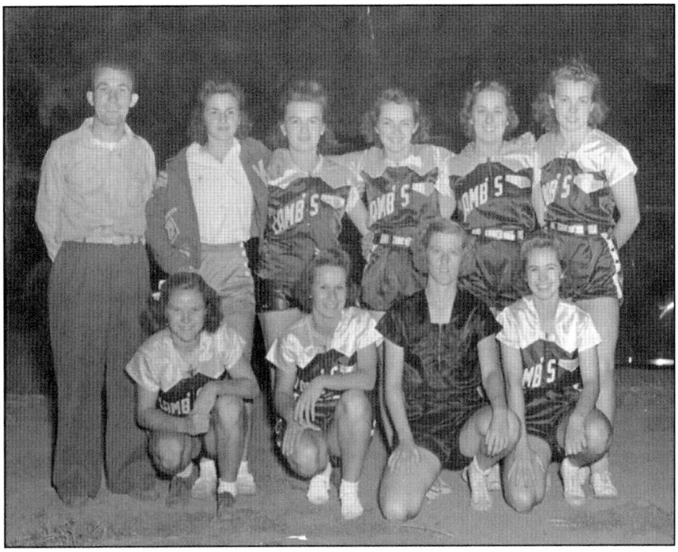

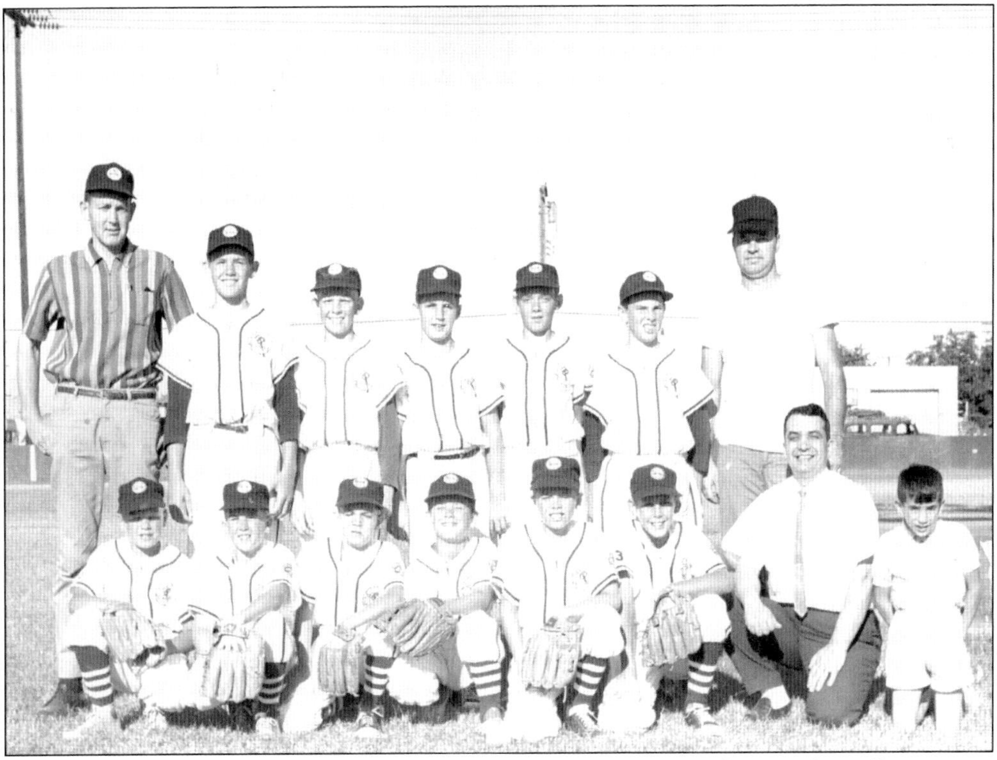

Born in Damascus, Syria, North Sacramento city councilman Joseph G. Halawe (first row on his knees) sponsored a Woodlake softball team and named it after his restaurant, Lil Joe's, at 1710 Del Paso Boulevard. Next to Joseph Halawe is his son, George Halawe, who now runs the family restaurant along with daughter, Nadia Halawe. Lil Joe also sponsored an ice hockey team at Iceland. Joseph started a restaurant at the current location of Stoney Inn, a block from Iceland on the boulevard. Joseph moved his restaurant to the present location at 1710 Del Paso Boulevard, calling it Texas Chili, then Emerald Café in 1948 before settling on the name Lil Joe's. (Halawe family.)

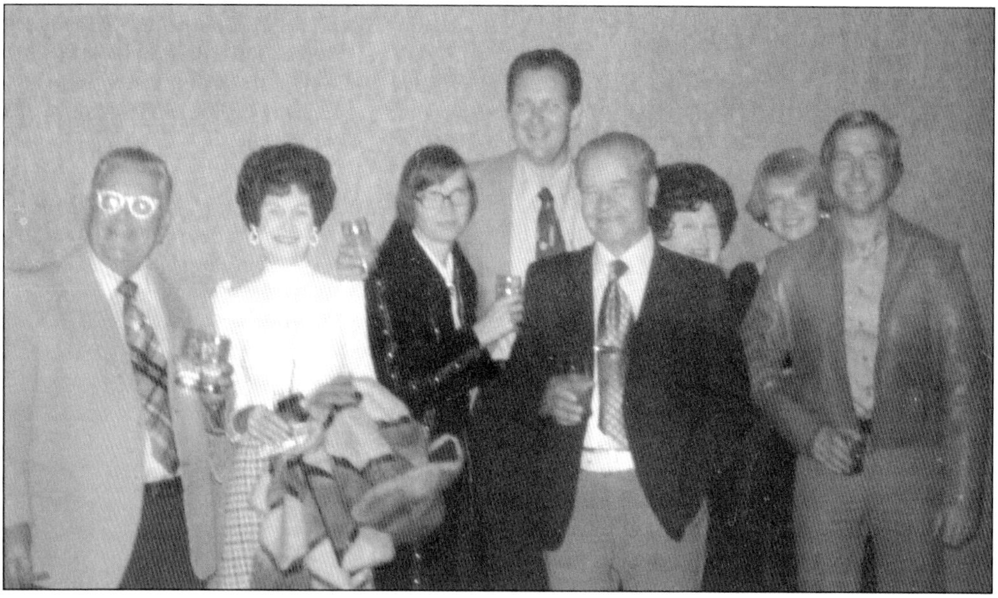

Sammy Powell (Sammy's Restaurant) celebrates with friends and family at North Sacramento's plush El Dorado Hotel in 1960. From left to right are Sammy (front and center and wearing a dark jacket); his wife, Zoe Powell (behind Sammy); Mrs. Gary Powell; and son Gary Powell, who died young. Sammy's is now run by a new family who opted to keep the name Sammy's to attract the loyal customers, such as city councilman Jay Grantland Johnson, who is seen below. (Hansen-Nickless.)

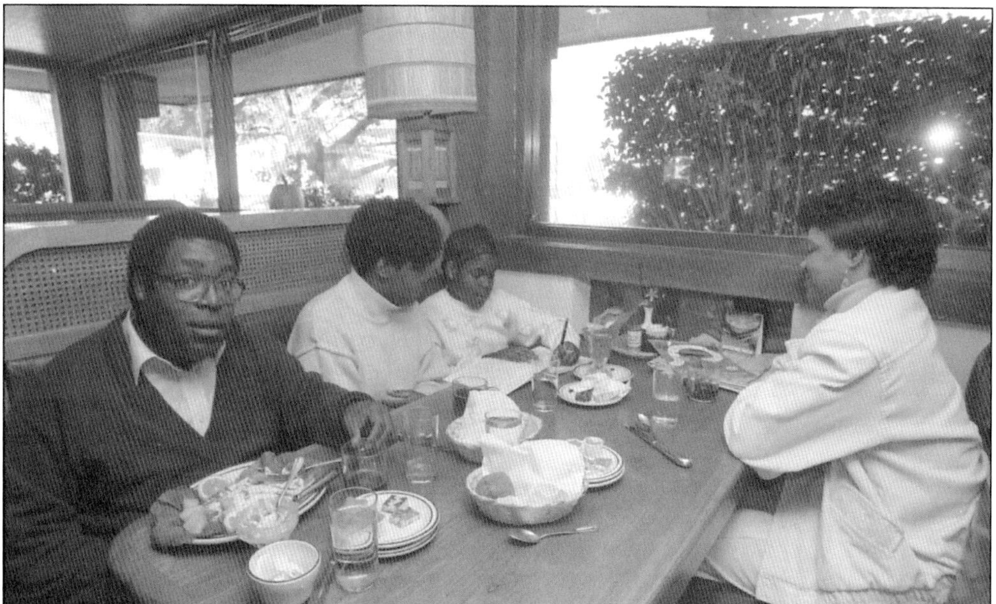

On the far left is city councilman Jay Grantland Johnson, the first black city councilman for the north area, enjoying with his family a Sunday meal at Sammy's Restaurant in April 1986. Opening in 1944, Sammy's is located at 2021 Del Paso Boulevard. Sammy Powell had the unusual luck to hold a liquor license and opened his first restaurant in 1935 adjacent to Taber's Furniture at 1819 Del Paso Boulevard, as seen in the photograph on page 118. (SAMCC.)

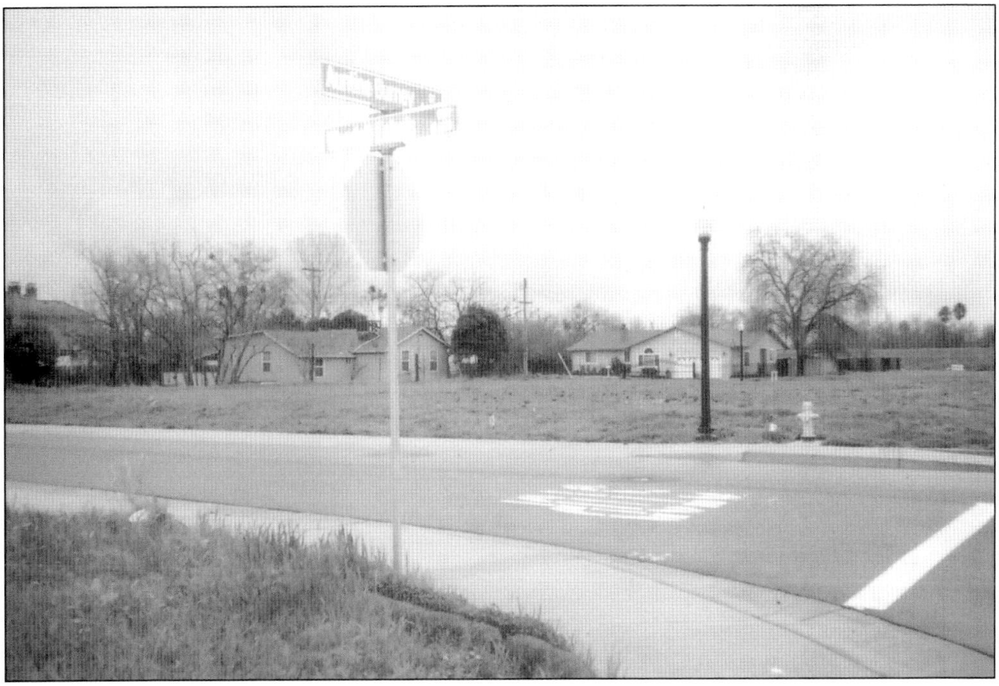

Here is a modern-day image of Wendell Echols Way, a street named in honor of the North Sacramento pioneer. (Ehrenreich-Risner.)

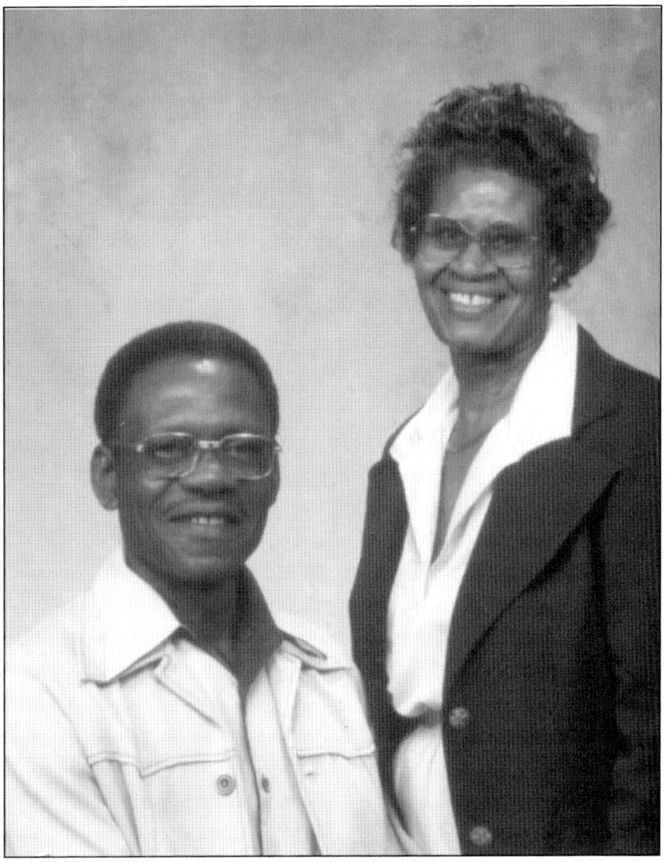

The Echolses pose for a portrait in 1980. The streets shown above in the north area is named Wendell Echols Way for Wendell's long service to the school district and his work in the community. (SAMCC.)

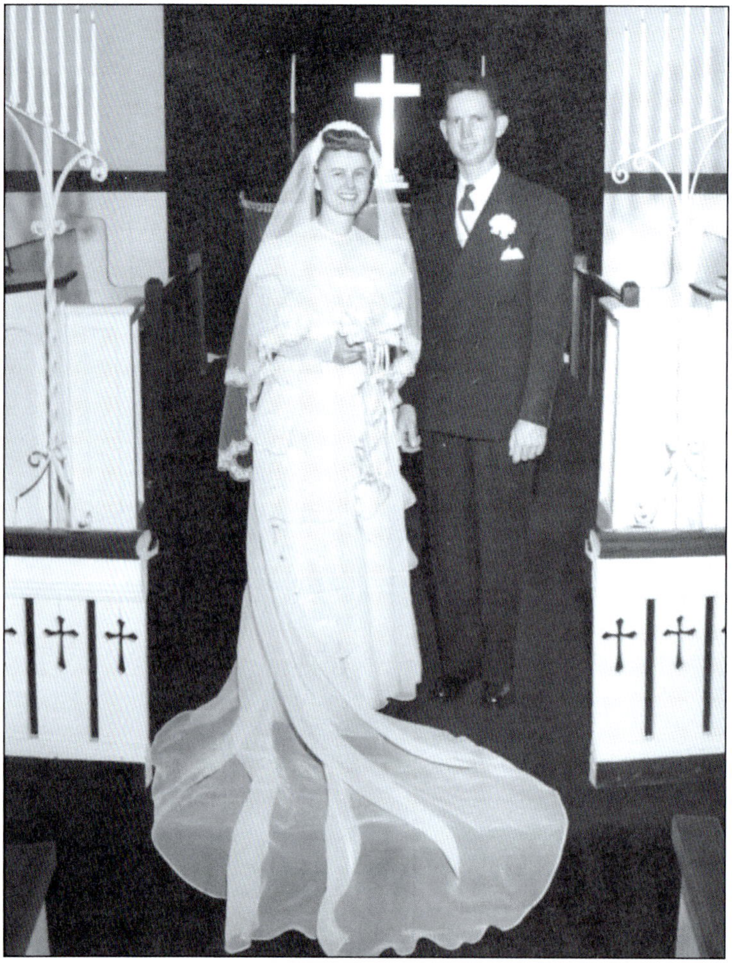

Alice E. Johnson, city clerk of North Sacramento, became the bride of Auburn Erickson on January 29, 1950, in the Epworth Methodist Church of North Sacramento. (Erickson-Nastal.)

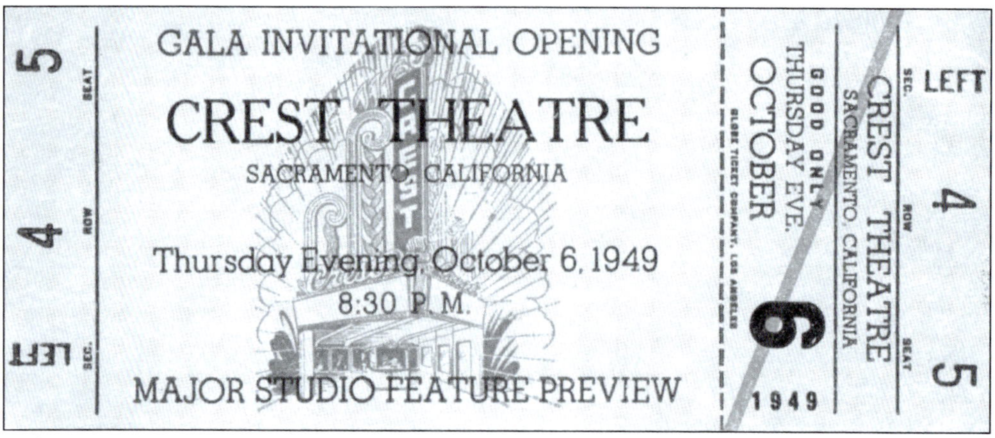

Auburn Erickson was shy and took the opportunity of the opening of the Crest Theatre on October 6, 1949, to ask Alice E. Johnson out on a date. Erickson Construction Company built the Crest Theatre and received this gold ticket. (Erickson-Nastal.)

Betty Bryan took this portrait of her friend John Holden in all his Masonic regalia. Holden was editor of the *North Sacramento Journal*, located at 1503 Del Paso Boulevard. Ca 1935. (Risse: Betty Bryan.)

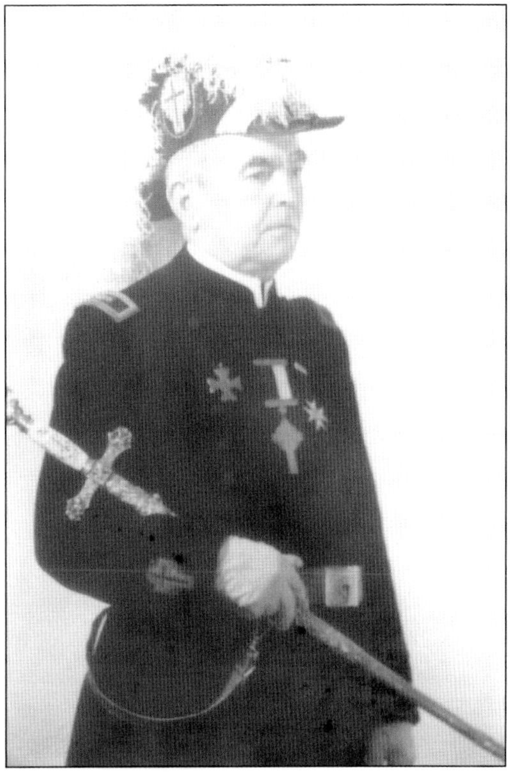

Attendees of the Johnson-Erickson wedding included North Sacramento dignitaries like fire chief Louis Cassaglia; Judge John. L. Missall; his wife, Evelyn Johnson Missal; Alice's sister; and police officer Jack Rea, who was later shot in the line of duty. Erickson Construction remodeled the church. (Erickson-Nastal.)

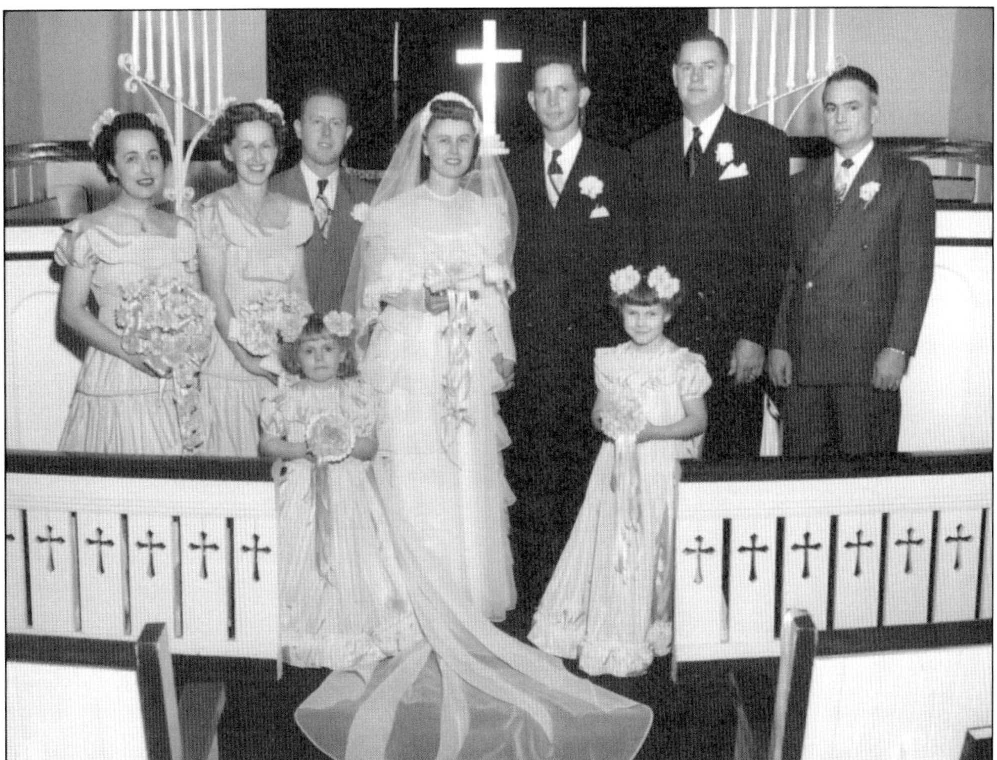

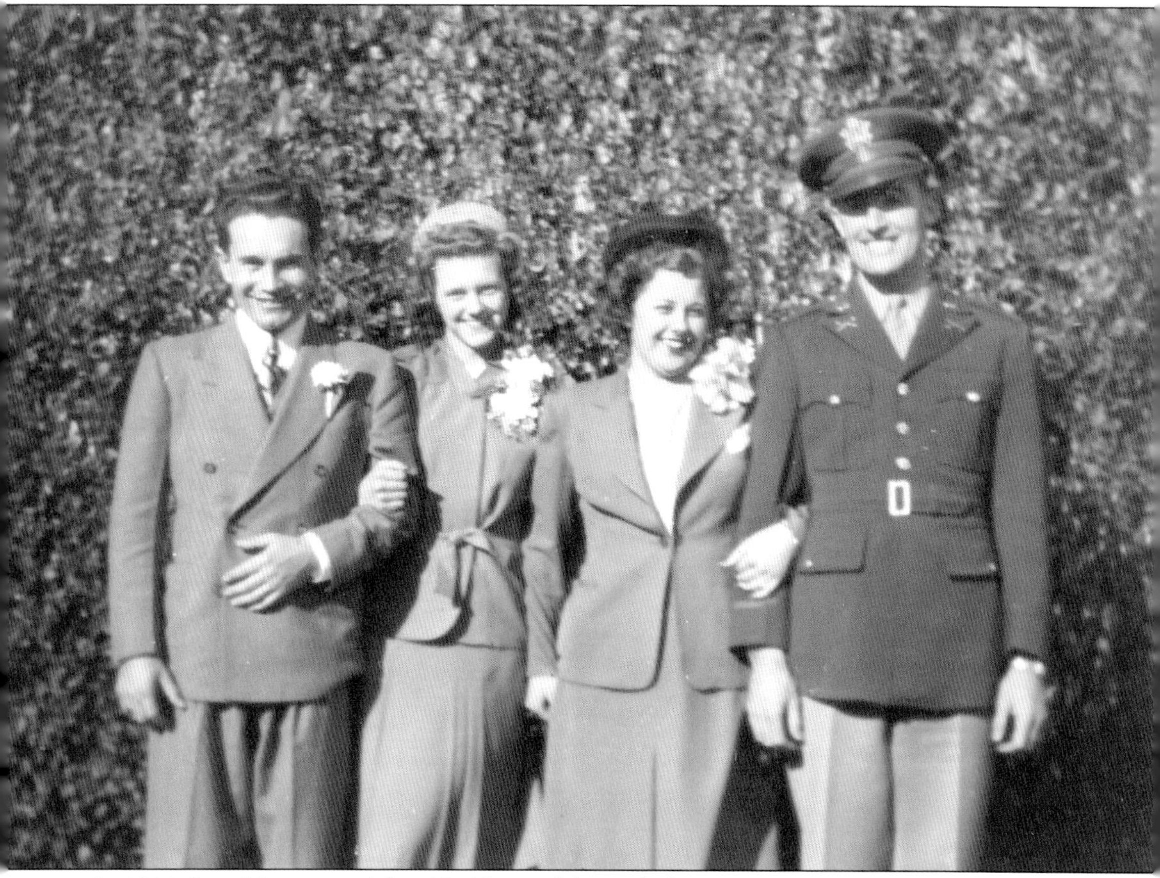

In 1944, Lois Hansen and Jess Nickless celebrate before Jess returns to active duty during World War II. From left to right are two unidentified people, Lois Hansen-Nickless, and Jess Nickless. On November 8, 1942, Lt. Donald Hansen was reported missing in Guadalcanal. Lois never saw her brother again. (Hansen-Nickless.)

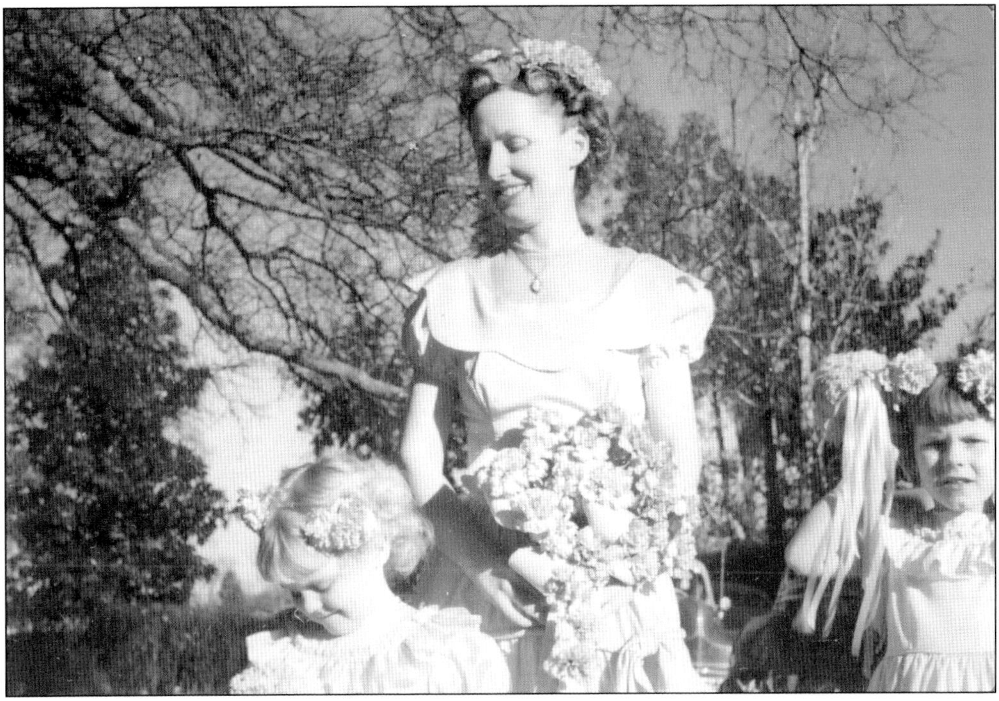

Jo Alice (left) participates in a wedding as a flower girl near the family's Woodlake home in this c. 1953 image. (Erickson-Nastal.).

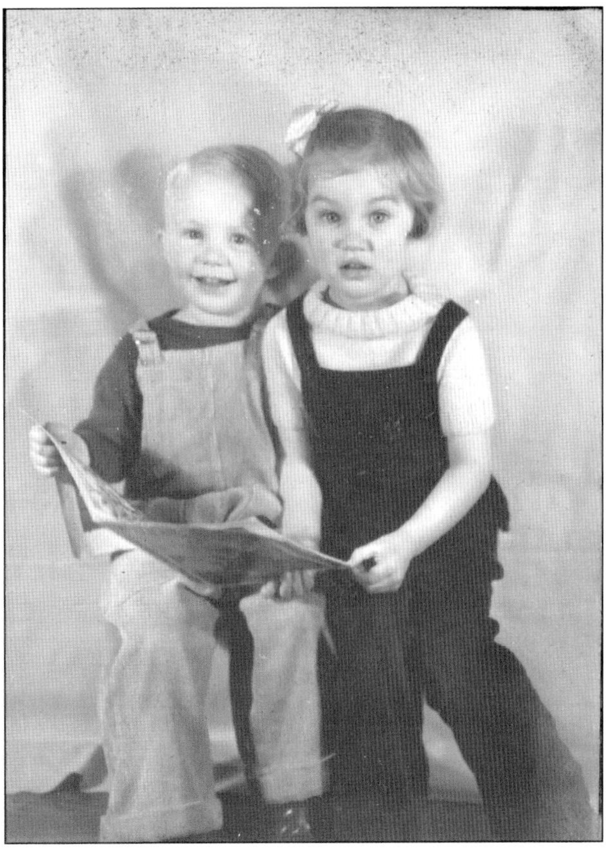

From left to right, Fred Roth is read a story by his best friend Leora (Kaufer) Matranga, pictured around 1936. (Roth.)

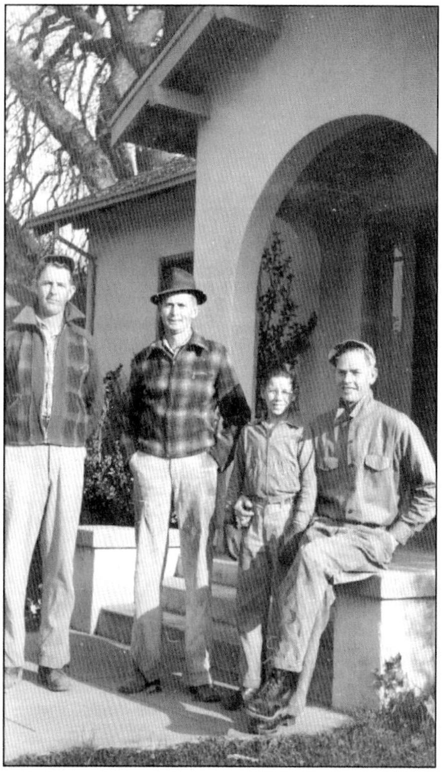

From left to right, Harry, Axel "Pop," Bob Frago, and Frank Erickson are outside the El Monte house in 1938. (Erickson-Nastal.)

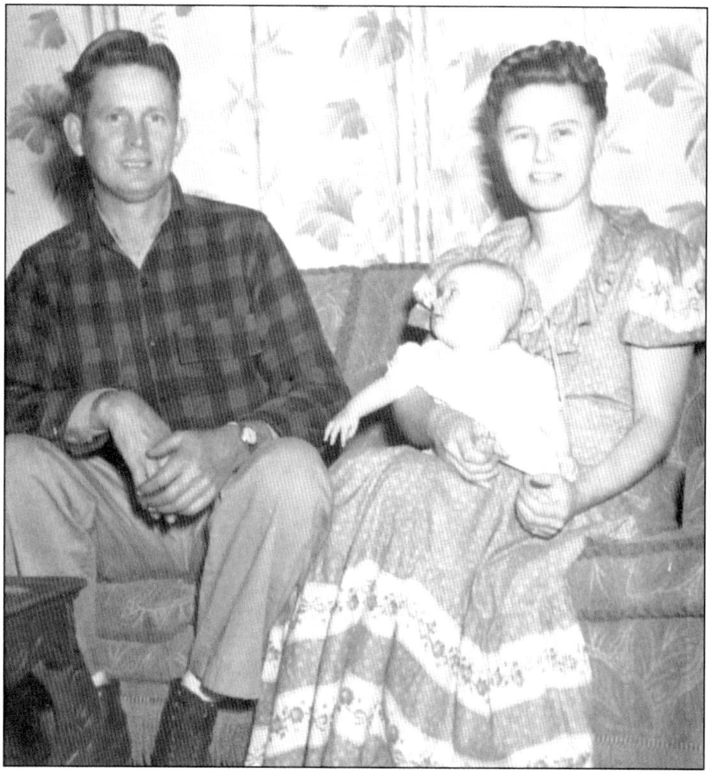

Baby Jo Alice Erickson only has eyes for daddy. Pictured from left to right around 1953 are Auburn "Babe" Erickson, Alice Johnson Nastal, and baby Jo Alice. (Erickson-Nastal.)

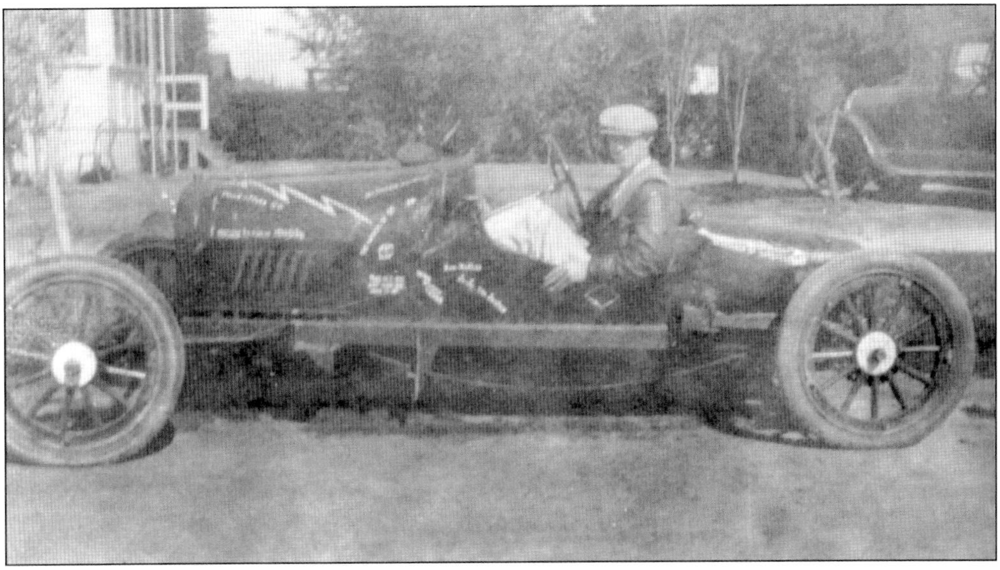

Axel Erickson sits in his roadster in the driveway of the house he built on Pope Avenue in the back of the Del Paso Country Club around 1914. (Erickson-Nastal.)

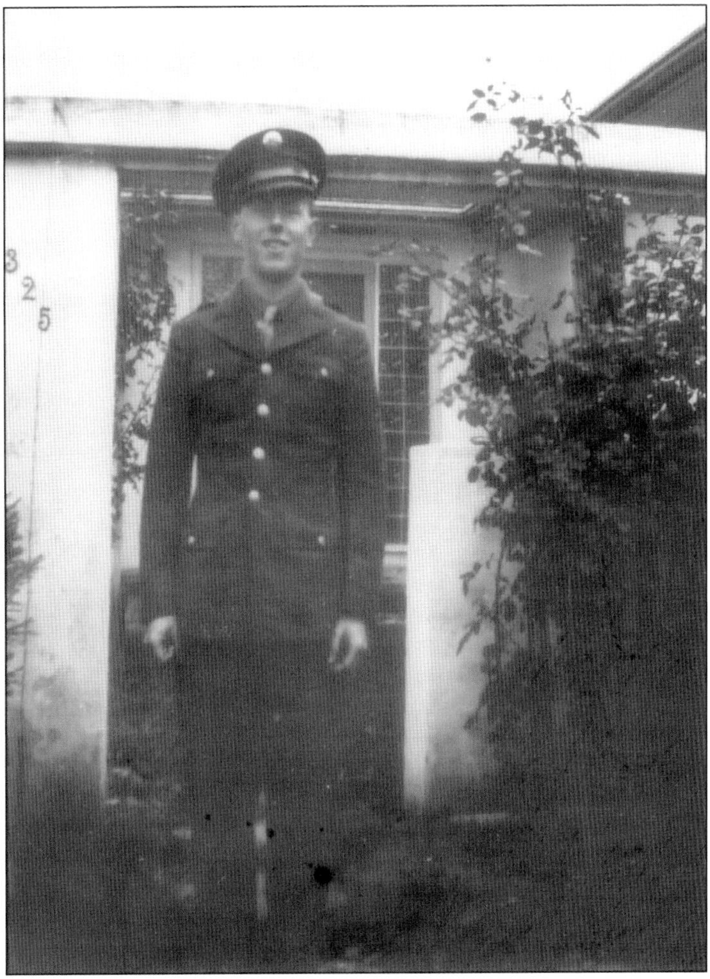

Pfc. Bob Johnson prepares for his departure from 325 Lochbrae Road in North Sacramento. Bob, brother of the Johnson girls and Alice Johnson Erickson, met action in World War II. A boating aficionado, Bob drowned in the American River. This photograph was taken around 1942. (Erickson-Nastal.)

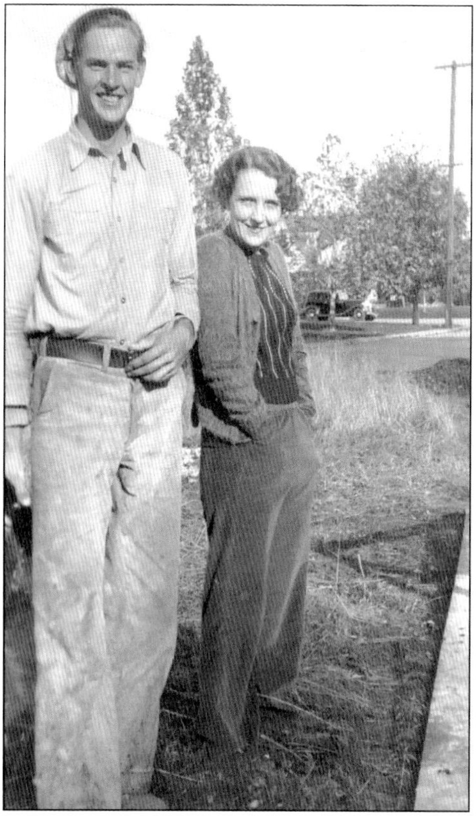

Frank Erickson and his beautiful wife stand outside the beginnings of a home in North Sacramento around 1938. (Erickson-Nastal.)

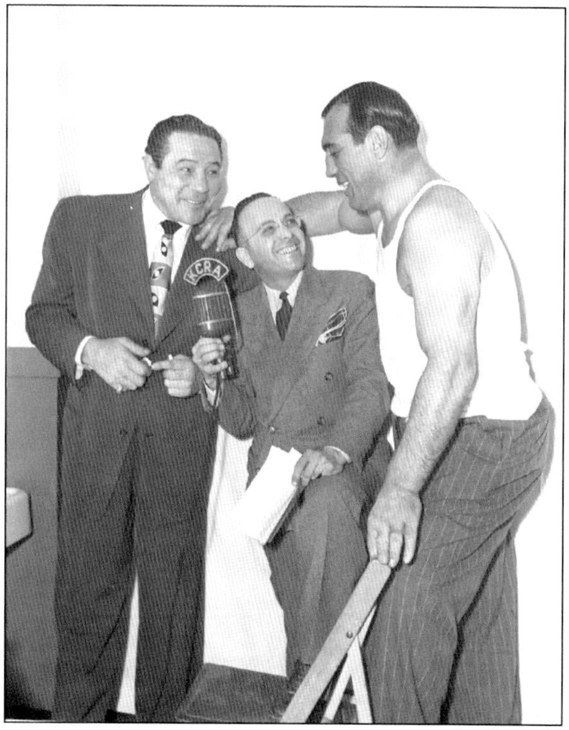

Max Baer, Steve George, and Primo Carmera are pictured around 1949. Max and his brother Buddy Baer lived on Lochbrae Avenue in North Sacramento. Fred Steinkamp, Woodlake resident for 67 years, was good friends with Jerry Cameron. Jerry's brother, Larry Cameron, was broke and met up with Max Baer, who funded his opening of the Pontiac dealership on the boulevard. Margaret Fish Smith remembers seeing Max Baer walking down the boulevard and always being astonished at his huge size and how he filled out the space of door jambs. (Sacramento Room, Sacramento Public Library.)

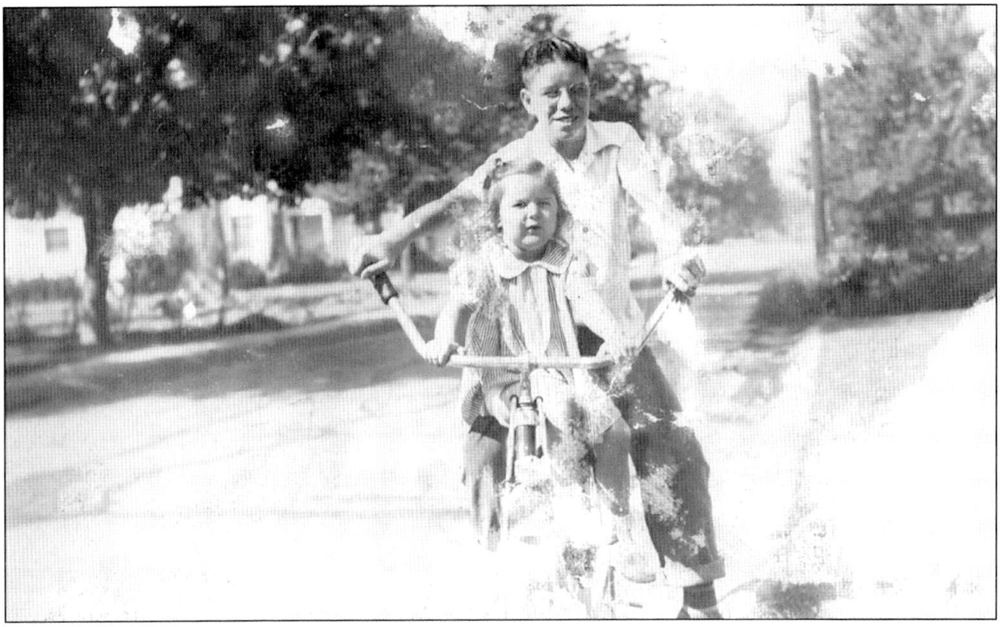

On September 26, 1944, Bob bikes his sister JoAnne over to the Erickson house, where they were steady visitors. (Erickson-Nastal.)

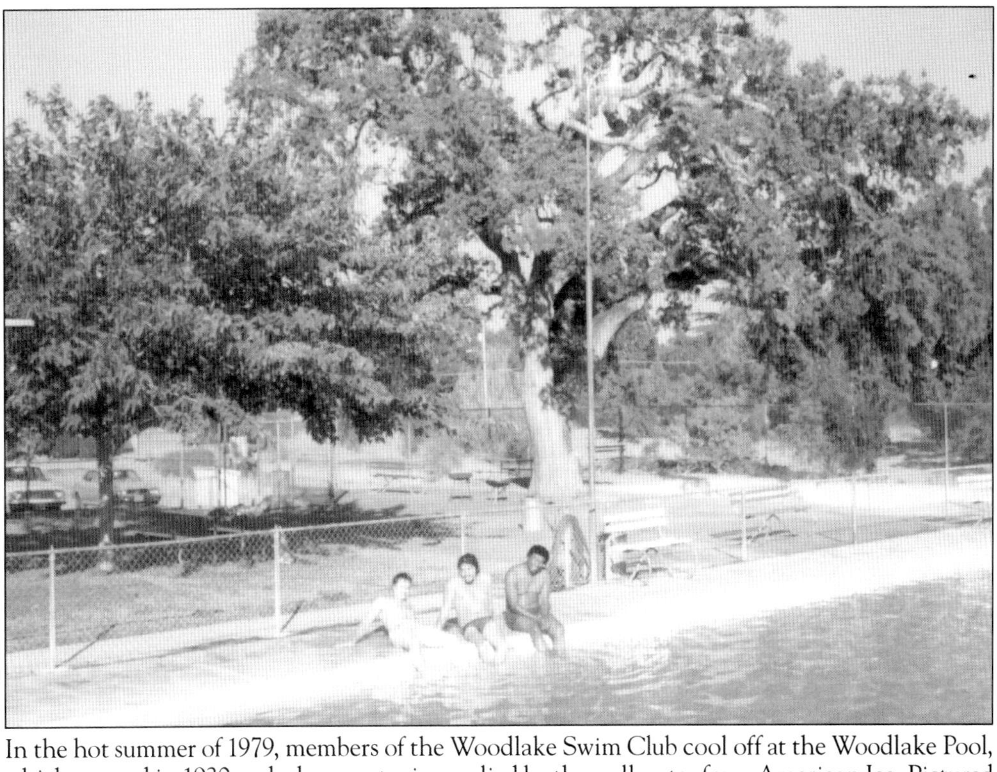

In the hot summer of 1979, members of the Woodlake Swim Club cool off at the Woodlake Pool, which opened in 1920 and whose water is supplied by the well water from American Ice. Pictured from left to right are Frank Paulo, Serfio Rodriguez, and Warner James (Erickson-Nastal.)

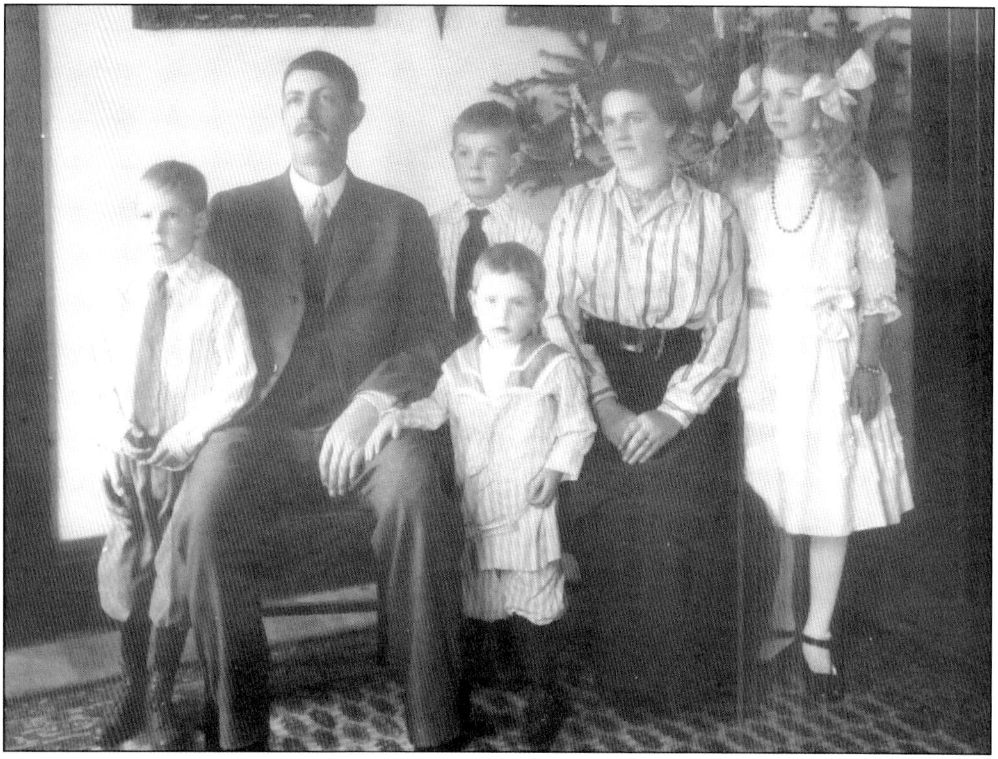

An Erickson family portrait taken on Pope Avenue in 1916 pictures (from left to right) Frank, Axel, Harry, Auburn (with hand on Axel's knee), Mama, and Nellie Erickson. (Erickson-Nastal.)

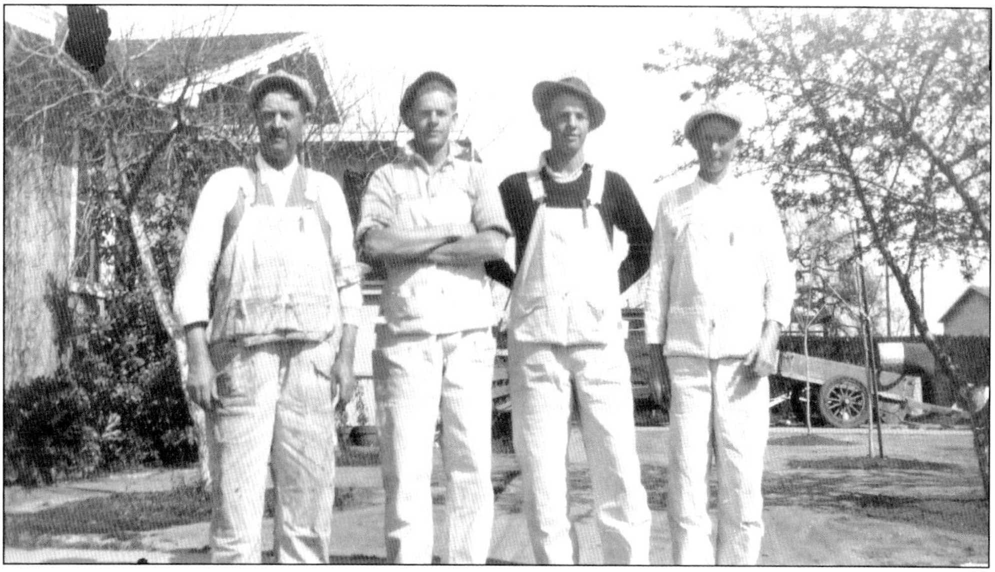

All "grow'd" up and ready for work, the Erickson boys join "Pop" outside the 1924 El Monte house on their way to construct another building for North Sacramento. From left to right in this *c.* 1929 photograph are Axel Erickson, Frank Erickson, Harry Erickson, and Auburn "Babe" Erickson. (Erickson-Nastal.)

In August 1936, on Darina Avenue in North Sacramento, the Johnson brood stands with their mother after the death of Mr. Johnson, the well digger and their father. Pictured clockwise from top left are Alice (Johnson Erickson), Addie (mother), Mildred (Johnson Roundtree), Evelyn (Johnson Missall), and Bob Johnson, who later drowned in a boating accident on the American River. (Erickson-Nastal.)

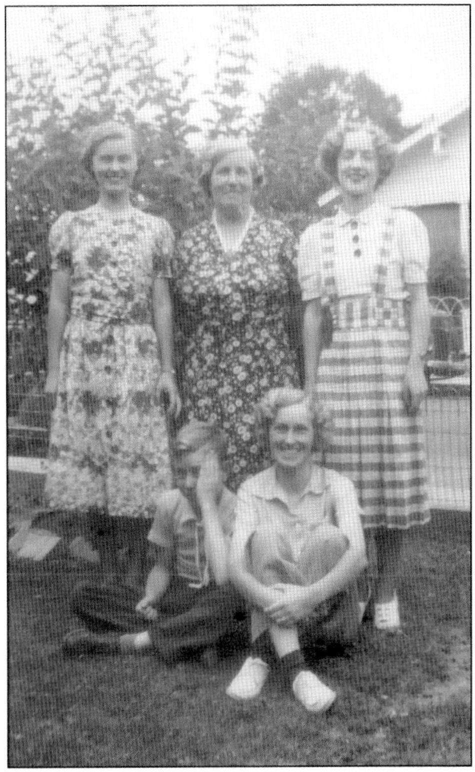

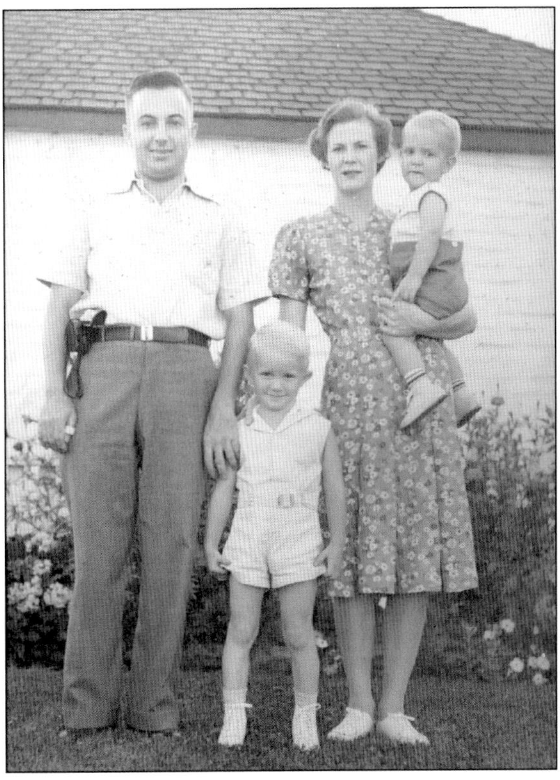

The Roth family poses for a c. 1930 photograph outside their Woodlake home. From left to right are Capt. Fred Roth of the North Sacramento Fire Department, Robert Roth, Olga Roth (first and only female North Sacramento City councilwoman and North Sacramento mayor) holding Fred "Fritz" Roth. The couple also had two girls, Dorothy and Louise. (Roth.)

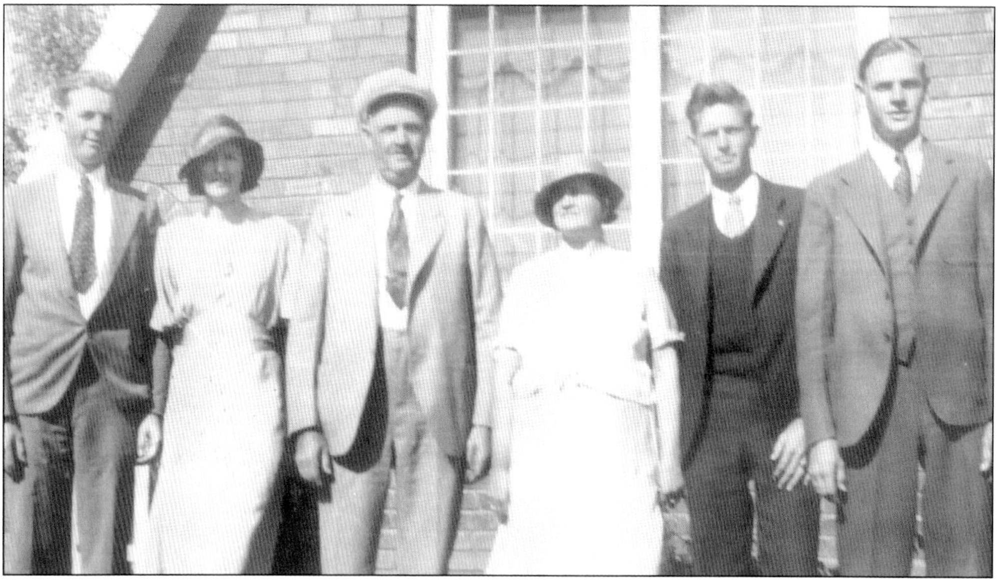

The Erickson family congregate in 1940 outside the Woodlake home they built on Forrest Street. Pictured from left to right are Harry, Nellie, Axel, Olga, Auburn, and Frank Erickson. (Erickson-Nastal.)

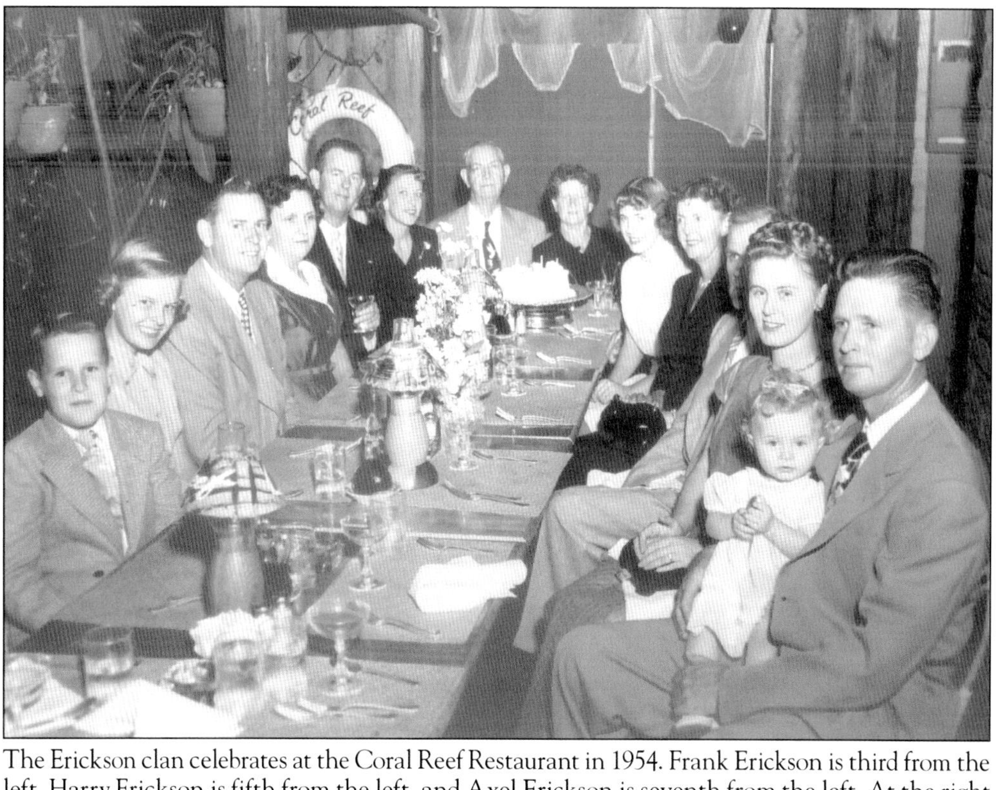

The Erickson clan celebrates at the Coral Reef Restaurant in 1954. Frank Erickson is third from the left, Harry Erickson is fifth from the left, and Axel Erickson is seventh from the left. At the right side of the table, Auburn (Babe) sits with Jo Alice on his knee beside Alice Johnson Erickson.

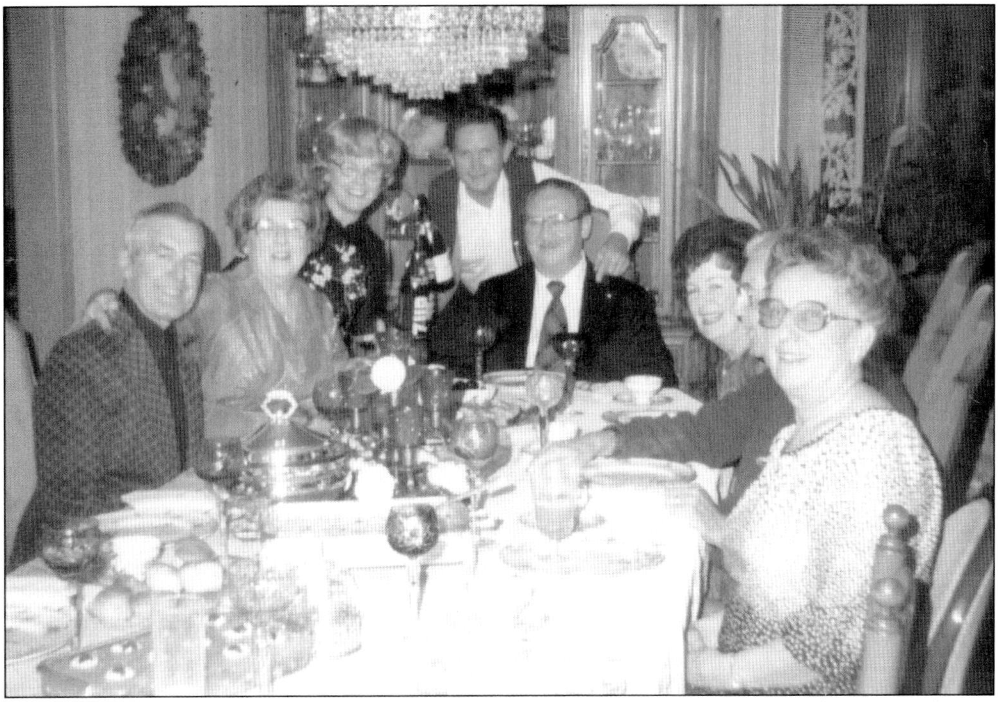

Lois and Jess Nickless enjoy a New Year's Eve in 1979 at Auburn and Alice Johnson Erickson's Woodlake home on Garden Avenue. From right to left at the table are Jess Nickless, Evie McPherson, Alice Erickson, Babe Erickson, Mr. McPherson, Annah Carlisle, Lee Carlisle, and Vera Lundberg. (Hansen-Nickless.)

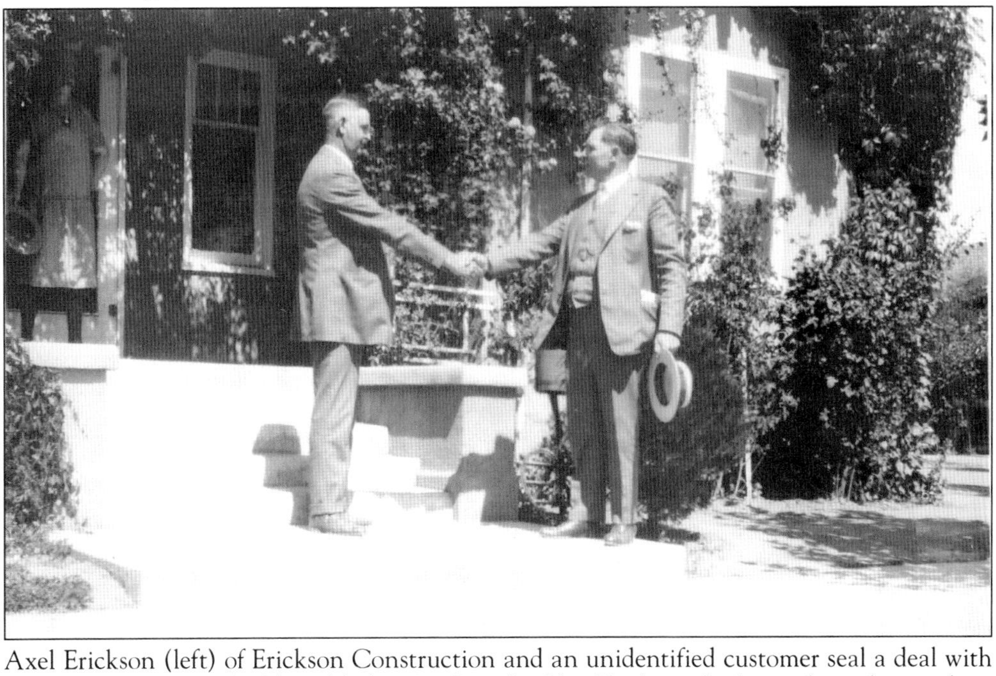

Axel Erickson (left) of Erickson Construction and an unidentified customer seal a deal with the company's proverbial handshake. Axel's wife, Olga Erickson, looks on from the porch in this *c.* 1940 photograph. (Erickson-Nastal.)

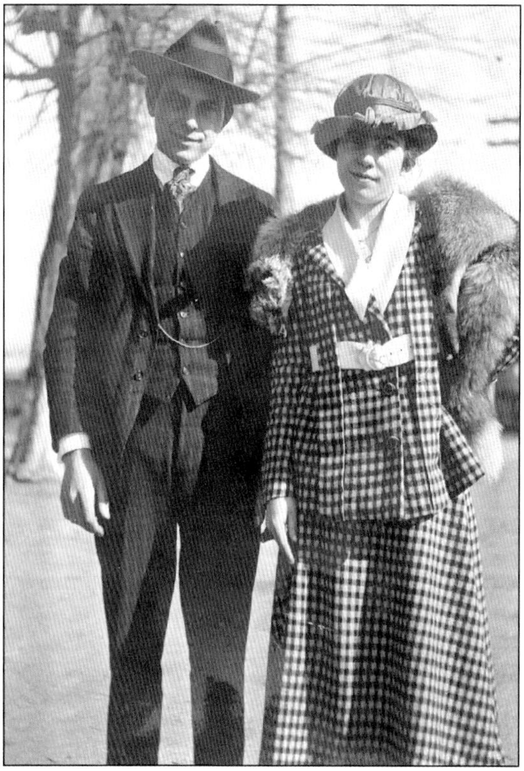

Pictured here around 1925 are William Kerth Sr. and Emily Kerth, just before their move to North Sacramento. (Kerth.)

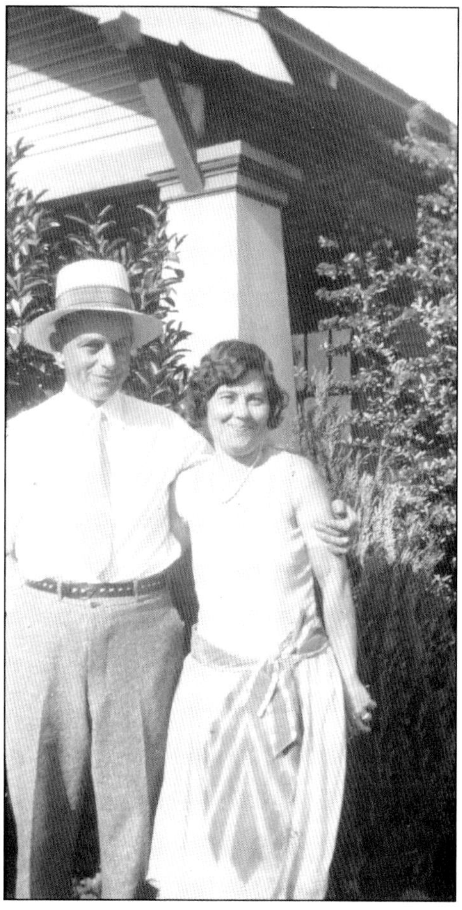

William Kerth Sr. and Emily Kerth are pictured around 1935 at their home on Grove Avenue and Barrette Street in North Sacramento. (Kerth.)

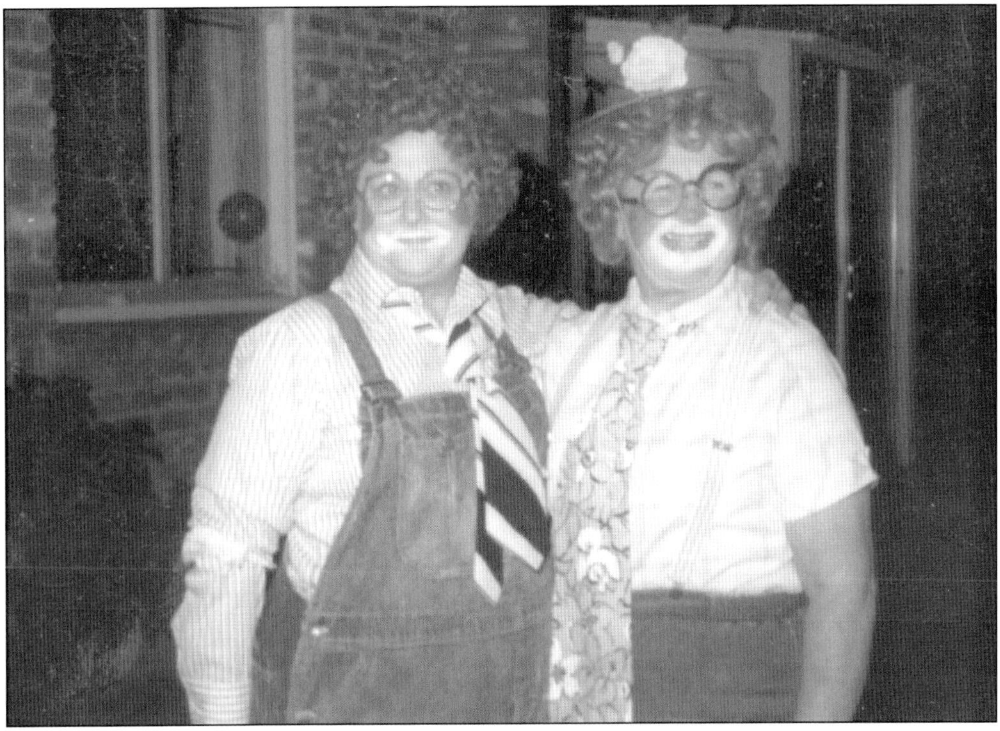

Lois Hansen Nickless (left) clowns around with Betty Palmilu at the Erickson house in Woodlake for the annual barbecue around 1983. (Hansen-Nickless.)

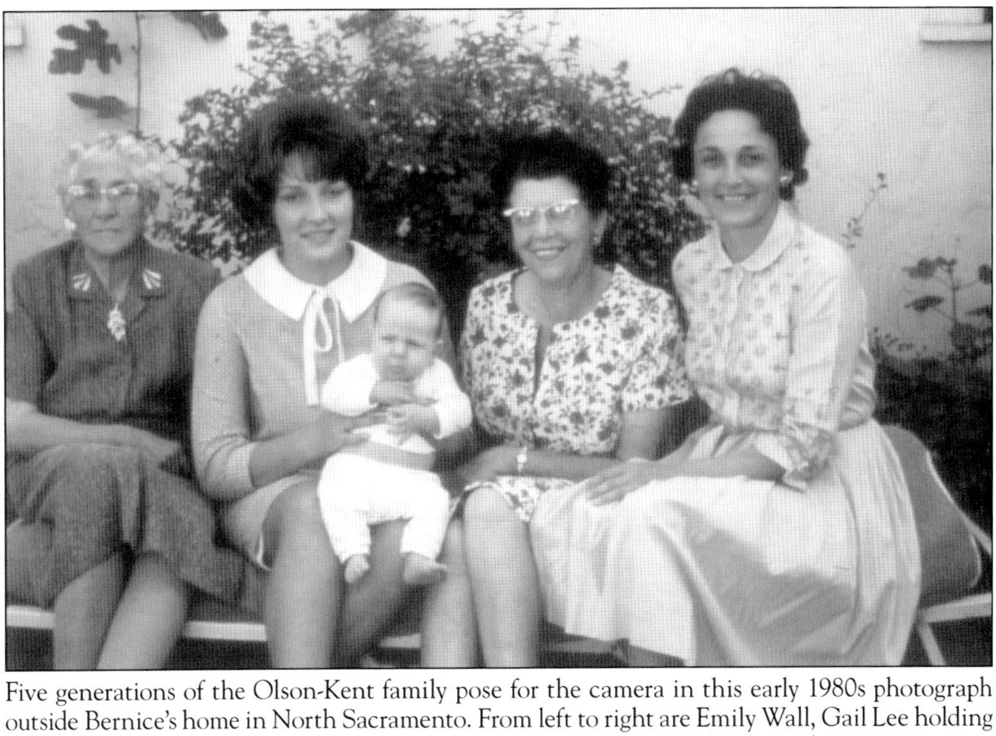

Five generations of the Olson-Kent family pose for the camera in this early 1980s photograph outside Bernice's home in North Sacramento. From left to right are Emily Wall, Gail Lee holding baby Richard Lee, Evelyn Ruth Olson, and Bernice Olson-Kent. (Olson-Kent.)

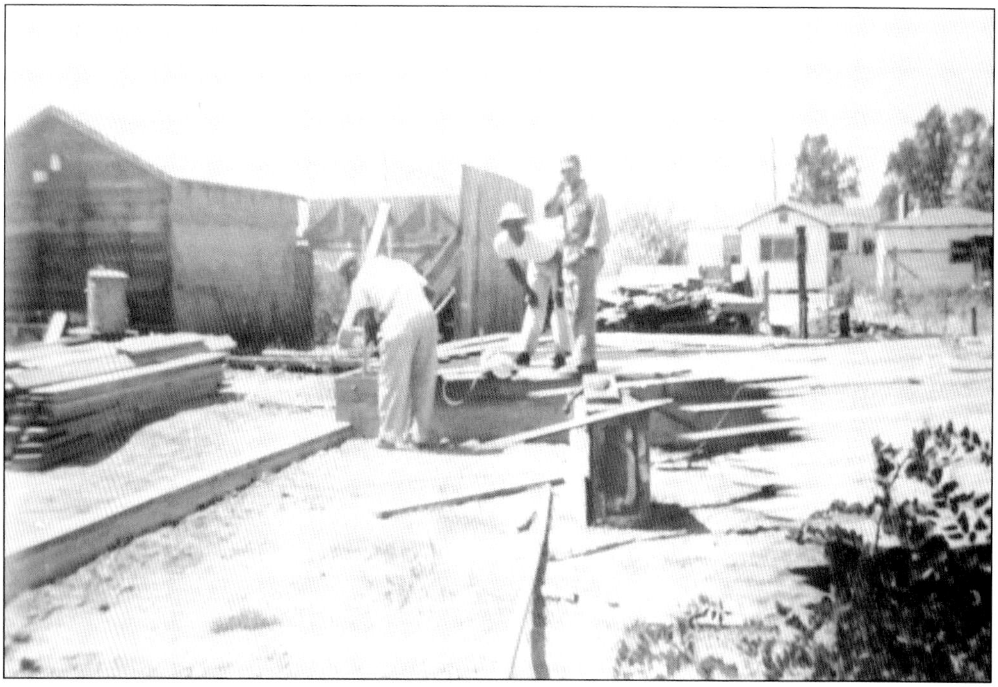

Members of the Peeler family and a neighbor work on the foundation for the Peeler house in Del Paso Heights around 1953. (SAMCC.)

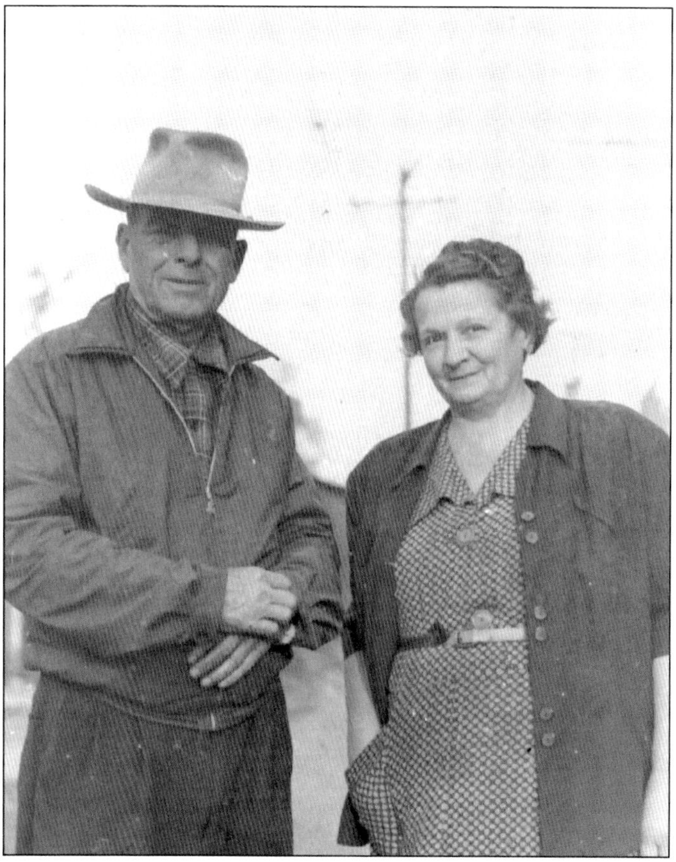

Richard D. Taber Sr. and Olga Taber of Taber's Furniture take a moment to pose along the boulevard around 1940. The Tabers lived at 1017 Del Paso Boulevard until 1930. (Taber.)

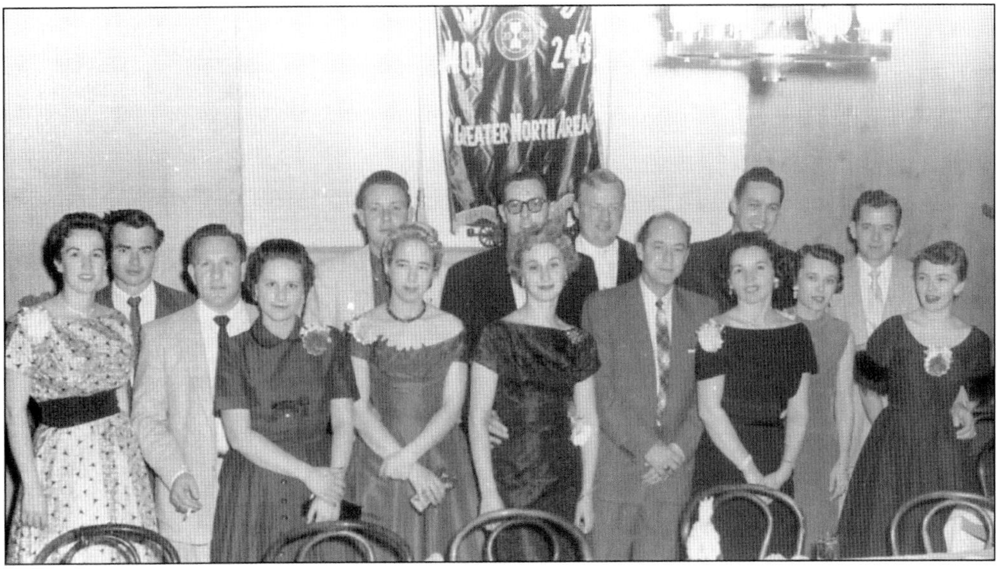

Pictured on the far right in 1956 are Dick Taber (Taber's Furniture) and his wife, Eldene. They were members of the North Area chapter of the 20-30 club. (Taber.)

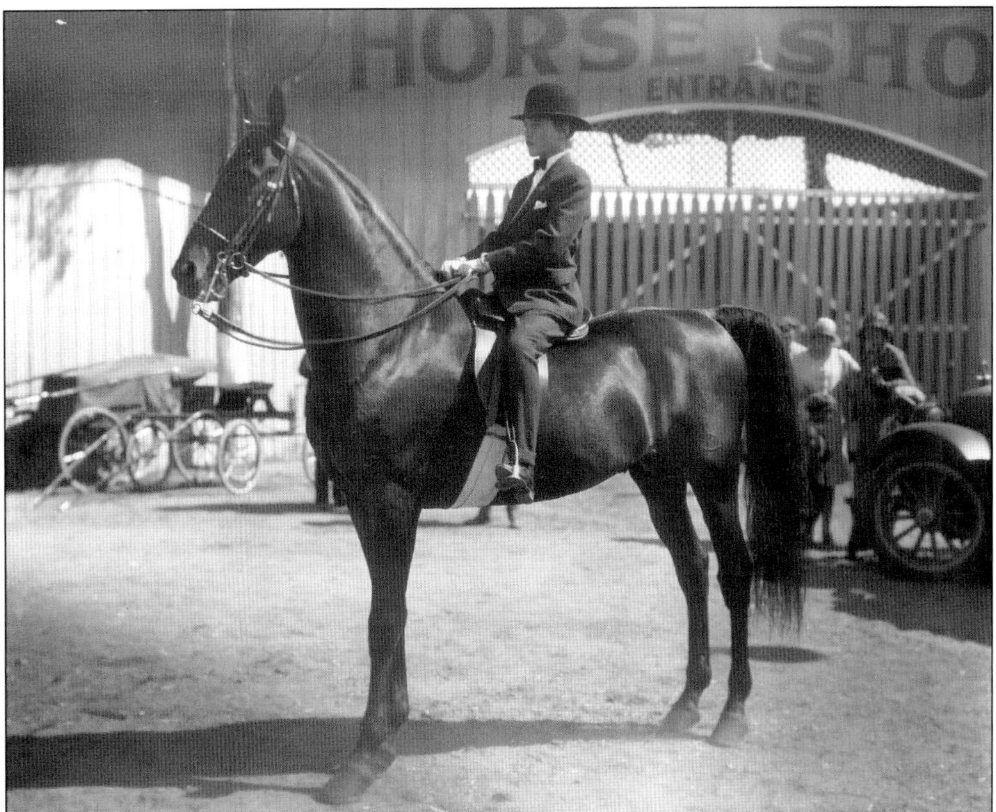

Around 1925, a young Barbara Worth prepares for the English-style competition at the old State Fair grounds. The location of her stables can be seen today with her name emblazoned above the old barn behind Del Paso Park. (SAMCC-McCurry.)

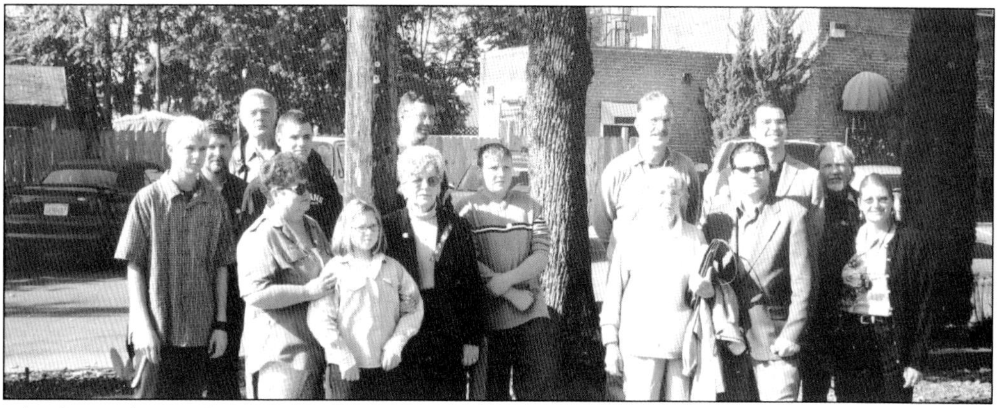

The descendants of North Sacramento police chief Erskin Fish stand under his tree at the far north end of Woodlake Park. Fish was fatally shot in the line of duty. The tree was planted in his honor to commemorate his service to North Sacramento and is tended by the Woodlake Garden Club. North Sacramento officer Jack Rhea was shot and killed by a burglar on January 3, 1954, and an obelisk in Woodlake Park commemorates his and Fish's life and service, along with other officers. (Fish Smith.)

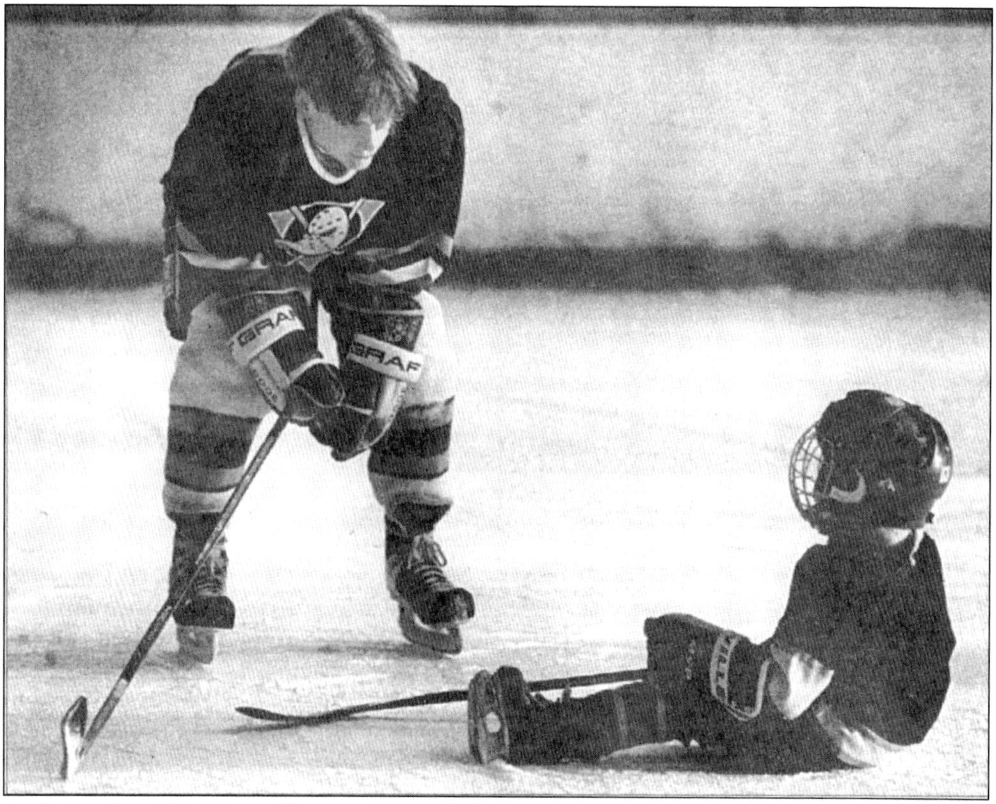

At Iceland in 1994, Ryan Ehrenreich, 12, left, leans over to give his younger brother Kevan, 5, advice during the youth hockey skills class at Iceland. Ryan helps coach the kids. The rink suffered a five-alarm fire in March 2010, but the community rallied and 500 volunteers cleaned up the debris. The city is funding a portion of the rebuilding for this landmark site established 1940. (Ehrenreich-Risner.)

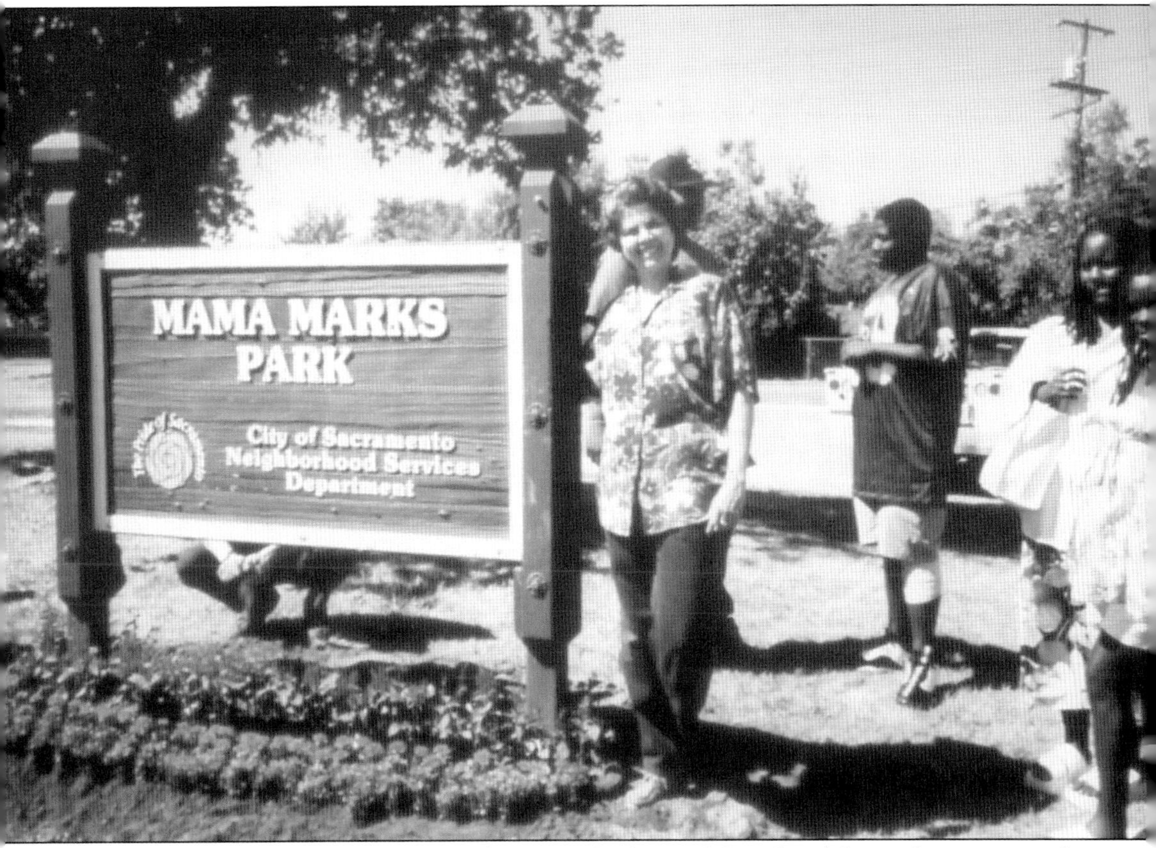

North area activist and longtime resident Fran Barker and friends celebrate the opening of Mama Marks Park. In 1970, Mama Marks had a dream that inspired her to feed the hungry in the north area. Before her death in 1991, "Mama" had spent over 20 years doling out 100 meals a day to the hungry in the community. Fran Barker and other citizens lobbied for a park in Mama's name. (SAMCC.)

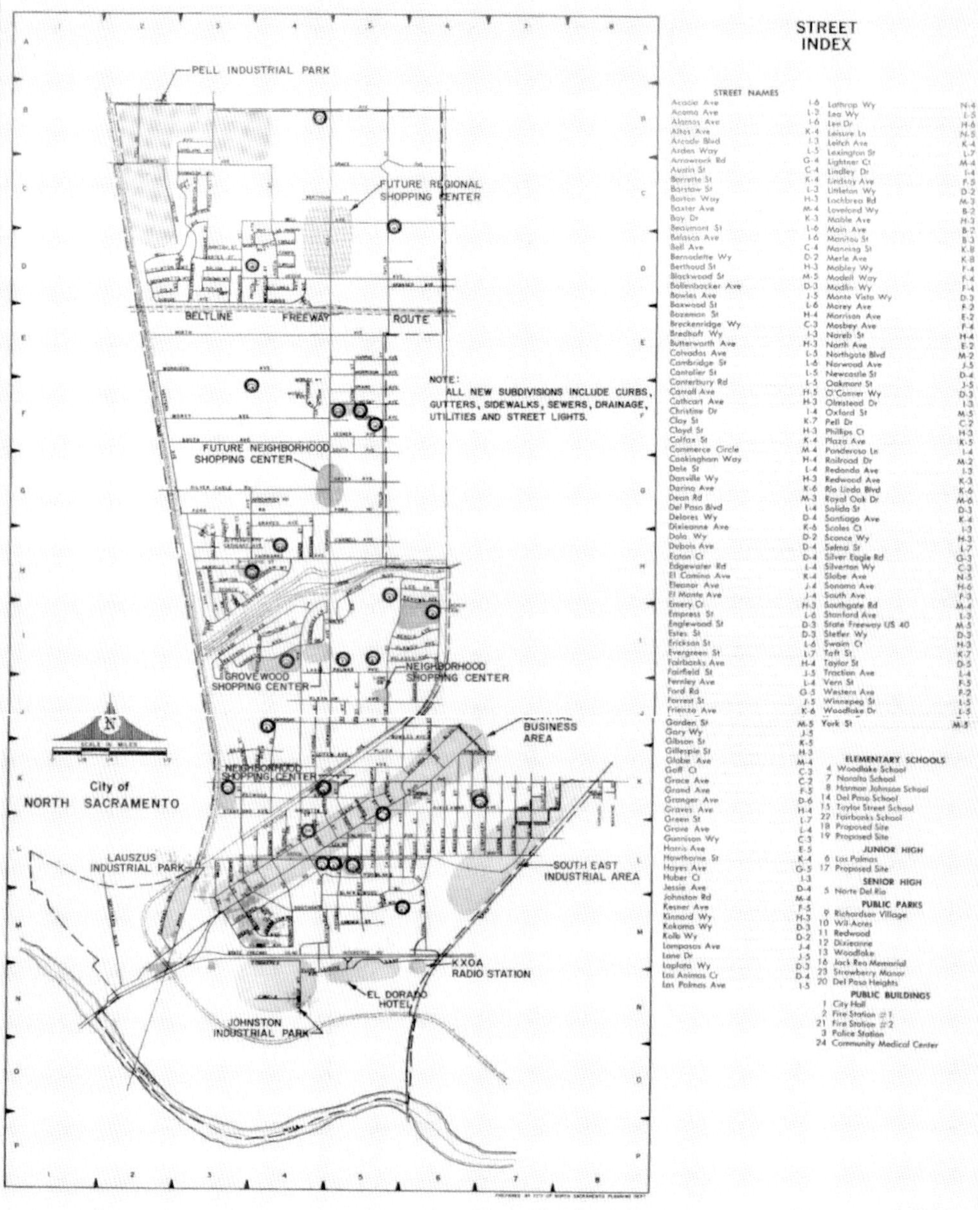

IMPORTANT PHONE NUMBERS	
City Hall	WA 2-3447
Police & Fire, Business	WA 5-3552
Emergency	WA 5-2727
Water Dept., Business	WA 2-3447
Emergency	WA 2-7893
Municipal Court	IV 3-6681
Community Medical Center	WA 5-2771

POPULATION	
1950	6,220
1953	7,500
1957	9,200
1960	12,960
1963	15,000 projection

ASSESSED VALUE		Revenue Sales Tax
1956	$14,076,135	
1957	14,038,860	148,554
1958	15,421,335	167,206
1959	17,207,280	222,223
1960	20,161,320	233,029
1961	23,941,415	189,576
to County level of Assessment		
1962	20,682,890	242,704
1963	22,467,180	326,423

DOLLAR VALUE OF BUILDING PERMITS	
1958	$1,274,697
1959	2,935,019
1960	3,101,505
1961	2,657,481
1962	3,492,227

In 1960, the City of North Sacramento created a map to celebrate the area's growth. The map hung on the wall in the city council office. (North Sacramento Chamber of Commerce.)

Six

Along the Boulevard

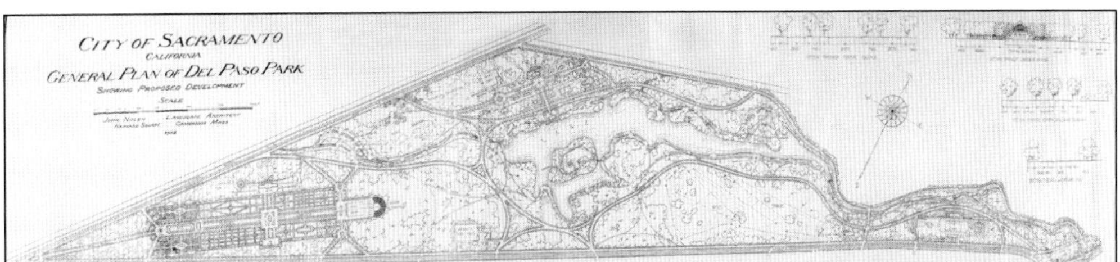

In 1914, the City of Sacramento hired the firm that created Central Park to design a recreational site called Del Paso Park on Auburn Boulevard along the International Highway 49. Del Paso Boulevard was a leg of Highway 49, albeit a one-lane dirt road requiring motorists to close the gate at the entrance to keep the cows from straying. In an effort to attract buyers to the area, in 1911, the City of Sacramento had donated the land for the park that would include a zoo, a Greek theater, formal gardens, a lake and boathouse, a golf course, a baseball field, a bridal path, a bowling green, a carousel, and acres of picnic grounds. North Sacramento Land Company donated the land between the American River and the new Del Paso Park for a four-lane "grand boulevard" (i.e., Del Paso Boulevard) to facilitate travel to the park and to attract business to North Sacramento, thereby establishing today's wide Del Paso Boulevard. A modified version of the grand Del Paso Park exists today. (SAMCC.)

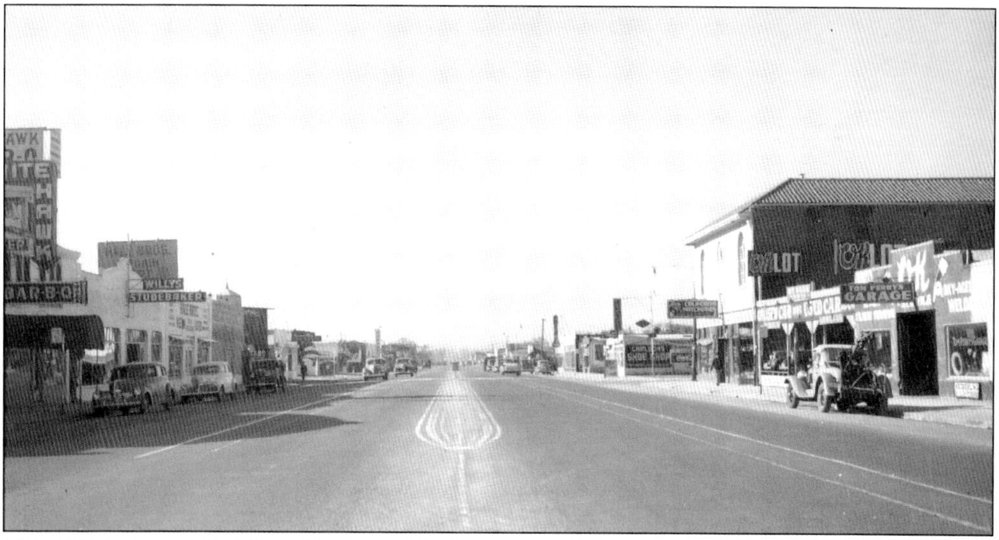

This 1940 view of Del Paso Boulevard looking toward Sacramento shows Ray Martin's Used Car dealership on the right. Ray would become owner of the Studebaker dealership for North Sacramento. His family still resides in Woodlake. Next to Ray Martin's is the California Hatcheries on the Masonic Temple's bottom floor, where Del Paso Antiques is today. On the left is the Nite Hawk Saloon, which stands today. Willy's Studebaker, which Ray Martin would take over and transfer across the street to his location, is to the right of the saloon. Also toward the left is Texas Chili, Joe Halawe's second diner before moving Lil Joe's, which is at a different location on the boulevard. (SAMCC.)

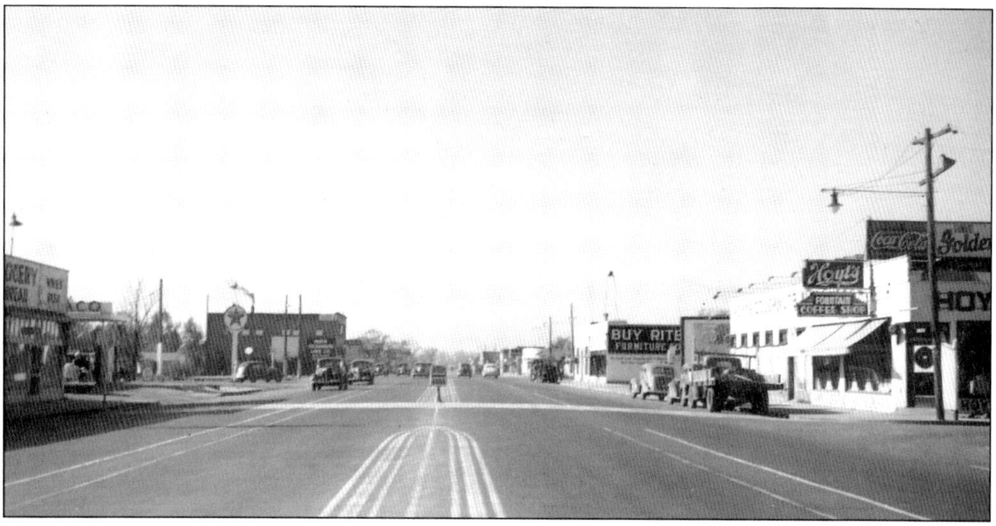

This 1940 image of Del Paso Boulevard looking toward Sacramento depicts the central location of Hoyt's Doughnut Shop on the left. Hoyt had the idea for a moving sidewalk for the boulevard, but due to finances the city was unable to incorporate his ahead-of-his-time innovation. Max Baer, as well as other locals, would congregate at Hoyt's for a good cup of coffee and a warm doughnut. (SAMCC.)

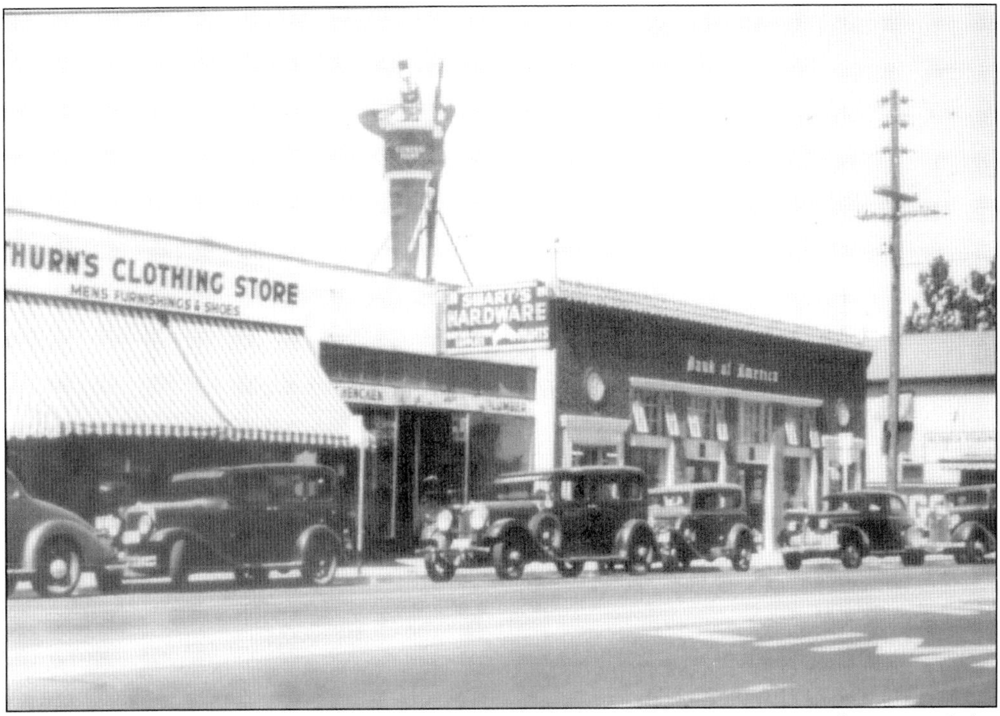

Note the parallel parking in front of Thurn's Clothing Store, Swart's Hardware, and the Erickson Building housing the Bank of America in this c. 1940 image. Several times the city switched between diagonal and parallel parking for safety concerns. (North Sacramento United Methodist Church.)

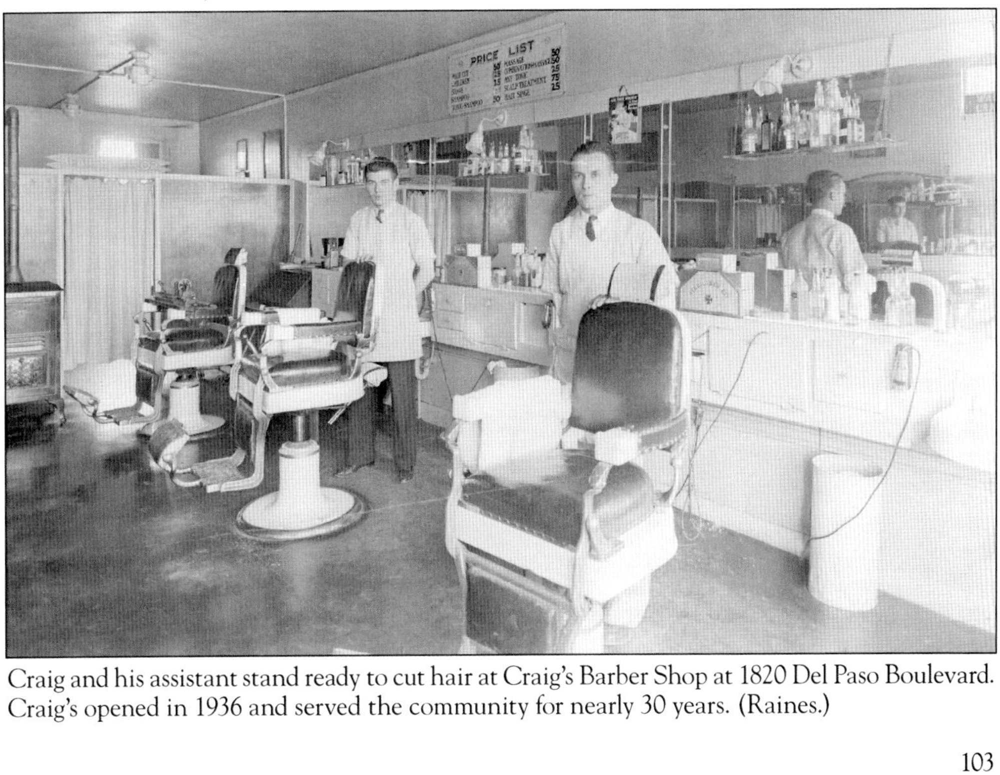

Craig and his assistant stand ready to cut hair at Craig's Barber Shop at 1820 Del Paso Boulevard. Craig's opened in 1936 and served the community for nearly 30 years. (Raines.)

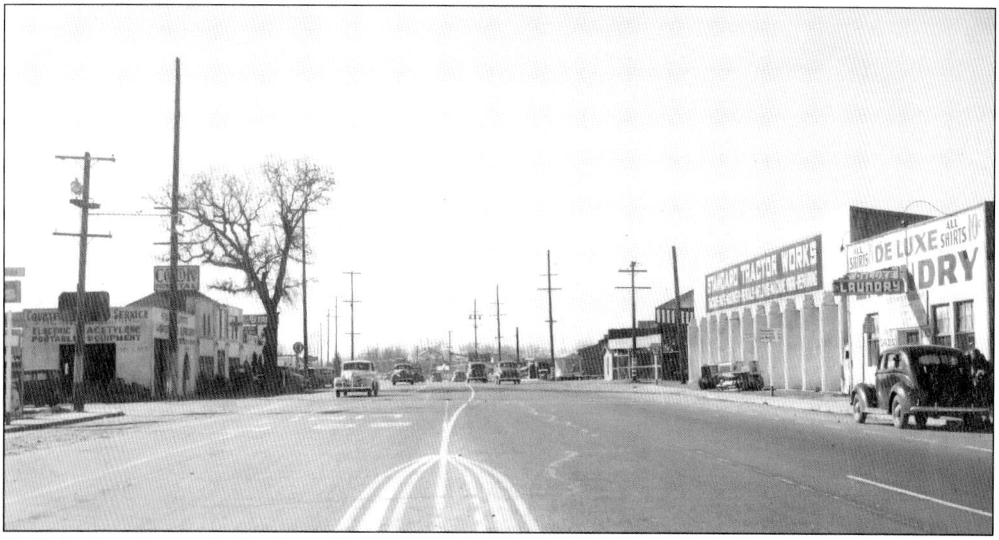

Still further down the boulevard toward Sacramento, the image depicts the four-lane highway. On the right is Standard Tractor Works in front of the old Liberty Iron Works building. Cook Veterinarian Hospital (different family from Cook's Hardware) is on the left under the tree at the base of the boulevard. (SAMCC.)

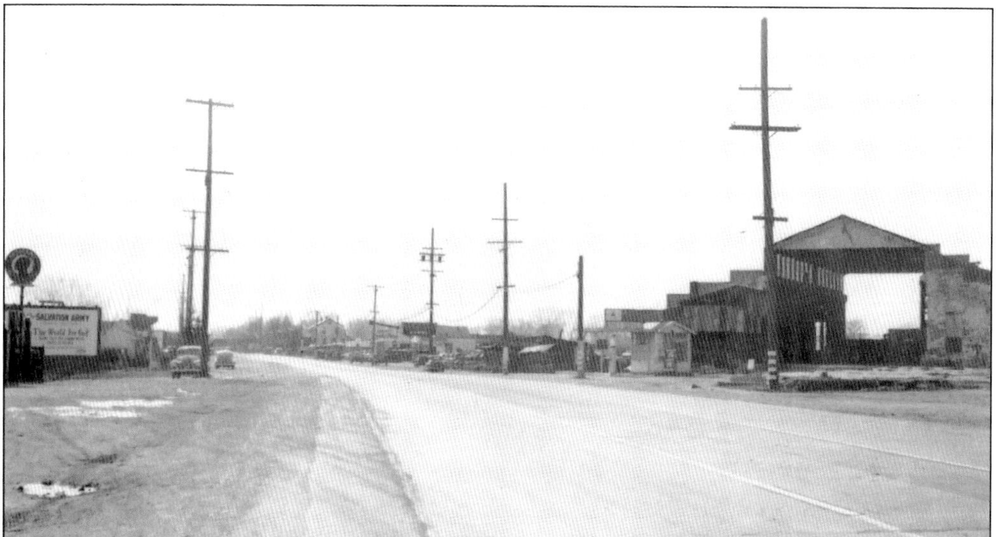

Pictured around 1940, the Kraft's Flying A Service Station sits in front of the empty shell of the Liberty Iron Works foundry. Further down, almost at the base of the boulevard, is Beacon service station. On the left is Mohawk Gasoline service station. As the Lincoln Highway, an international highway, the boulevard abounded with service stations and auto dealerships. Until the 1960s, most gas stations were called "service stations." In the center of the photograph at the base of the boulevard is the Lauszus family's (Subway Truck Parts) white house, which stands today. (SAMCC.)

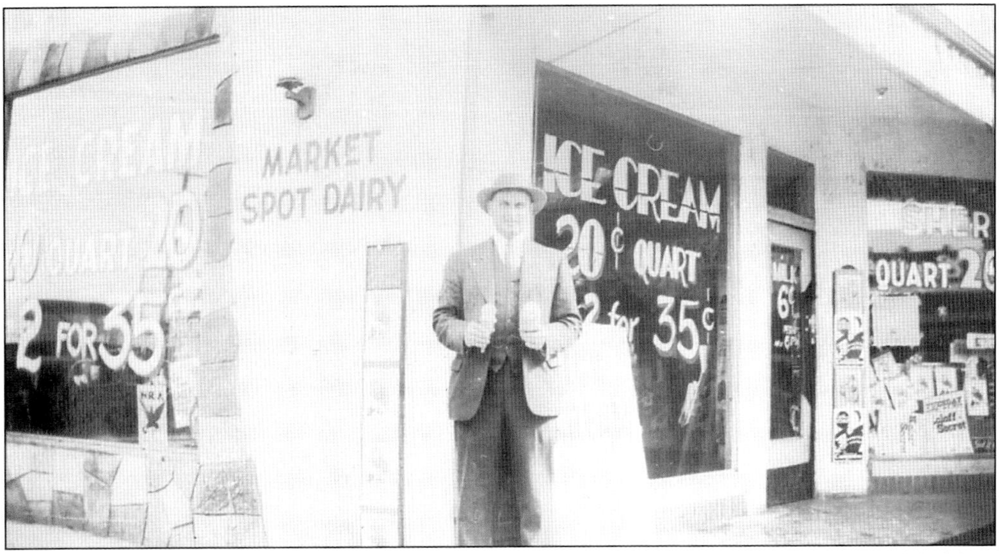

In 1938, E. W. Boudier stands in front of the Market Spot Dairy on Del Paso Boulevard holding two ice creams on a hot summer's day in North Sacramento. (SAMCC.)

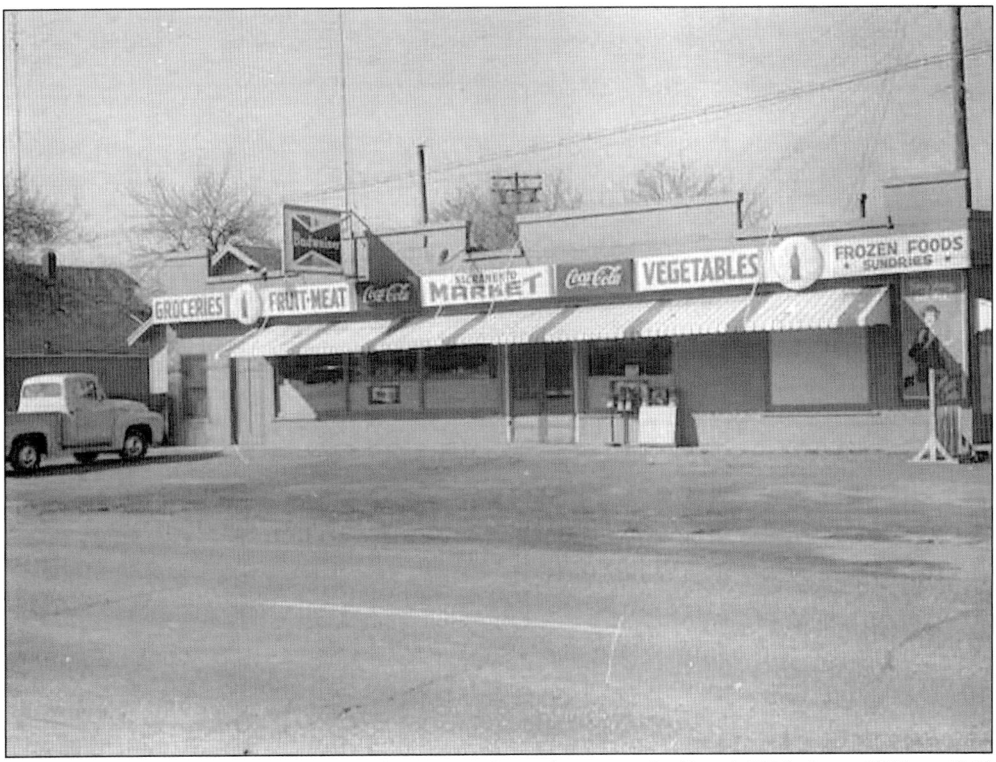

The Sacramento Market at 3089 Del Paso Boulevard was run by Frank Wah from 1955 to 1965 to meet the needs of North Sacramentans. The building exists today. This photograph was taken around 1955. (Leong-Wah.)

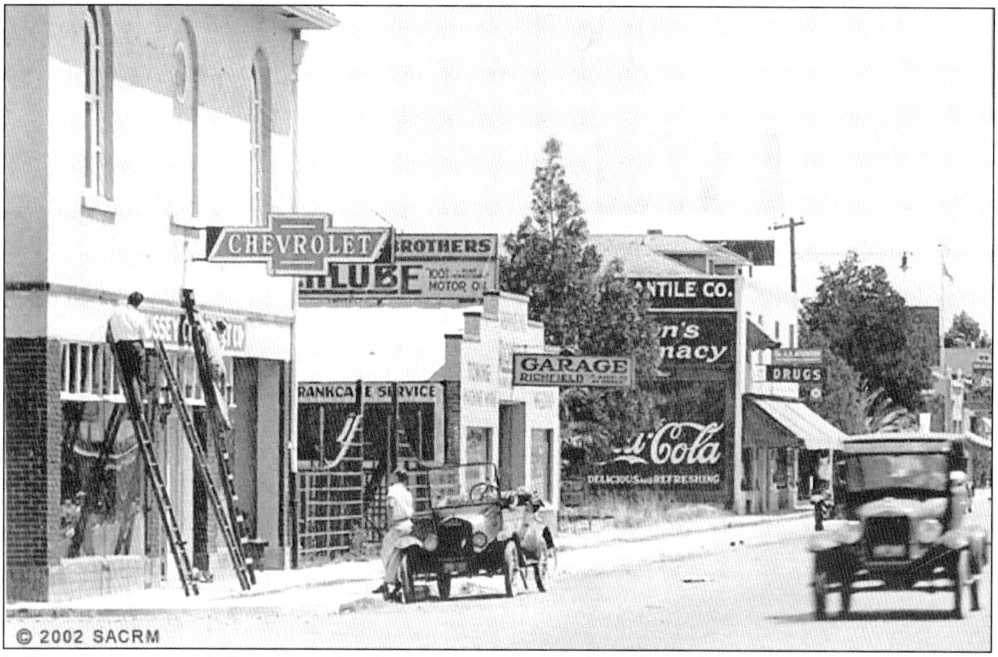

When the Masonic lodge opened in North Sacramento, the Chevy dealership was on the bottom floor. Lodges require two floors, since meetings cannot be held on the ground level. To the left of the Coca-Cola sign would be the Ray Martin Studebaker dealership. This photograph was taken around 1926. (Sacramento Room, Sacramento Public Library.)

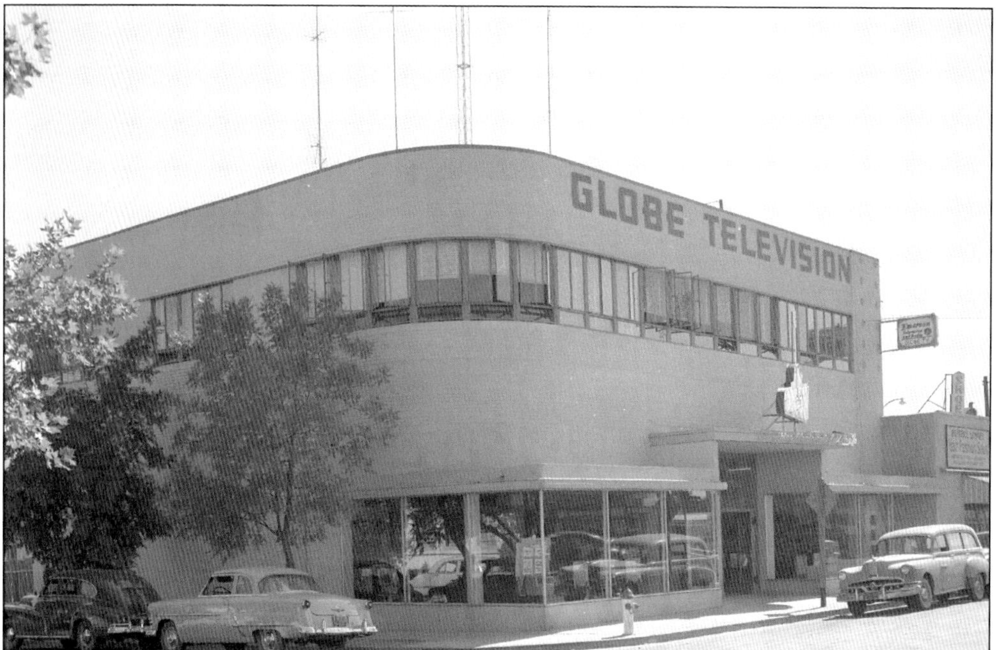

Globe Television stands proudly with its streamline moderne facade. When television came into being, North Sacramentans embraced the new media, which caused a slowing of business for the Grand and Del Paso Theatres on the boulevard, around 1955. (SAMCC.)

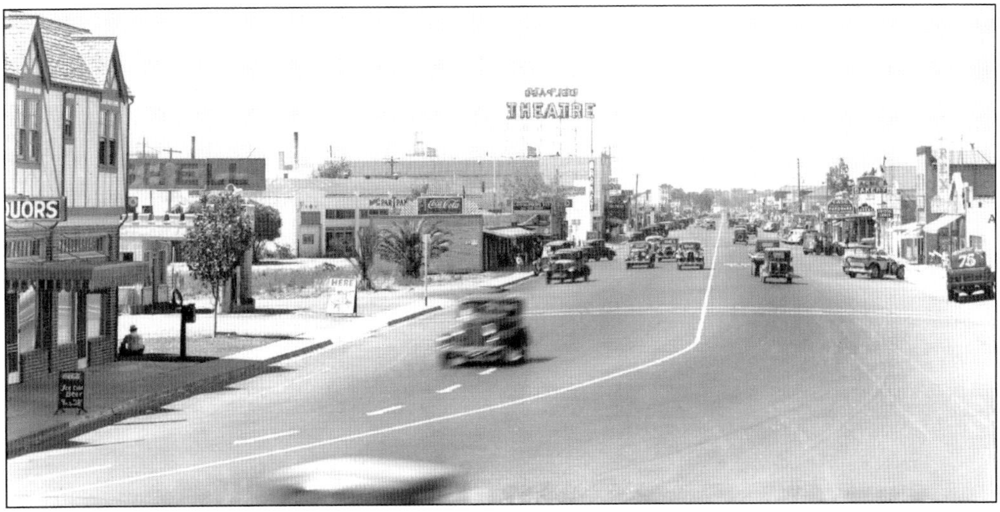

Turning down the corner toward Sacramento onto the boulevard, Shell Service Station is on the left with the Nehi Bottling Company behind it. Under the awning by the Coca-Cola sign to the right of the palm trees is a black newspaper boy calling out to potential buyers. Diagonal parking is now in use. (SAMCC.)

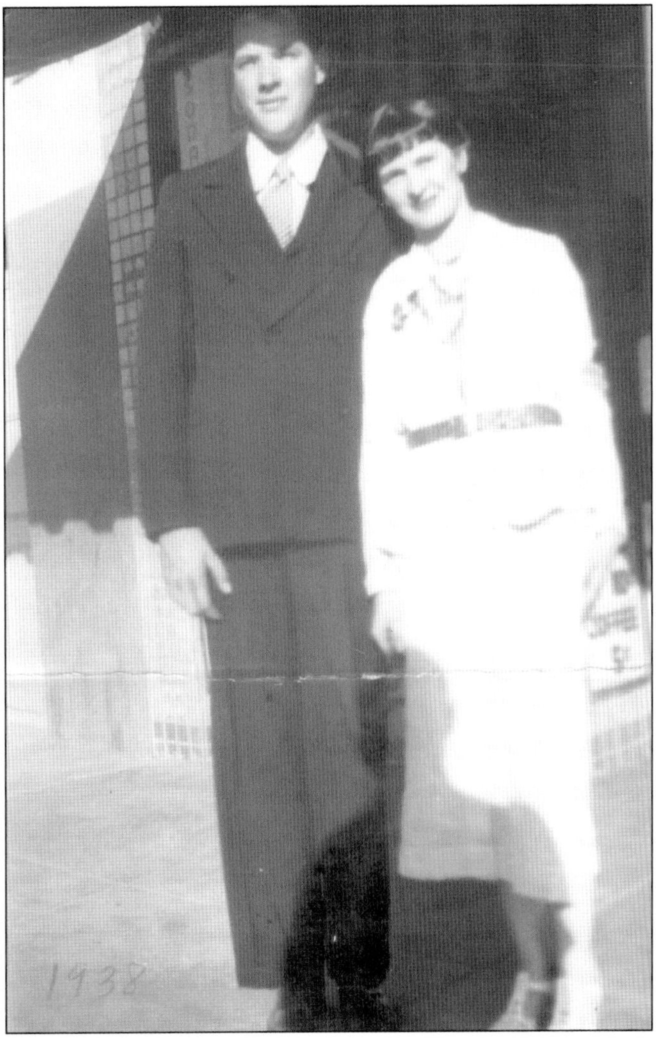

Betty Ollie Pontius (1905-) married her third husband, Rae Bryan, the love of her life, as evidenced by their longevity as a couple. The newly wedded lovers stand in front of Betty's Candyland in 1938 at 2116 Del Paso Boulevard where coffee is 5¢. Betty inscribed "taken in front of my store 'Betty's Candyland' and North Sac Photo Supply 2116 Del Paso Blvd N. Sacramento Cal. I closed this store on April 4th 1939. We had only been married a few months." (Risse: Betty Bryan.)

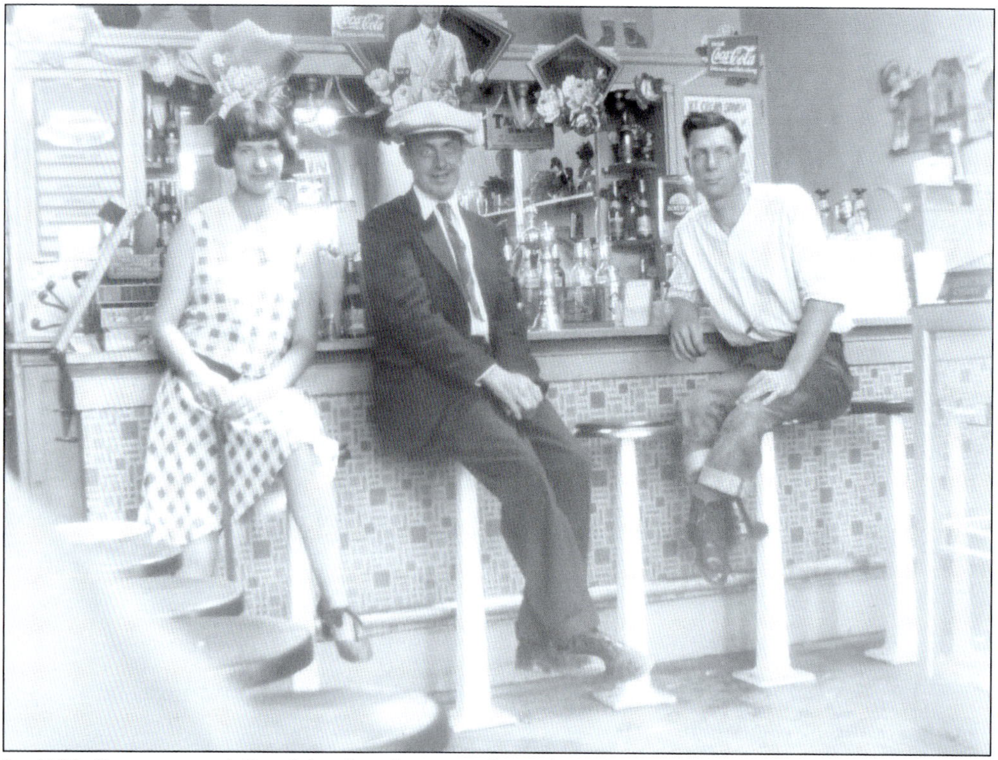

In 1930, Betty opened Candyland and is joined on the right by Billie Bass and an unidentified customer. Buying candy before going next door to the Del Paso Theatre, the kids, Margaret Fish Smith remembers, called her Betty "Boop" because she looked like the sexy cartoon character. (Risse: Betty Bryan.)

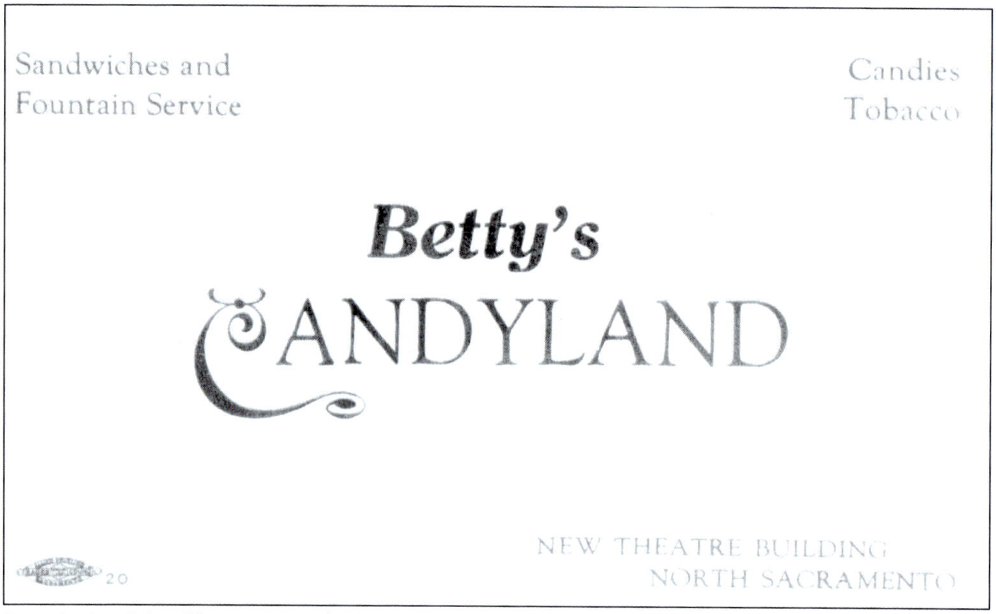

Betty's Candyland business card advertises sandwiches and fountain service in the New Theatre Building. Betty's first shop was in the Old Theatre Building. (Risse: Betty Bryan.)

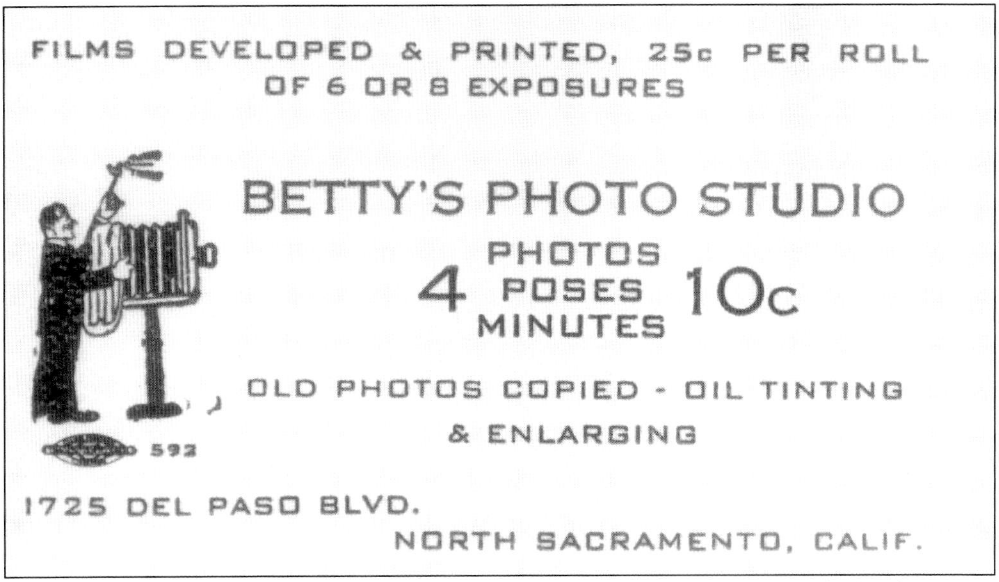

A true entrepreneur, Betty had dual businesses on the boulevard. A woman before her time, she offered 4 photos 4 poses in 4 minutes for 10¢ at 1725 Del Paso Boulevard. Never reported at community functions, as announced in the *North Sacramento Journal*, perhaps she was less than accepted by the wives. (Risse: Betty Bryan.)

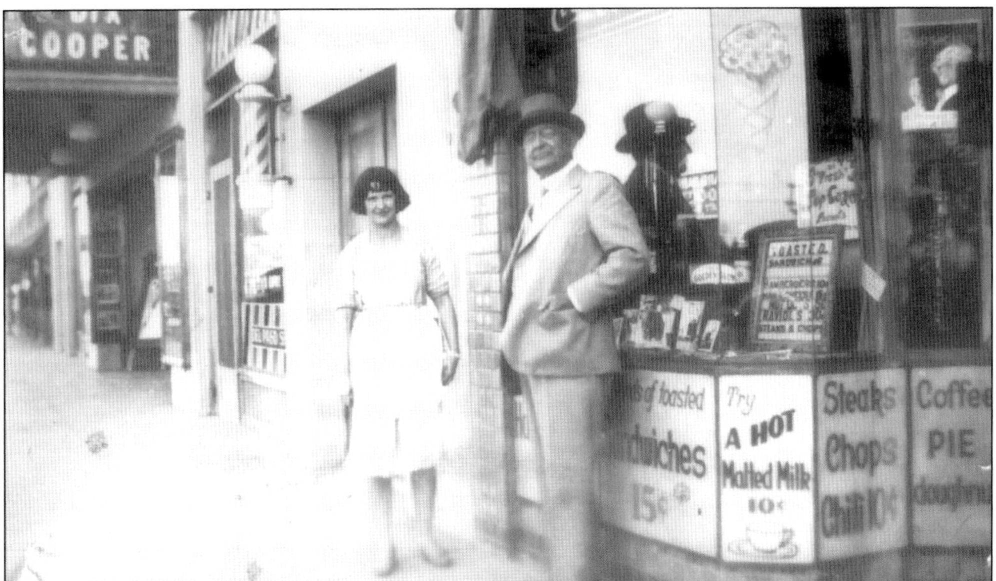

Outside Betty's Candyland next to the new building, Del Paso Theatre, Betty "Boop" hobnobs with her best buddy, John Holden, editor of the *North Sacramento Journal* around 1938. (Risse: Betty Bryan.)

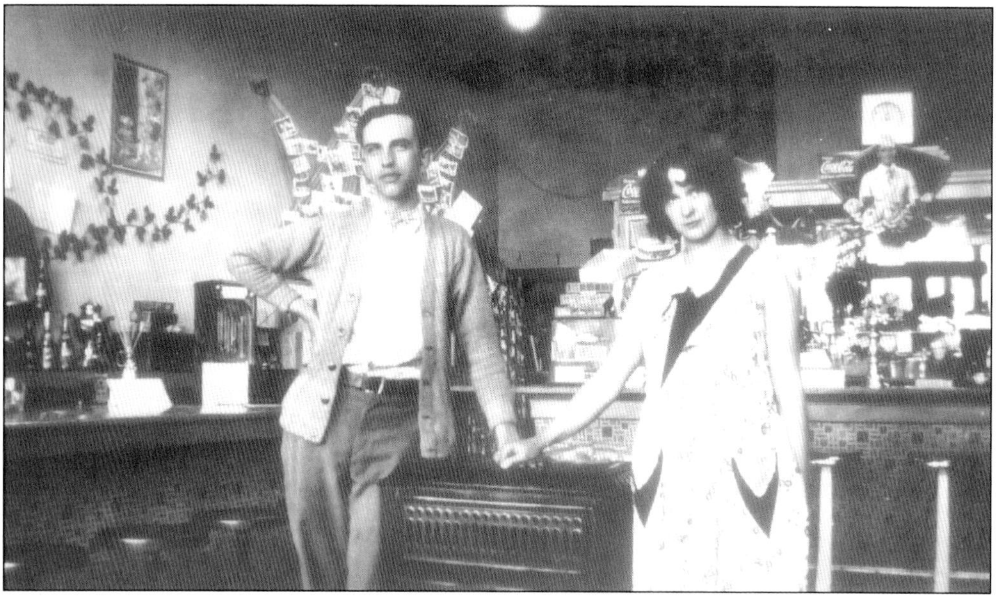

Betty and her third husband, Charles E Newth, are pictured in 1932 at her store located at 2116 Del Paso Boulevard. The inscription reads, "I had this store there for about 12 years till 1939." (Risse: Betty Bryan.)

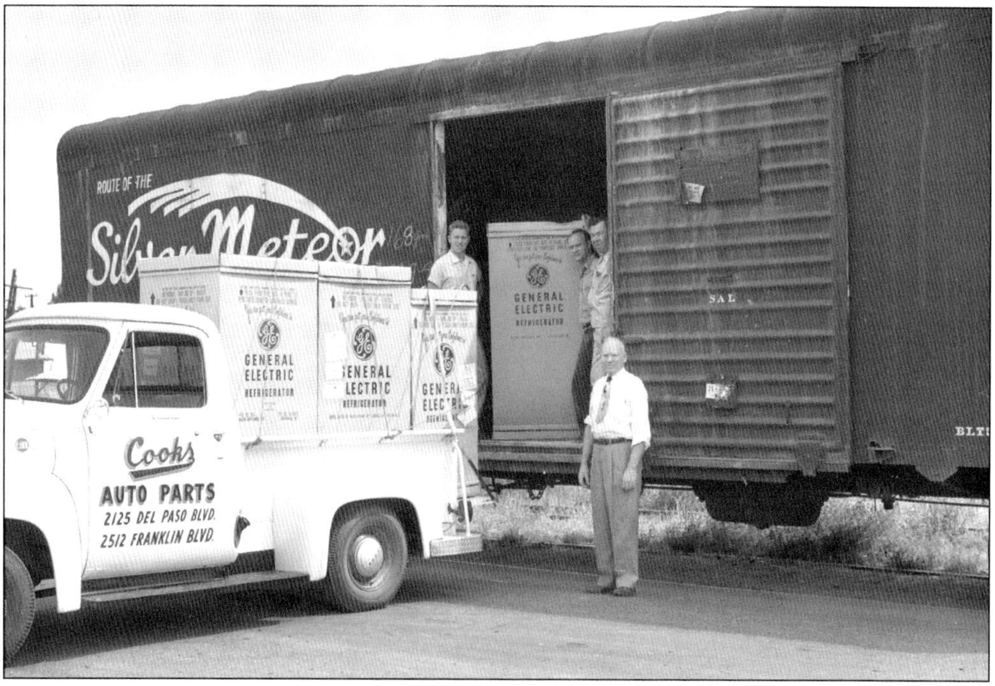

Roscoe D. Cook Sr. stands below as his son, Dale Cook (at left inside the door), and two helpers unload the newest GE refrigerators for the new Cook's Hardware Store on 2125 Del Paso Boulevard. This is the old Wroolie's Corner location at Del Paso Boulevard and Rio Linda Boulevard from the 1920s. (Cook family.)

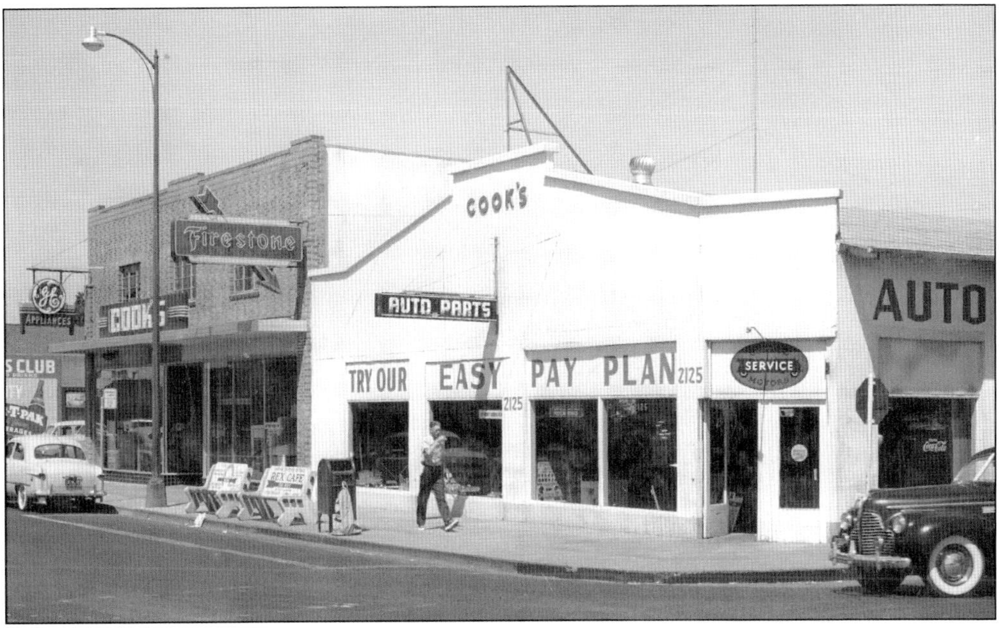

Seeing the automotive needs of motorists on the boulevard, Cook opened as an auto parts store at Wroolie's Corner (Rio Linda and Del Paso Boulevard) in 1952. Wroolie opened his store at this site in 1910 before incorporation of North Sacramento. An eager customer winds his way up the boulevard to 2125 Del Paso Boulevard and Cook's Auto Parts. Cook's Hardware, the attached brick building, opened a few years later, around 1954. (Cook family.)

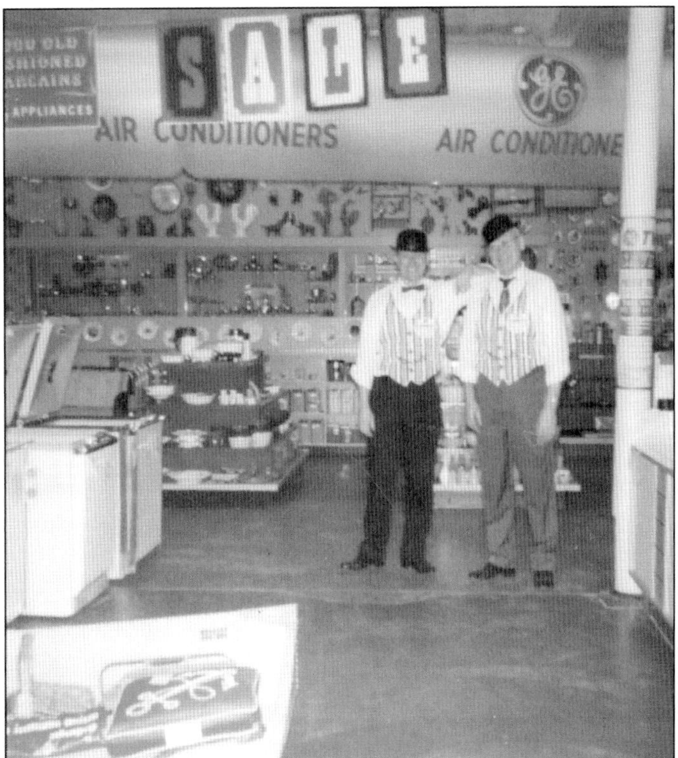

Pictured around 1960, Dale Cook (left) and his dad and founder of Cook's, Roscoe D. Cook, get ready for a big sale in the store. Four out of five of Dale's children, Steve, Cindy, Joni, and Sue, have taken active parts in the present location at 2125 Del Paso Boulevard so that expansion into other areas of sales could be possible. Cook's is an Ace hardware store, which also carries televisions, stereos, videos, satellite dishes, major appliances, furniture, housewares, sporting goods, and toys. Cook's continues to sell automobiles, tires, and parts, as well as smog checks and auto repair. (Cook family.)

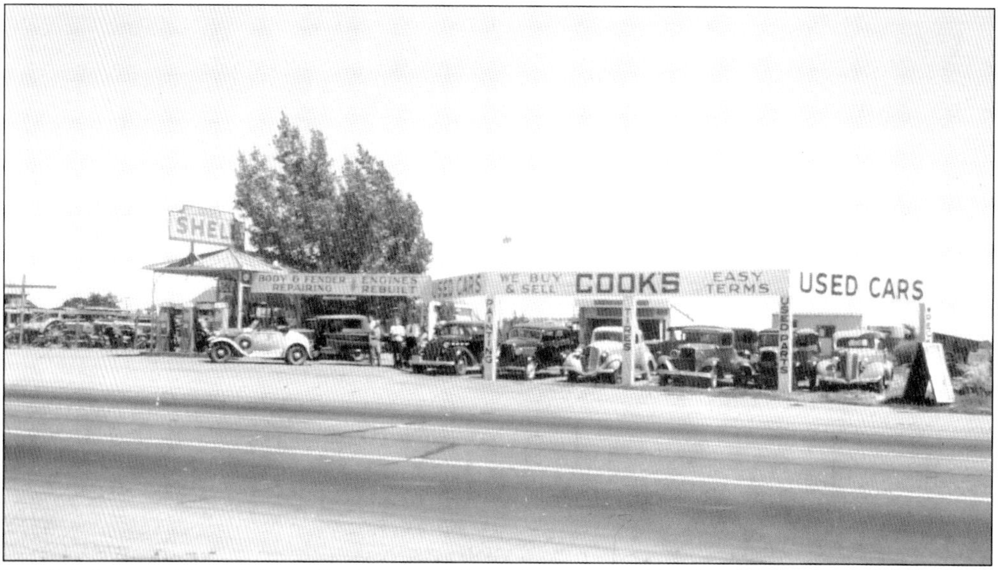

In 1936, Roscoe D. and Susie Cook started doing business in North Sacramento by buying the Graham new car dealership. He then bought a used car lot to supplement his Shell Service Station at the base of North Sacramento Avenue with the help of his sons, Roscoe Jr. (killed in World War II) and Dale. Roscoe Sr. kept up his contact with World War I veterans who became steady customers. This photograph was taken around 1939. (Cook family.)

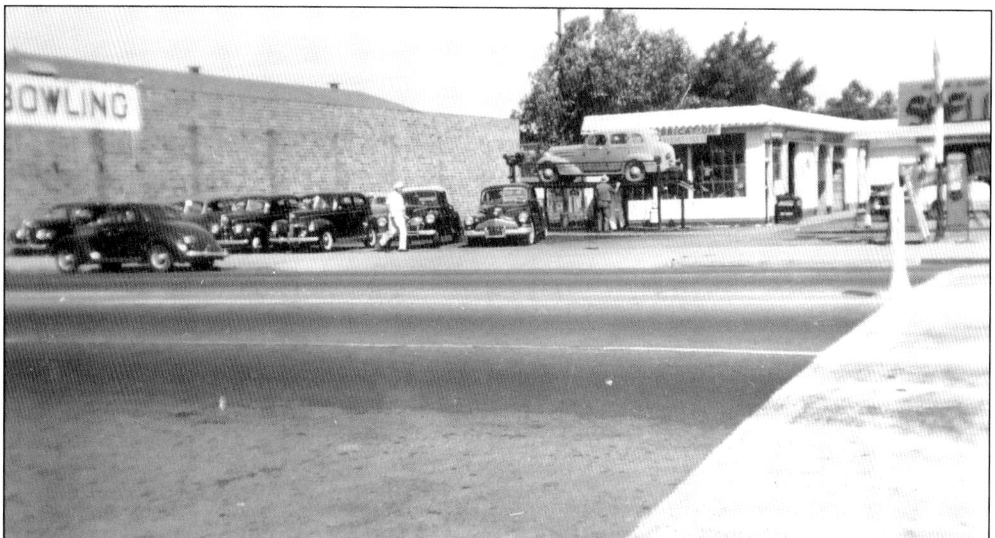

In 1941, when the state decided to build a highway overpass (Highway 160) at his site, Cook took over the Shell dealership at Del Paso Boulevard and Orange Avenue. This photograph was taken around 1942. (Cook family.)

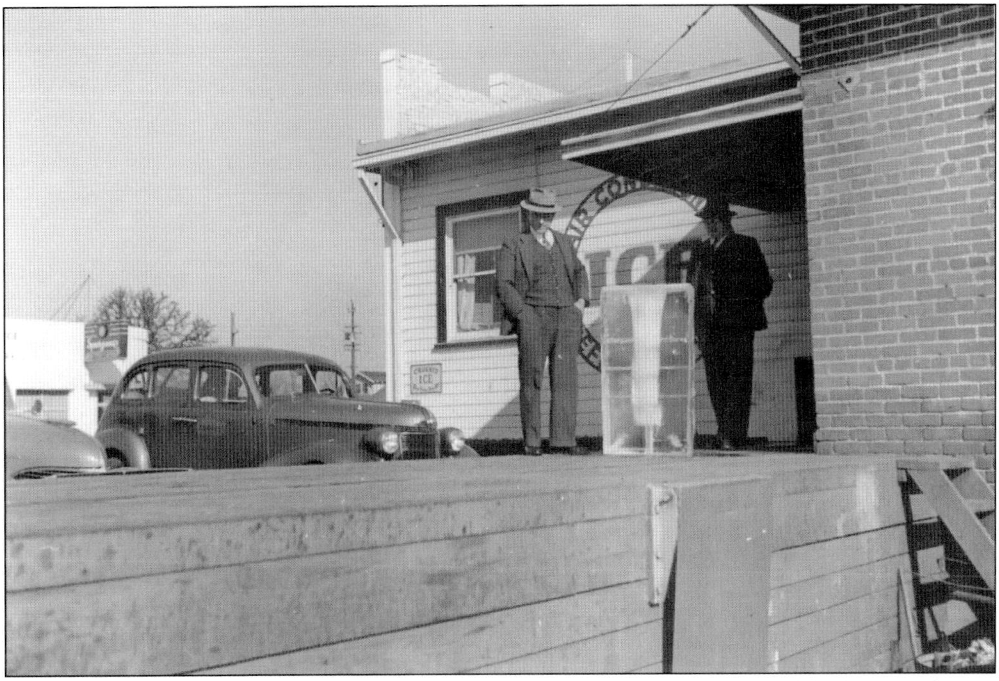

William "Pop" Kerth stands on the dock of his American Ice with a tall ice block, around 1929. American Ice continues a thriving business today and continues to supply water to the Woodland Swimming Pool and to Iceland. (Kerth.)

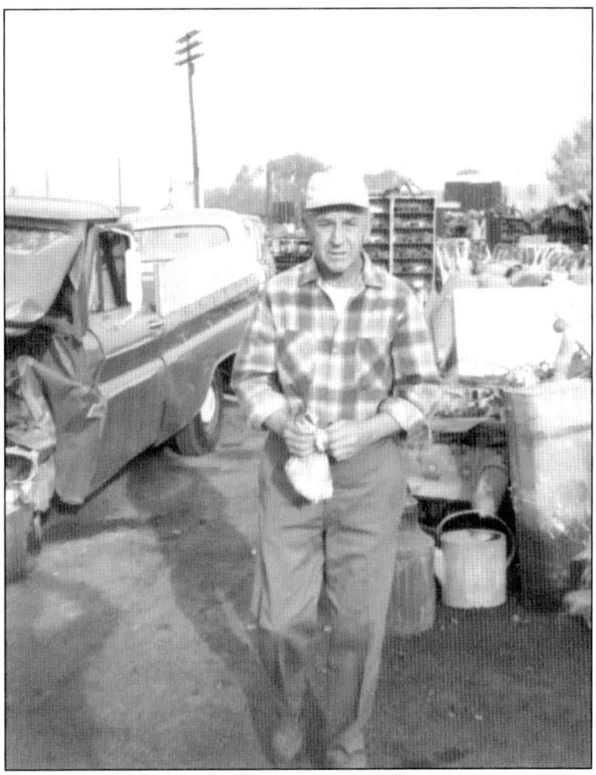

The son of the founder of Subway Parts at the base of Del Paso Boulevard, Herman Lauszus Jr. looks over his inventory, around 1955. (Lauszus.)

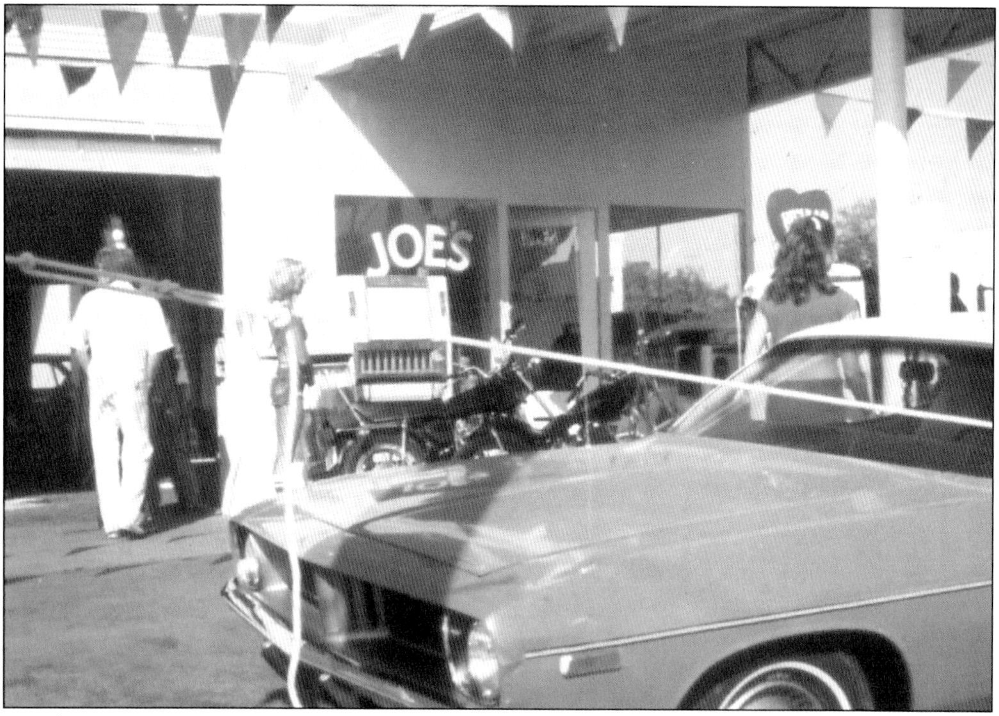

North Sacramento went Hollywood for the production of "Gas Pump Girls," a B-movie that saw the makeover of a service station on the boulevard. This photograph was taken around 1960. (SAMCC.)

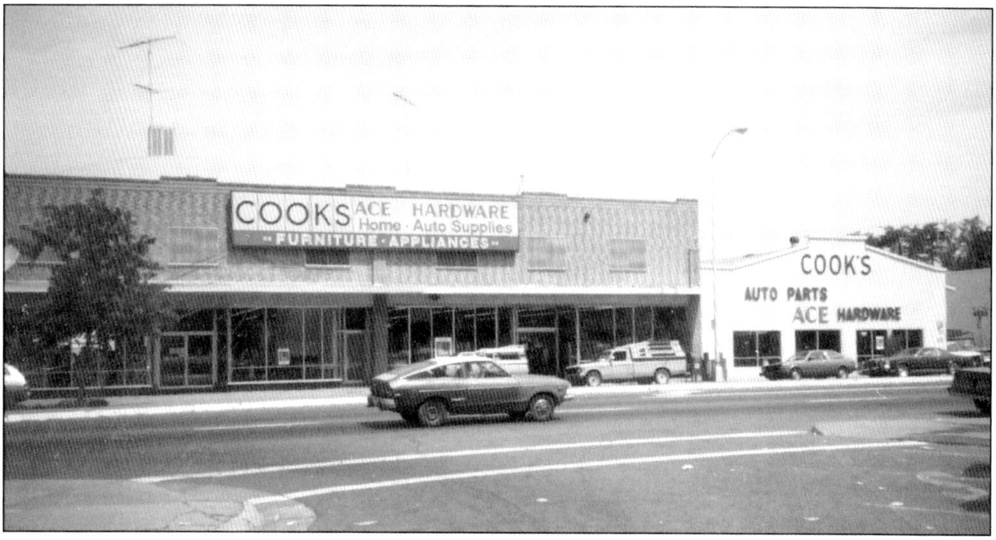

Cook's Hardware expanded from the original Wroolie's Corner site at Rio Linda and Del Paso Boulevard to the adjacent building. To the left of the Cook's Ace Hardware signage at 2109 Del Paso Boulevard was Crest Upholstery, which became the current home of the North Sacramento–Hagginwood branch of the Sacramento Public Library when the North Sacramento branch moved from 492 Arden Way. Dale Cook, the owner of the property, leased the building to the city and donated the janitorial services to the library that opened to the public in 1987. (Cook family.)

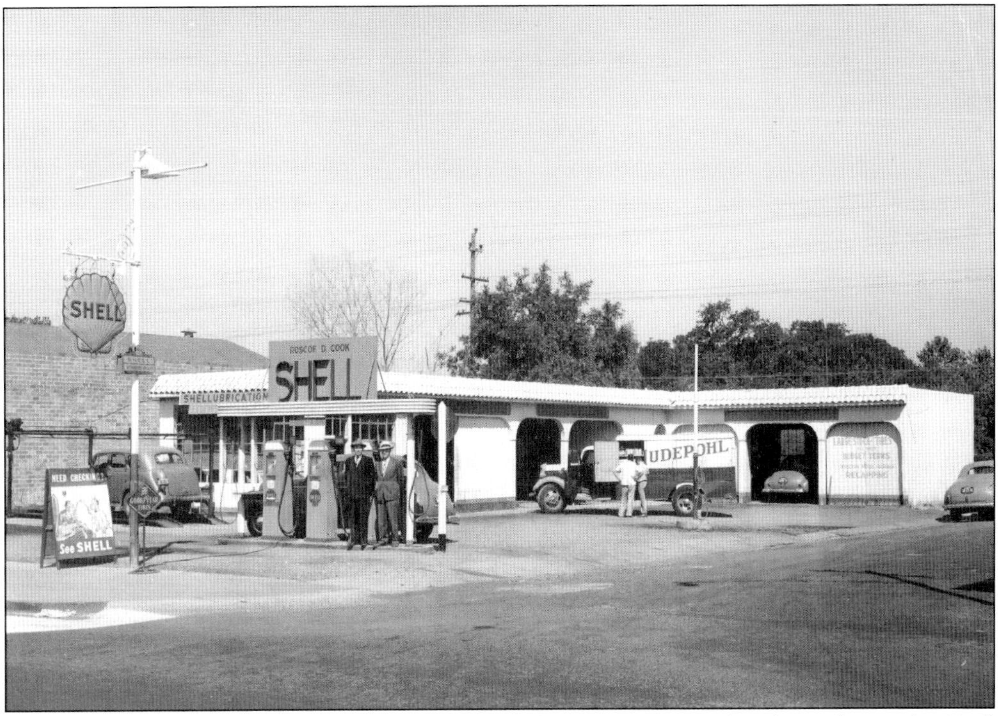

Roscoe Cook (at left) meets with R. Martin, the Shell representative, when he took over the Shell dealership at Del Paso Boulevard and Orange around 1942. (Cook family.)

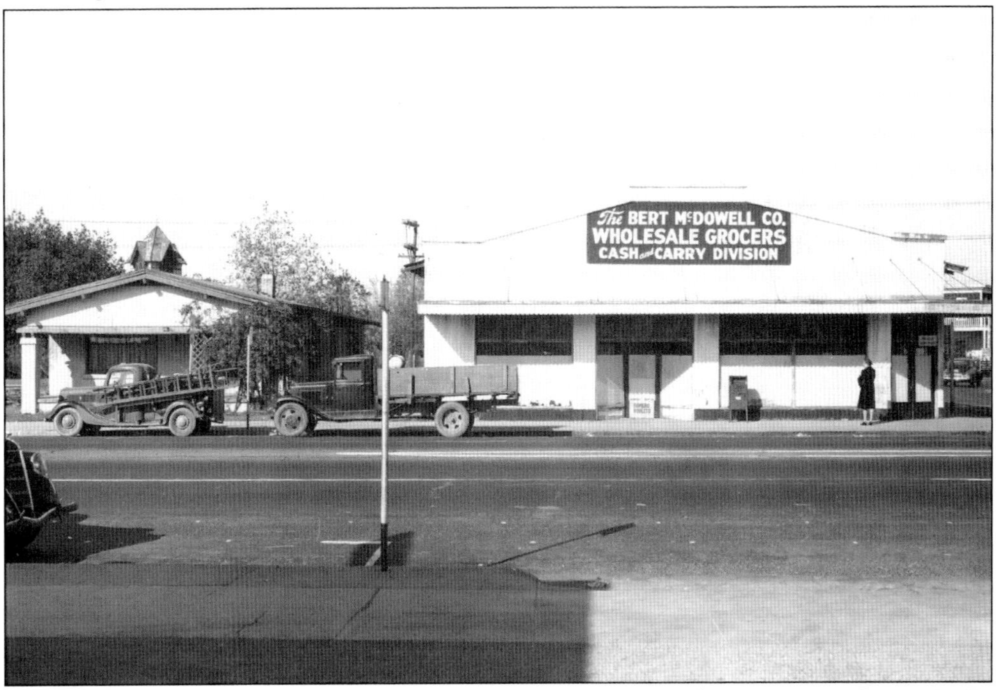

Pictured here is another view of Bert McDowell's grocers at Wroolie's Corner in the 1940s. To the left in the background is the Epworth Church steeple. The house on the left was the rental for Bob Kent's family. (Cook family.)

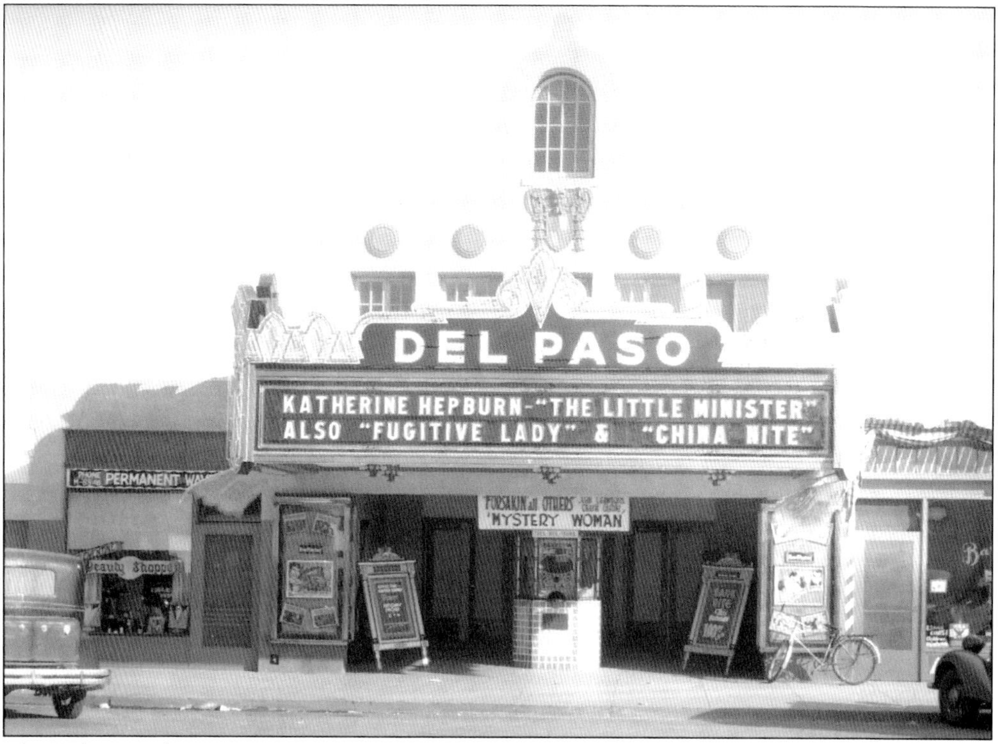

The Del Paso Theatre, pictured around 1935, was the queen of Del Paso Boulevard and the most likely place for the open-air theater and the adjacent lot where Max Baer's sparred. Erickson Construction built the theatre. (Berg.).

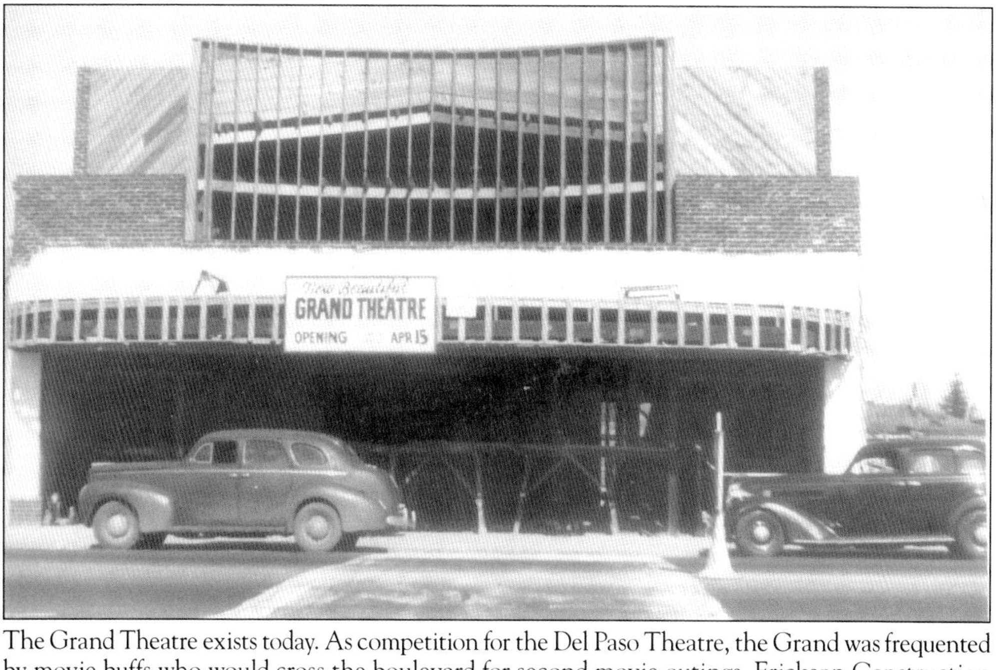

The Grand Theatre exists today. As competition for the Del Paso Theatre, the Grand was frequented by movie buffs who would cross the boulevard for second movie outings. Erickson Construction was involved in building the theater, pictured here around 1940. (Erickson-Nastal.)

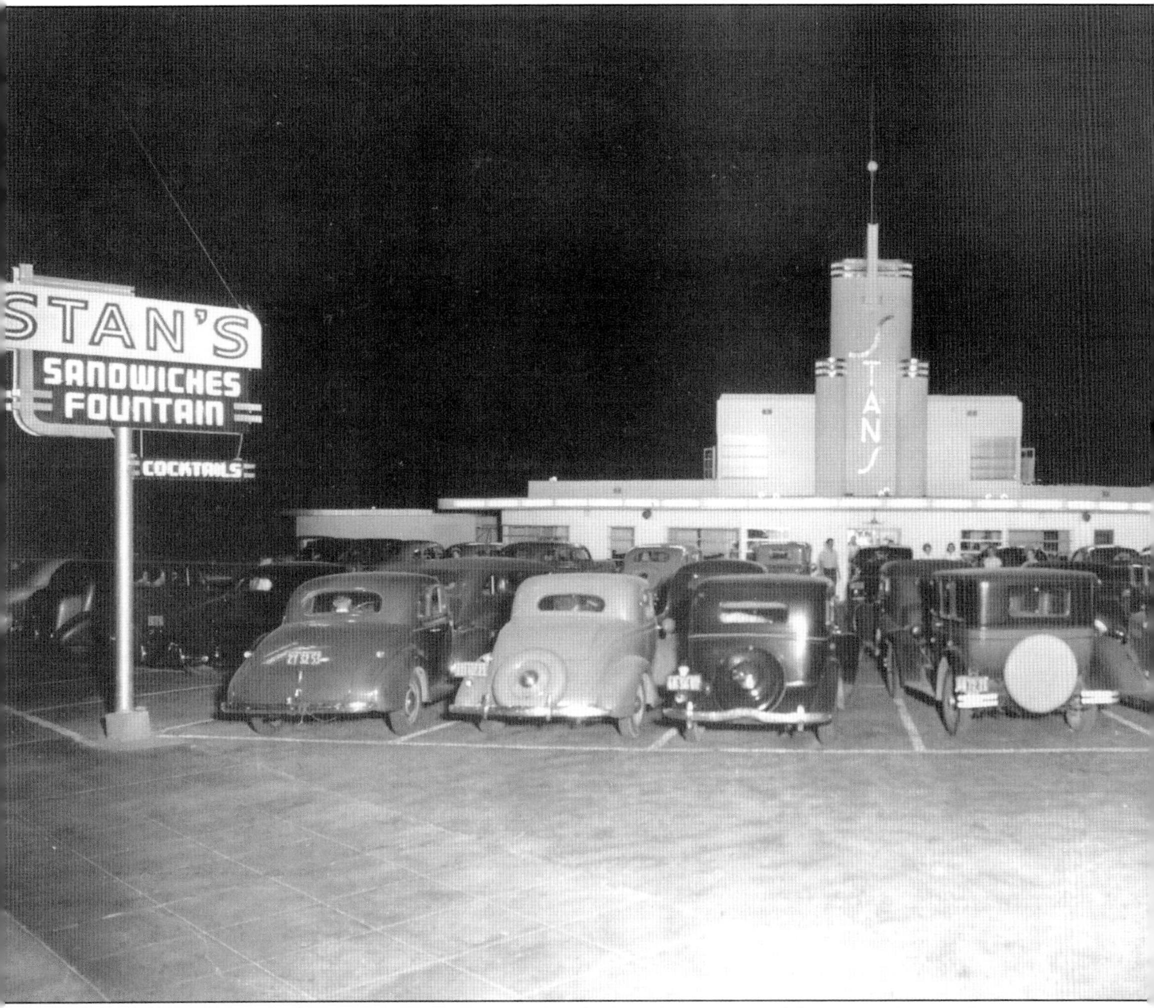

"Kapra City," as North Sacramento is known by the locals, was a world unto itself. On the corner of El Camino and Del Paso Boulevard, Stan's was the teen hot spot in the 1940s and 1950s, to many parents' chagrin. This photograph was taken around 1948. (Sacramento Room, Sacramento Public Library.)

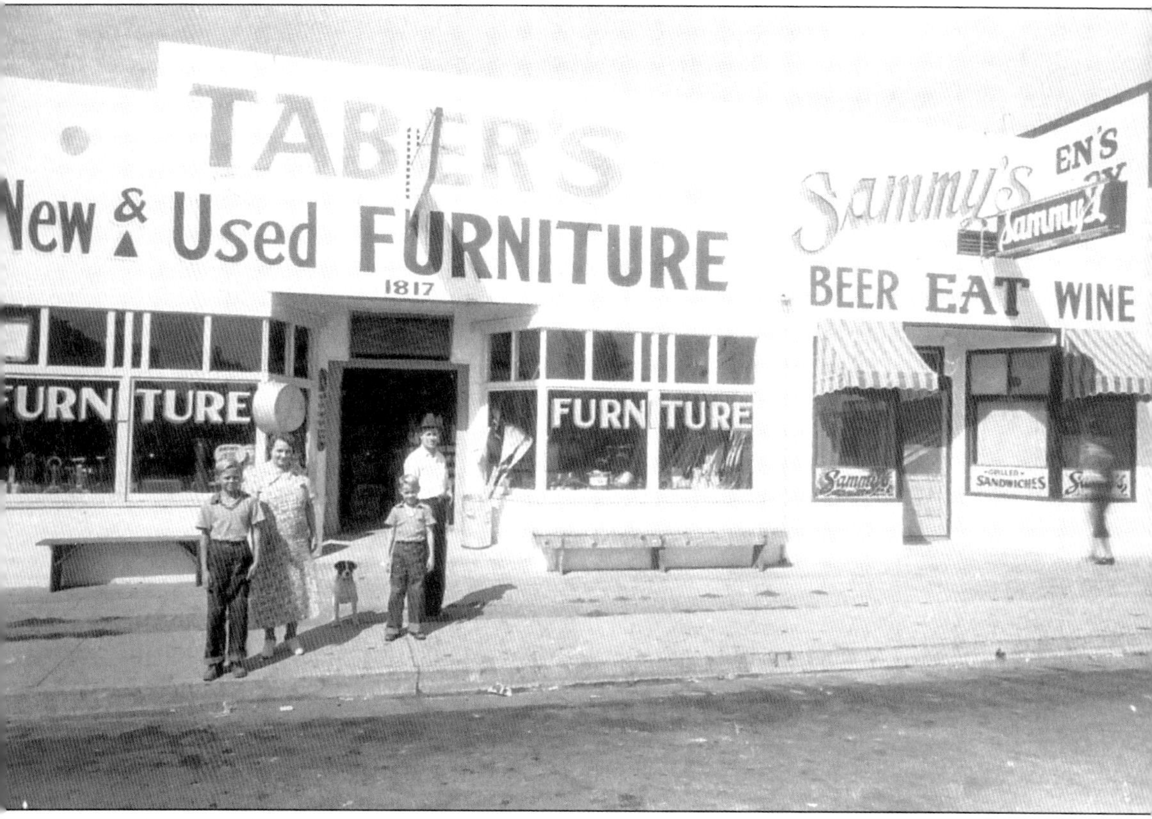

Members of the Taber clan stand outside their store at 1817 Del Paso Boulevard in 1934. From left to right are Dick Taber, his mother Mrs. Taber, the family dog, Bob Taber, and Richard D. Taber Sr. Richard D. Taber Sr. began his furniture business at this location in 1925. Dick and Bob carried on the business in the same location, as did their children. Note that the original Sammy's at 1819 Del Paso Boulevard was adjacent to Taber's Furniture around 1935, before Sammy Powell moved the restaurant to its new location up the boulevard. Sammy had the unusual fortune to possess a liquor license at this time and was able to offer alcoholic beverages. (Taber family.)

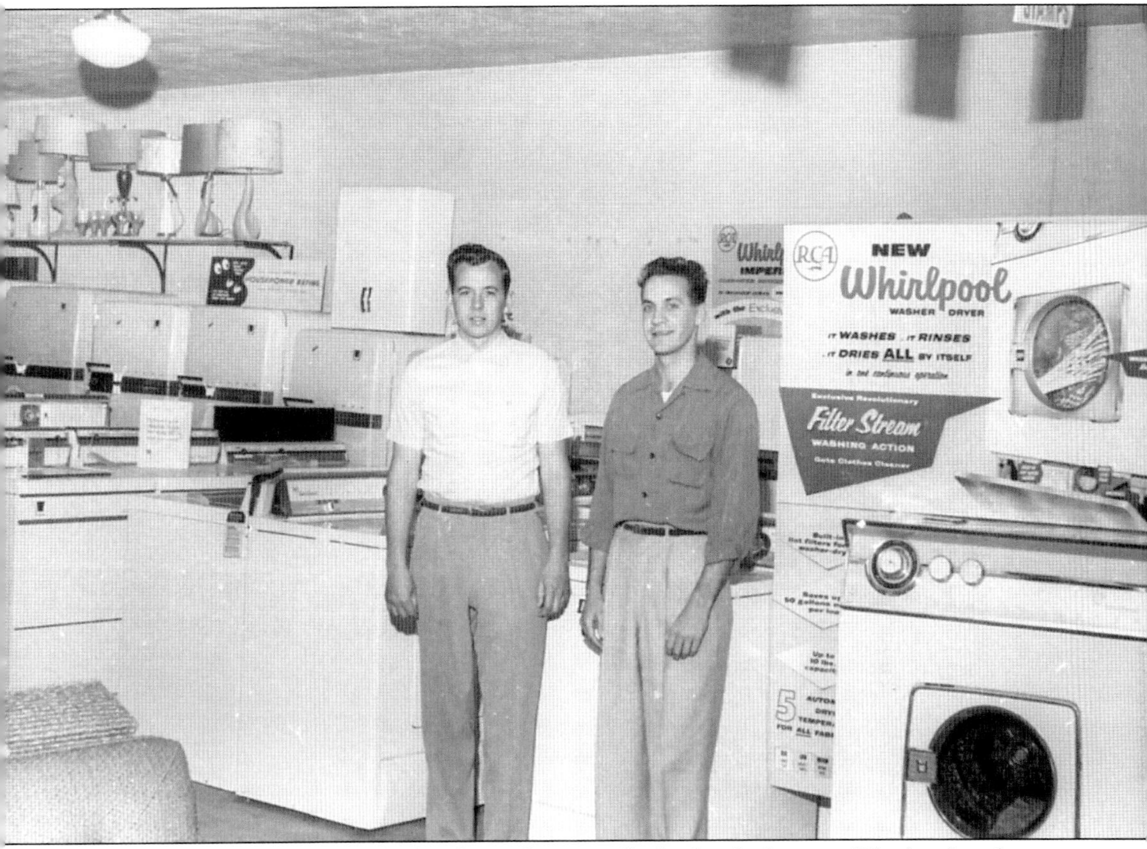

Inside Taber's, Dick Taber and his brother Robert proudly display the latest in Whirlpool appliances around 1956. (Taber family.)

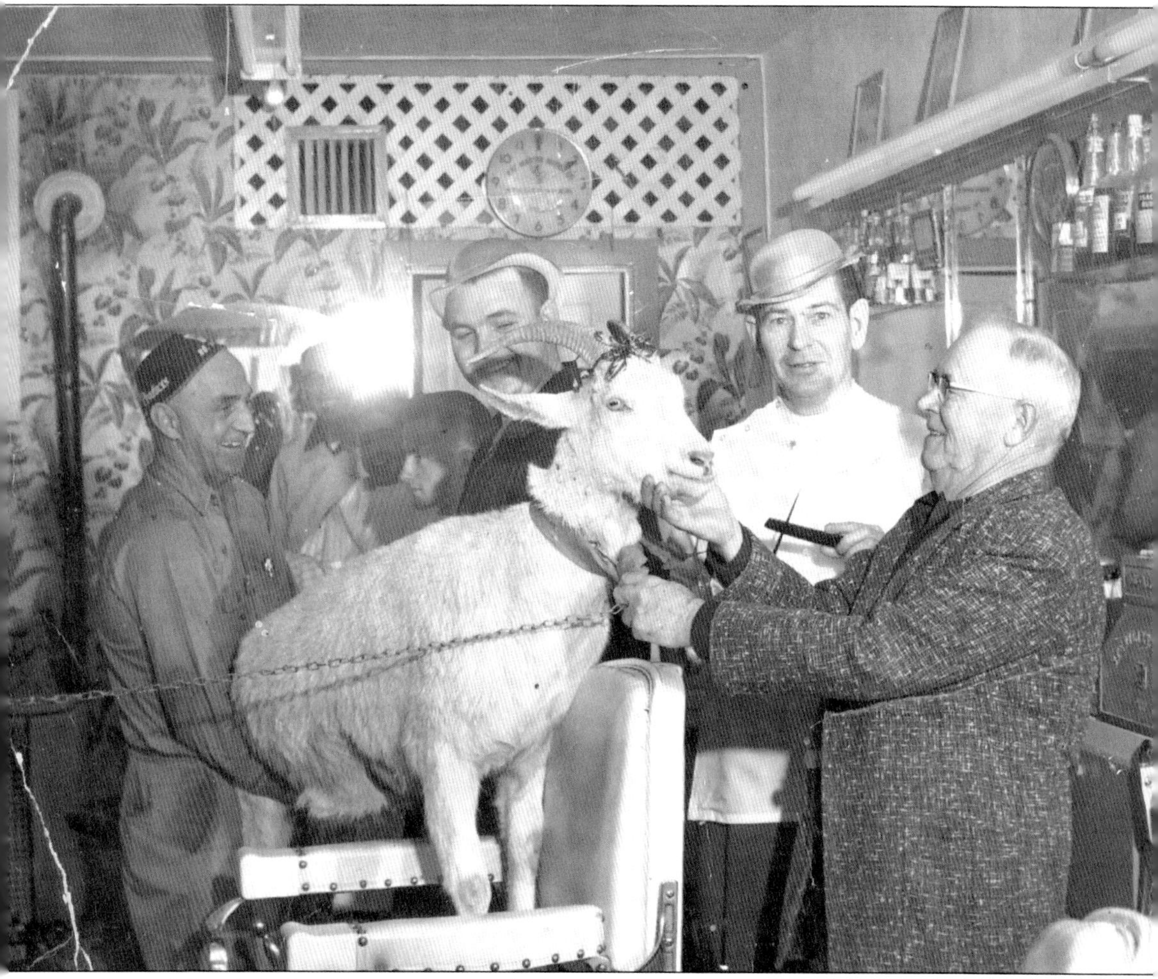

Craig of Craig's Barber Shop cut hair on the boulevard beginning in 1935. Trimming the whiskers of his customer Mr. Goat at his shop on 1820 Del Paso Boulevard in 1950, Craig is surrounded by amused North Sacramentans. (Raines.)

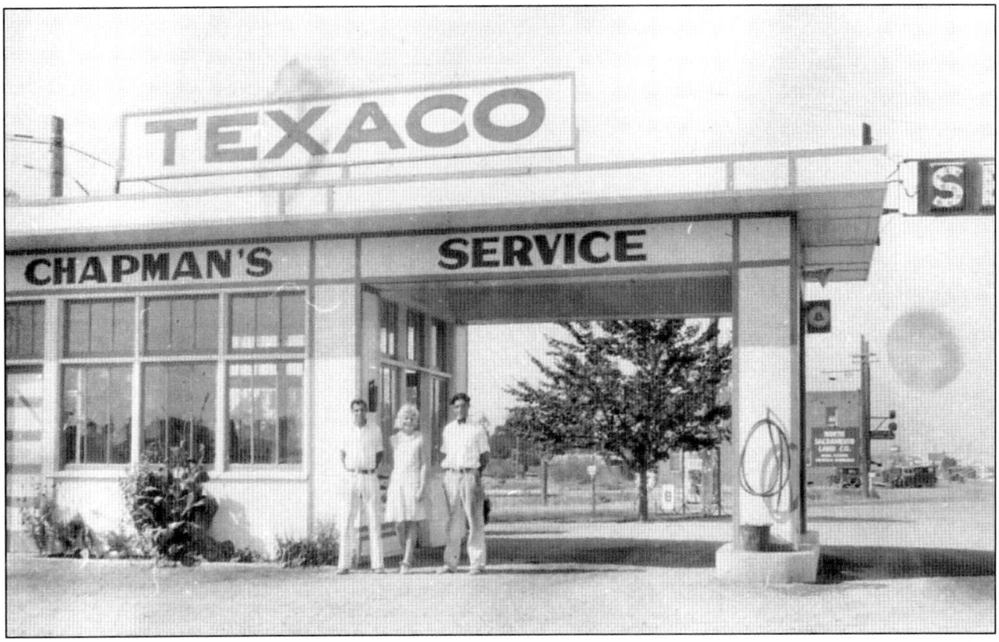

Virgil Chapman (left) and his wife, Susie (center), owned the Texaco service station at 1500 Del Paso Boulevard, which was bought from the prior owners, Fraser and Doyle, around 1927. (SAMCC.)

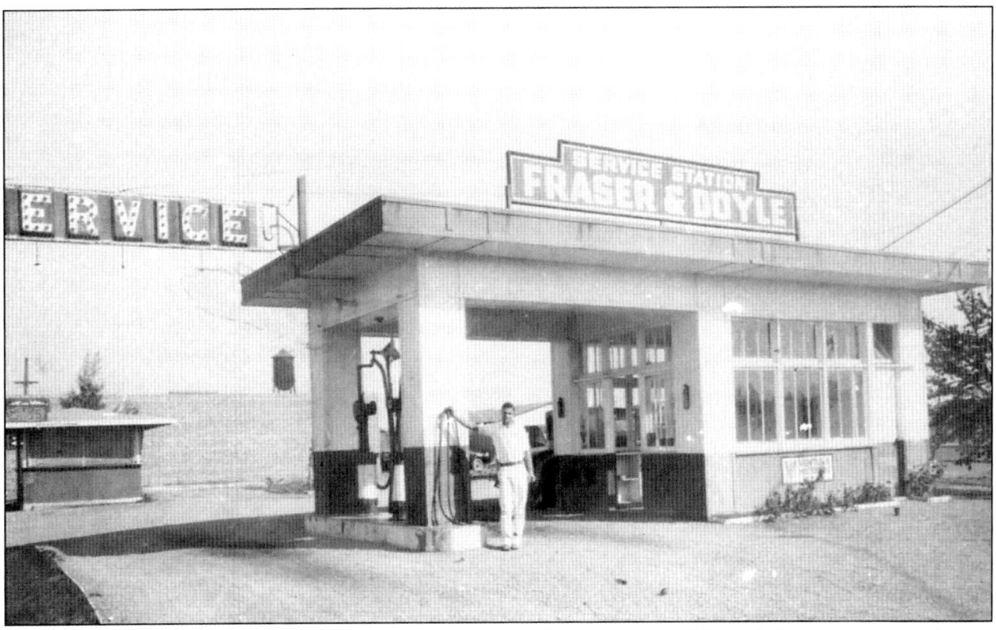

Virgil Chapman stands outside his first gas station. Chapman loved North Sacramento and later developed a real estate business on the boulevard. His bust graces the boulevard, a gift to his memory from North Sacramento. (SAMCC.)

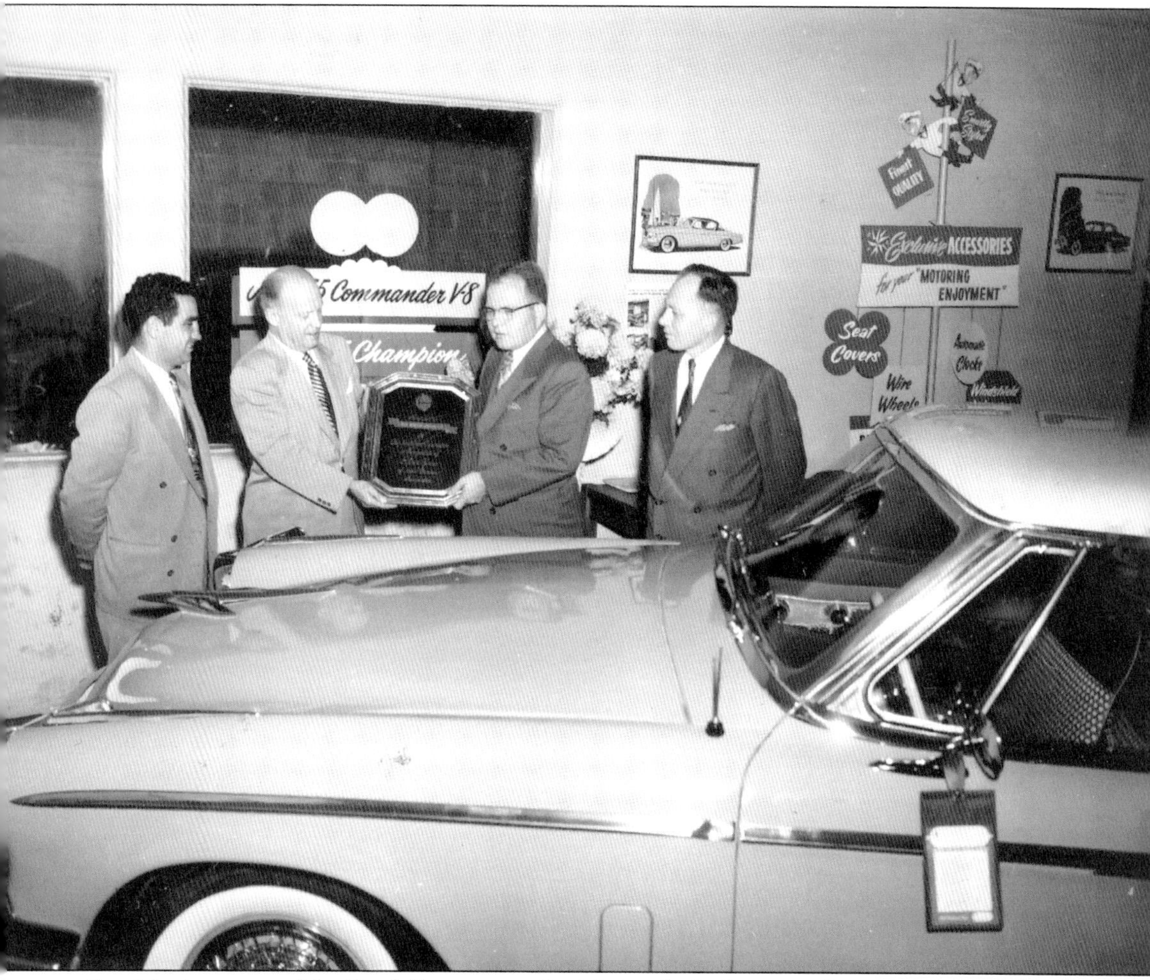

Ray Martin, owner of the North Sacramento Studebaker dealership, proudly receives an award from Studebaker, around 1955. Martin's dealership was adjacent to the Masonic lodge. (Raines.)

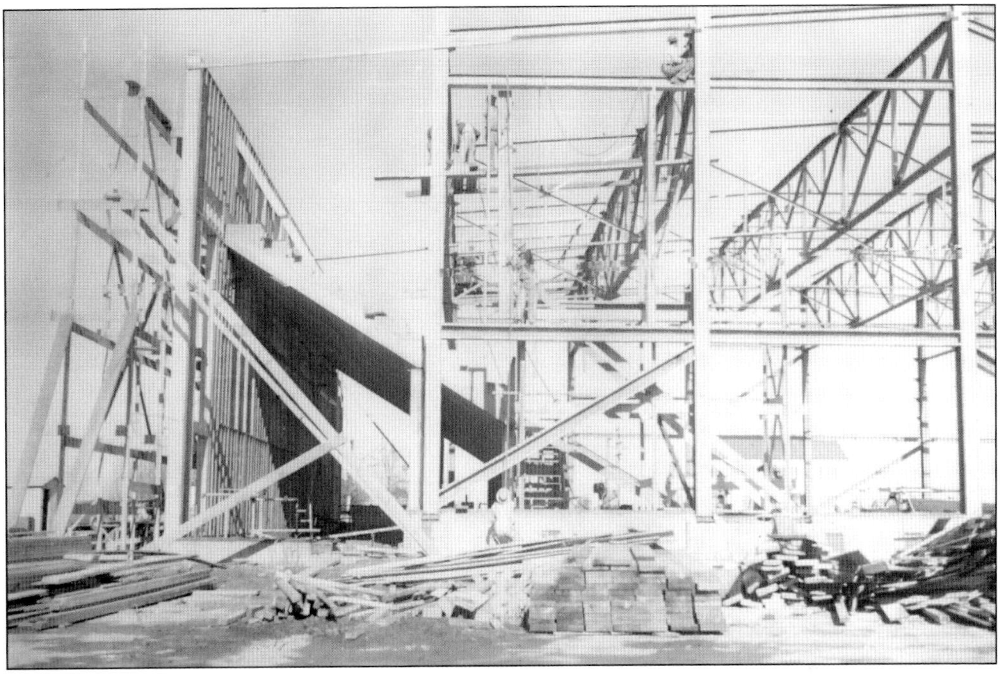

This image shows Iceland under construction in 1939 at its present 1430 Del Paso Boulevard location adjacent to American Ice. Iceland was designed by the prestigious architectural firm of Dean and Dean. Charles Dean's original drawings for Iceland included a four-tiered water fountain attached to the pylon atop Iceland, though it didn't make it off the drawing board due to the budget. Chris Lord runs the rink today.

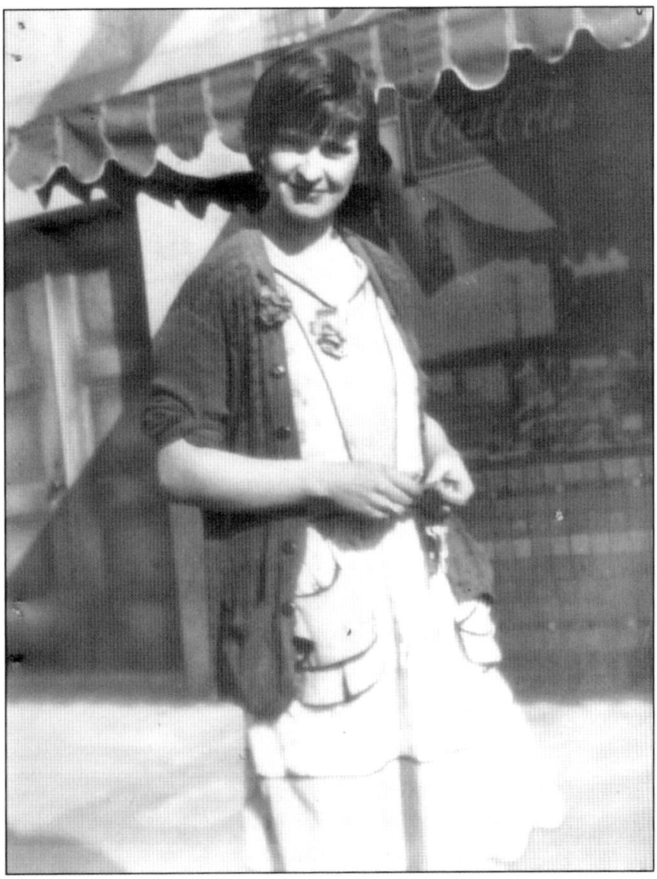

In 1931, pretty Betty "Ollie" Bryan poses in front of Betty's Candyland at 2116 Del Paso Boulevard. (Risse: Betty Bryan.)

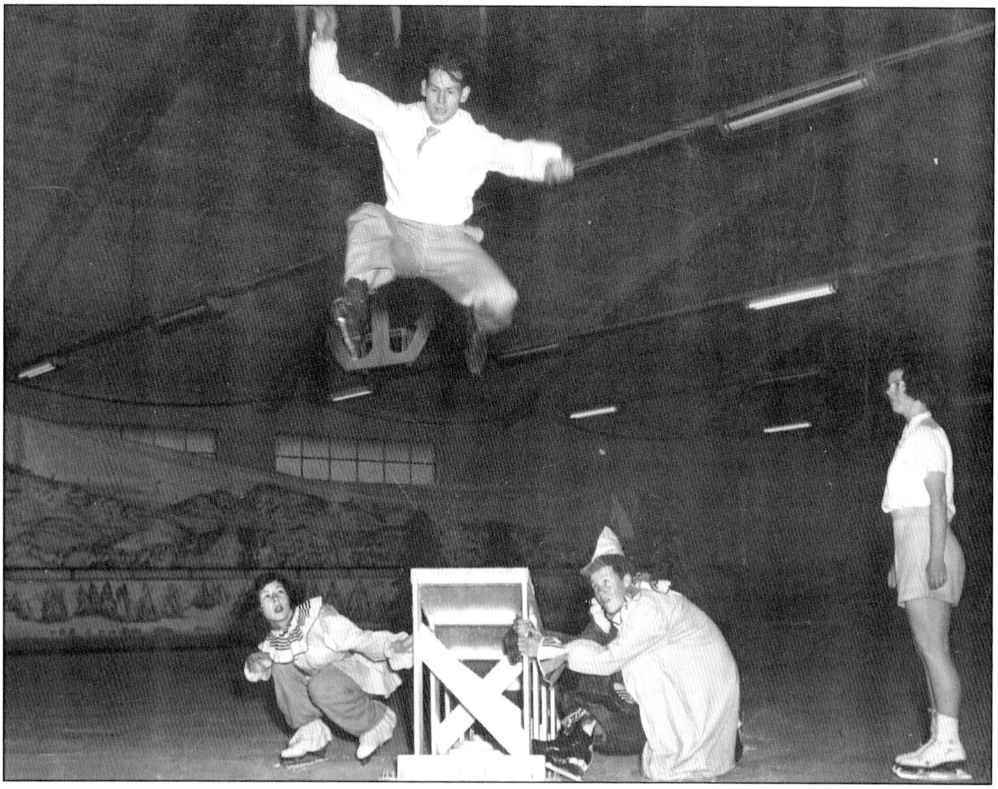

Acrobatics are part of the fun at Iceland. Pictured around 1950 is an impressive ramp-assisted jump, along with some expressions from the cowering co-participants, mixing concern and awe at this stunt. (Kerth.)

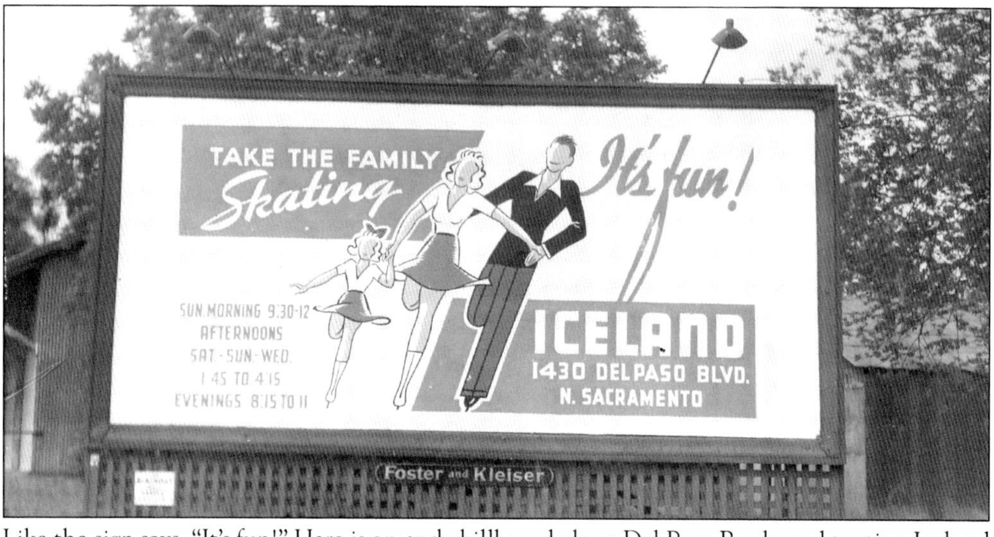

Like the sign says, "It's fun!" Here is an early billboard along Del Paso Boulevard touting Iceland around 1948. Iceland invites the family to come out for one of its many skating sessions. Now that owner Kerth had manufactured his own ice machine in "Snooky" the transformed jeep, he could afford more skaters sliding across the ice without worrying about the human labor needed for resurfacing. (Kerth.)

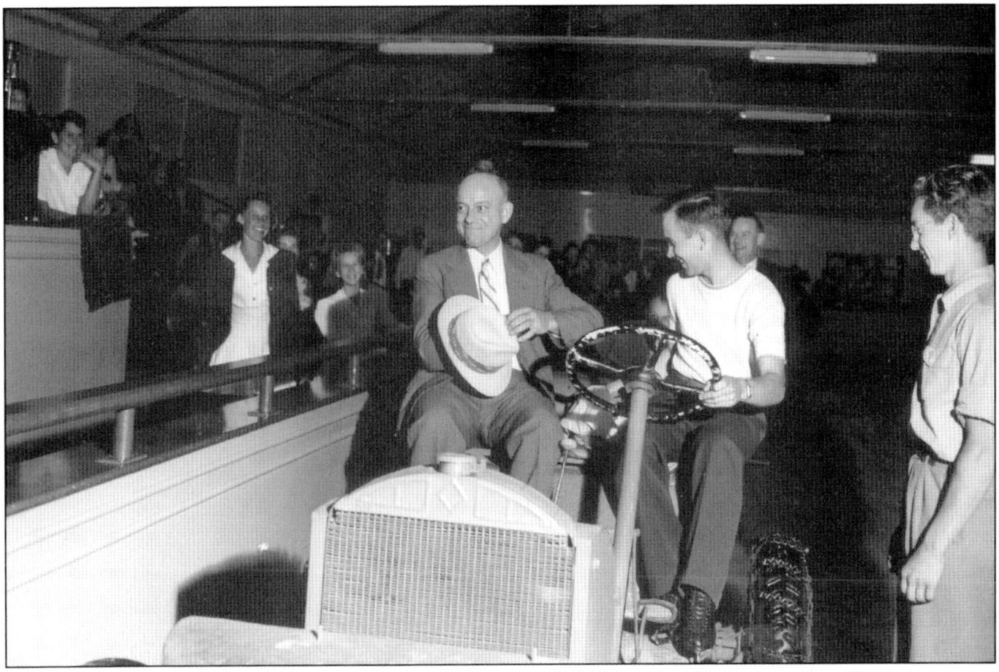

Inside his 1945 Iceland at 1430 Del Paso Boulevard, William Kerth Sr. beams as his son drives "Snoopy," a remodeled jeep made to clear the ice. Frank J. Zamboni later visited Kerth, and after watching a display of the invention went on to make millions with his own "Zamboni." (Kerth family.)

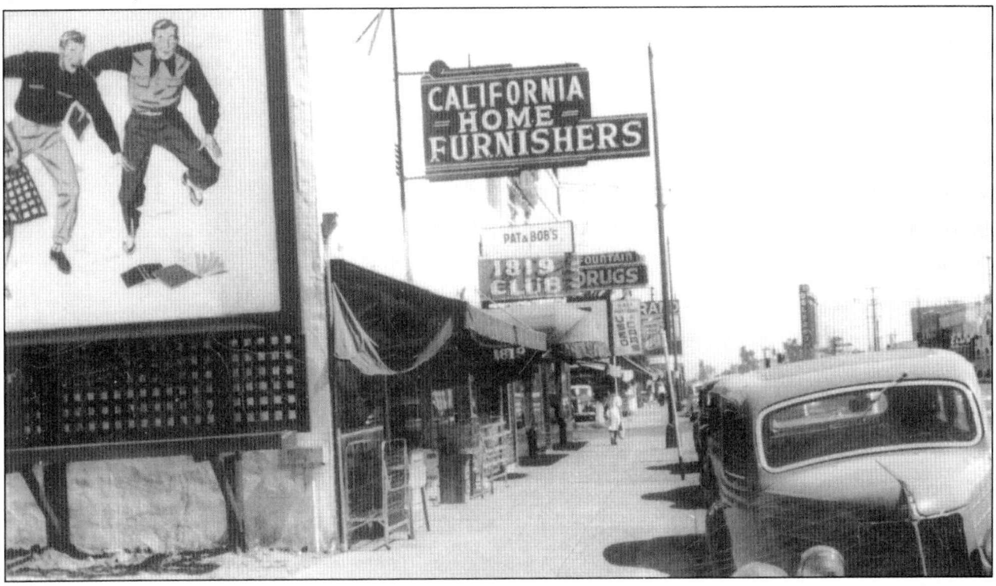

Behind the billboard is the original Taber's Furniture in 1940 advertising with the "California Home Furnishers" sign. Sammy's had moved to its current location at Cantalier Street and Del Paso Boulevard, and in its place was Pat and Bob's 1819 Club, a favorite hangout at—guess what—1819 Del Paso Boulevard. Note behind the fountain and a used cars sign is the "GRAND" theater, and across the street is the competing Del Paso Theatre. In 1968, Dick and Bob Taber expanded Taber's Furniture to include the vacant lot in front of this billboard. (Taber family.)

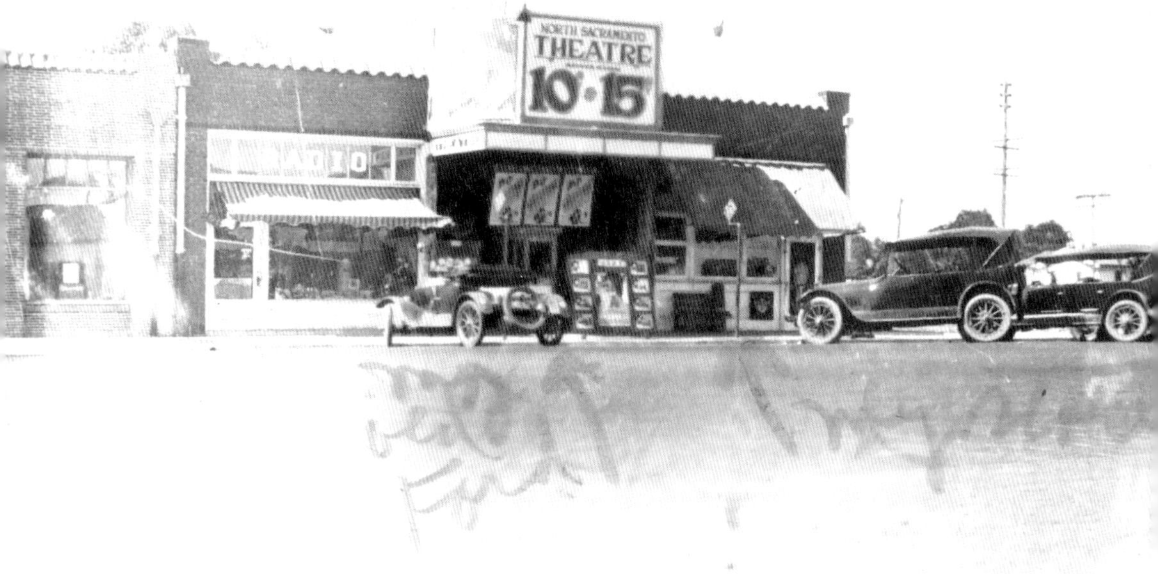

The original North Sacramento Theatre can be seen in this 1920s image of Del Paso Boulevard. Betty inscribed the words "My Old Ford" and "My Store" on the photograph. (Risse: Betty Bryan.)

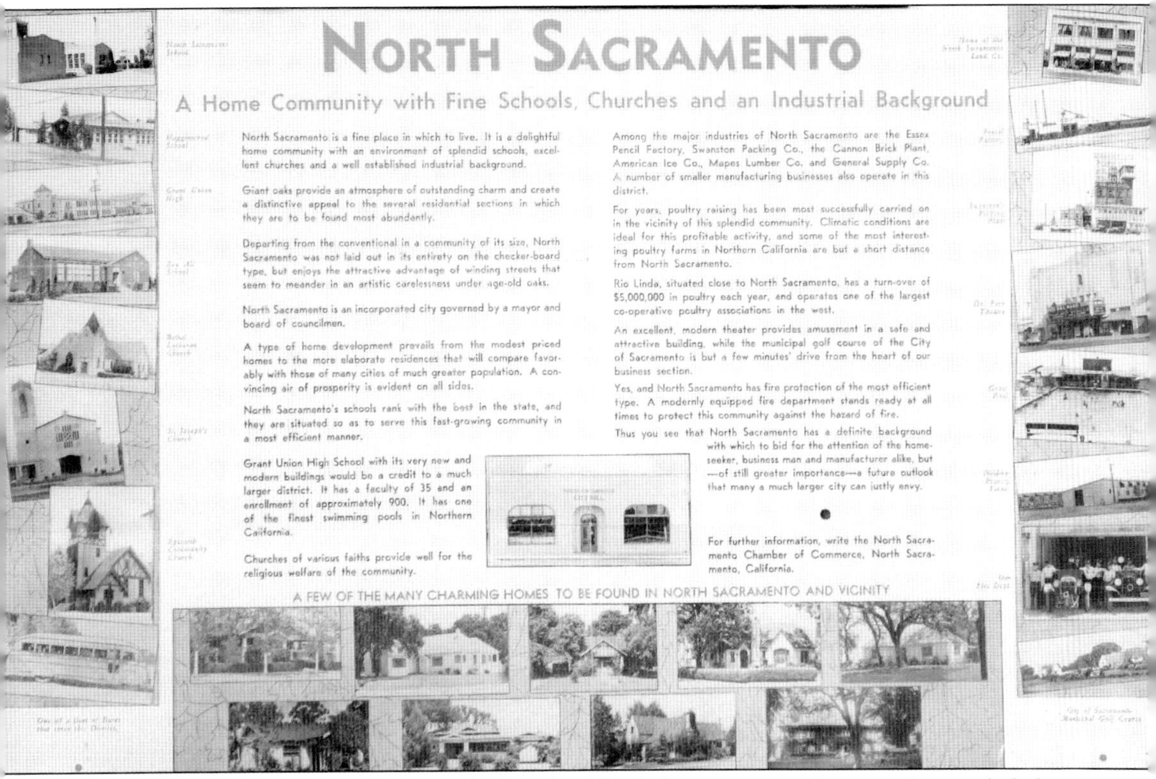

"A few of the many charming homes to be found in North Sacramento and vicinity" are included at the bottom of this promotional card from the North Sacramento Chamber of Commerce. Notable businesses, churches, theaters, and various destinations are showcased. "North Sacramento is a fine place in which to live. It is a delightful home community with an environment of splendid schools, excellent churches and a well establishd industrial background."

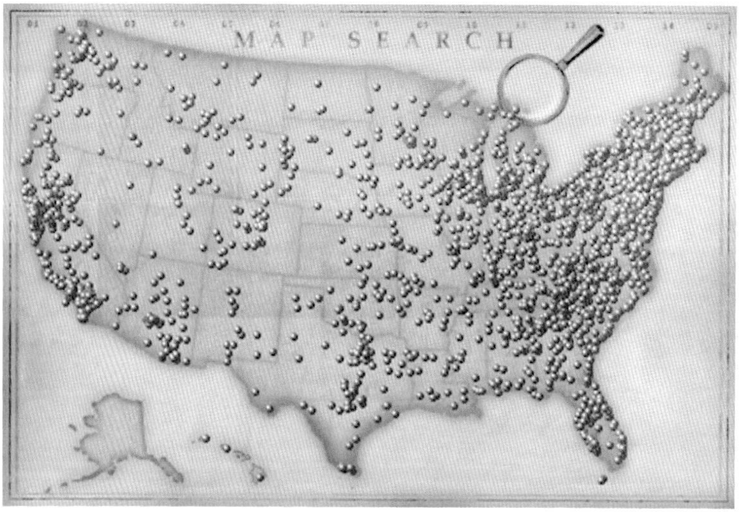
MAP SEARCH